Cricut®

by Kerri Adamczyk

Cricut® For Dummies®

Published by: **John Wiley & Sons, Inc.**, 111 River Street, Hoboken, NJ 07030-5774, www.wiley.com

Copyright © 2025 by John Wiley & Sons, Inc. All rights reserved, including rights for text and data mining and training of artificial technologies or similar technologies.

Published simultaneously in Canada

No part of this publication may be reproduced, stored in a retrieval system or transmitted in any form or by any means, electronic, mechanical, photocopying, recording, scanning or otherwise, except as permitted under Sections 107 or 108 of the 1976 United States Copyright Act, without the prior written permission of the Publisher. Requests to the Publisher for permission should be addressed to the Permissions Department, John Wiley & Sons, Inc., 111 River Street, Hoboken, NJ 07030, 201-748-6011, fax 201-748-6008, or online at http://www.wiley.com/go/permissions.

The manufacturer's authorized representative according to the EU General Product Safety Regulation is Wiley-VCH GmbH, Boschstr. 12, 69469 Weinheim, Germany, e-mail: Product_Safety@wiley.com.

Trademarks: Wiley, For Dummies, the Dummies Man logo, Dummies.com, Making Everything Easier, and related trade dress are trademarks or registered trademarks of John Wiley & Sons, Inc. and may not be used without written permission. Cricut is a trademark or registered trademark of Cricut, Inc. All other trademarks are the property of their respective owners. John Wiley & Sons, Inc. is not associated with any product or vendor mentioned in this book.

LIMIT OF LIABILITY/DISCLAIMER OF WARRANTY: THE PUBLISHER AND THE AUTHOR MAKE NO REPRESENTATIONS OR WARRANTIES WITH RESPECT TO THE ACCURACY OR COMPLETENESS OF THE CONTENTS OF THIS WORK AND SPECIFICALLY DISCLAIM ALL WARRANTIES, INCLUDING WITHOUT LIMITATION WARRANTIES OF FITNESS FOR A PARTICULAR PURPOSE. NO WARRANTY MAY BE CREATED OR EXTENDED BY SALES OR PROMOTIONAL MATERIALS. THE ADVICE AND STRATEGIES CONTAINED HEREIN MAY NOT BE SUITABLE FOR EVERY SITUATION. THIS WORK IS SOLD WITH THE UNDERSTANDING THAT THE PUBLISHER IS NOT ENGAGED IN RENDERING LEGAL, ACCOUNTING, OR OTHER PROFESSIONAL SERVICES. IF PROFESSIONAL ASSISTANCE IS REQUIRED, THE SERVICES OF A COMPETENT PROFESSIONAL PERSON SHOULD BE SOUGHT. NEITHER THE PUBLISHER NOR THE AUTHOR SHALL BE LIABLE FOR DAMAGES ARISING HEREFROM. THE FACT THAT AN ORGANIZATION OR WEBSITE IS REFERRED TO IN THIS WORK AS A CITATION AND/OR A POTENTIAL SOURCE OF FURTHER INFORMATION DOES NOT MEAN THAT THE AUTHOR OR THE PUBLISHER ENDORSES THE INFORMATION THE ORGANIZATION OR WEBSITE MAY PROVIDE OR RECOMMENDATIONS IT MAY MAKE. FURTHER, READERS SHOULD BE AWARE THAT INTERNET WEBSITES LISTED IN THIS WORK MAY HAVE CHANGED OR DISAPPEARED BETWEEN WHEN THIS WORK WAS WRITTEN AND WHEN IT IS READ.

For general information on our other products and services, please contact our Customer Care Department within the U.S. at 877-762-2974, outside the U.S. at 317-572-3993, or fax 317-572-4002. For technical support, please visit https://hub.wiley.com/community/support/dummies.

Wiley publishes in a variety of print and electronic formats and by print-on-demand. Some material included with standard print versions of this book may not be included in e-books or in print-on-demand. If this book refers to media that is not included in the version you purchased, you may download this material at http://booksupport.wiley.com. For more information about Wiley products, visit www.wiley.com.

Library of Congress Control Number is available from the publisher.

ISBN 978-1-394-30950-4 (pbk); ISBN 978-1-394-30952-8 (ebk); ISBN 978-1-394-30951-1 (ebk)

SKY10104905_050525

Table of Contents

INTRODUCTION 1
About This Book 1
Foolish Assumptions 2
Icons Used in This Book 2
Beyond the Book 3
Where to Go from Here 3

PART 1: GETTING STARTED WITH YOUR CRICUT 5

CHAPTER 1: **Welcome to the World of Cricut** 7
Cricut 101: What It Is and What It Does 8
Making Cool Stuff with a Cricut 8
Joining the Cricut Community 9

CHAPTER 2: **Choosing the Right Cricut for You** 11
The Cricut Maker Series 12
The Cricut Maker 4 12
The Cricut Maker 3 12
The Cricut Maker 14
The Cricut Explore Series 15
The Cricut Explore 4 15
The Cricut Explore 3 15
The Cricut Explore Air 2 16
The Cricut Joy Series 17
The Cricut Joy Xtra 17
The Cricut Joy 18
The Cricut Venture 19
Where to Buy a Cricut 21

CHAPTER 3: **Setting Up Your Cricut** 23
Firing Up Your Cricut 23
Syncing Your Cricut with Your Computer 24
Connecting via USB cable 24
Connecting via Bluetooth 25
Creating Your Cricut Account 27
Getting Cricut Design Space Up and Running 28
Meeting system and internet connection requirements 29
Installing Design Space on different devices 29
Navigating the Home screen 31
Finding and adjusting your settings 32
Saving for online or offline use 33

Table of Contents   **iii**

CHAPTER 4: ## Checking Out Cricut Tools and Materials 39

Looking at Tools and Accessories for All Cricut Machines........... 39
    Starting with the Cricut Essential Tool Set 40
    Considering other essentials 40
Choosing the Right Cricut Mat.................................. 41
    Distinguishing types of mats 41
    Picking the right size mat for your machine 42
Surveying Smart Materials..................................... 43
Cutting with Basic Blades...................................... 43
Writing and Drawing with Pens and Markers 44
    Looking at Cricut Pens and Markers......................... 45
    How to use Cricut Pens and Markers 45
Adding Accents with a Foil Transfer Kit 47
Making Lines with the Scoring Stylus 49
Staying Sharp with the Bonded-Fabric Blade 52
Trying Out Cricut Maker Series Tools 53
    QuickSwap tools 53
    Specialty blades.. 56
Picking the Right Heat Press 56
    Features to look for..................................... 57
    Types of heat presses................................... 58
    Heat press accessories 59
Customizing Items with Blanks 60

CHAPTER 5: ## Keeping Your Cricut in Top Shape 63

Cleaning Your Cricut Regularly 63
Changing Your Cricut Blade.................................... 64
    For Cricut Explore, Maker, and Venture machines............. 65
    For the Cricut Joy series 67
Cleaning Your Cricut Blade.................................... 67
Caring for Your Cricut Mats 68
Maintaining the Software and Firmware 69
    Updating Cricut Design Space software...................... 69
    Updating your Cricut's firmware 70
Calibrating Your Cricut 71
Troubleshooting Common Issues................................ 71
    Identifying cutting problems 71
    Resolving Design Space connectivity issues 72
    Applying advanced troubleshooting tips 72

PART 2: MASTERING CRICUT DESIGN SPACE..............73

CHAPTER 6: **Joining Cricut Access**......................75

Unlocking Exclusive Content with a Standard
Cricut Access Subscription.................................75
Checking Out Additional Cricut Access Subscription Types 77
Considering Other Options Besides Cricut Access.................77

CHAPTER 7: **Exploring the Cricut Design Space Canvas**..........79

Starting a New Project and Touring the Canvas...................80
Finding Inspiration: Projects and Images.......................81
Browsing the Projects library................................81
Looking through Images.....................................83

CHAPTER 8: **Designing in Cricut Design Space**..................85

Creating Cricut Projects in Design Space: The Basics..............86
Using Fonts and Designs Legally.............................87
Selling Cricut projects under the Cricut Angel Policy 88
Understanding personal versus commercial licenses 88
Avoiding copyright and trademark issues 89
Selling your Cricut creations safely.........................89
Uploading Your Own Designs 90
Filling Your Designs with Patterns...........................93
Applying pattern fills.....................................93
Uploading your own patterns..............................93
Working with Text...94
Finding and adding text 95
Installing your own fonts 96
Finding hidden font characters 97
Customizing fonts 98
Creating monograms 99
Visualizing Your Design with Templates and Guides.............100
Legacy Templates 101
Guides..103
Working with Layers 104
Discovering how to use layers............................105
Mastering key tools in the Layers Panel....................106
Setting the Correct Operations 113

CHAPTER 9: **Bringing Your Designs to Life**....................117

Saving and Sharing Projects................................117
Saving for offline use 118
Creating and managing Collections 118
Sharing your projects 118

Sending Your Design to Your Cricut 119
Introducing the Prepare screen. 120
Setting up your mat. 121
Checking out the Make screen 123

PART 3: PROJECTS USING PAPER AND CARDSTOCK 125

CHAPTER 10: Cutting Gift Tags 127
Checking Out Project Ideas Using Gift Tags. .127
Picking the Right Tools and Materials for Gift Tags 129
Choosing Your Gift Tag Method 130
Method 1: Simple cut 130
Method 2: Drawing and cutting. 131
Method 3: Print Then Cut. 132
Creating Gift Tags: A Step-by-Step Guide. 133

CHAPTER 11: Crafting Rolled Paper Flowers. 137
Exploring Project Ideas for Paper Flowers. 138
Choosing the Right Paper for Rolled Flowers 139
Exploring recommended paper types 139
Avoiding papers that don't work 139
Discovering Paper Flower Templates. 140
Searching Cricut Design Space for templates 140
Browsing third-party websites for templates 141
Choosing the Right Cut Size for Your Flowers. 142
Mastering Quilling Tools. 143
Using manual quilling tools 143
Trying electric quilling tools 144
Testing out alternatives to quilling tools 144
Rolling Paper Flowers: A Step-by-Step Guide 144
Gathering your materials. 145
Step 1: Designing your flower 145
Step 2: Cutting the flower. 146
Step 3: Rolling the flower 147
Step 4: Gluing the flower 148
Adding stems, leaves, and pistils. 148

CHAPTER 12: Making Cards 151
Starting Your Card-Making Journey 152
Celebrating all occasions 152
Building your skills. 152
Choosing between Insert Cards and Cutaway Cards. 153
Crafting Insert Cards. 153
Creating Cutaway Cards. 156
Picking the right size card. 156

vi   Cricut For Dummies

Gathering Materials for Card-Making...........................157
    Starting with the basics...................................157
    Enhancing with optional materials.........................158
    Using Cricut Card Mats...................................159
Making Cards with Your Cricut: A Step-by-Step Guide...........160
    Step 1: Finding a project.................................160
    Step 2: Creating a template...............................162
    Step 3: Adding your designs...............................165
    Step 4: Adjusting operations..............................166
    Step 5: Preparing to make your card.......................167
    Step 6: Loading your material onto the mat................168
    Step 7: Loading your tools and mat........................169
    Step 8: Making your project...............................170
    Step 9: Assembling your card..............................171

PART 4: VINYL AND HEAT TRANSFER PROJECTS.........173

CHAPTER 13: Working with Vinyl...........................175

Exploring Vinyl Project Ideas.................................176
Avoiding Surfaces Vinyl Doesn't Stick To.....................177
Checking Out Types of Vinyl..................................177
    Deciding between permanent and removable vinyl.........178
    Exploring specialty vinyl for unique designs..............178
    Using Smart Vinyl for mat-free cutting....................179
Weeding Vinyl to Reveal Your Design..........................179
Using Transfer Tape..181
Gathering Your Materials for Vinyl Projects..................182
Working with Vinyl: A Step-by-Step Guide.....................183
    Step 1: Designing your project............................183
    Step 2: Preparing the materials...........................184
    Step 3: Loading and cutting the vinyl.....................185
    Step 4: Weeding the excess vinyl..........................186
    Step 5: Applying transfer tape............................186
    Step 6: Transferring your design..........................186
Caring for Your Vinyl Projects...............................187

CHAPTER 14: Layering Vinyl for Colorful Designs.........189

Choosing the Right Vinyl for Layering........................190
    Sticking with the easiest vinyl to layer..................190
    Avoiding vinyl that's hard to layer.......................190
    Layering dark colors last.................................190
Working with Multilayered Designs in Design Space............191
    Ungrouping layered designs................................191
    Deciding the stack order..................................192
    Considering the maximum number of layers..................192
    Simplifying designs with the Slice tool...................193

Exploring Layering Techniques 194
Layering from bottom to top 194
Layering from top to bottom 194
Using registration marks for precise layering 195
Layering with parchment paper 200

CHAPTER 15: Using Heat Transfer Vinyl 203
Exploring HTV Project Ideas 203
Checking Out Types of HTV 204
Finding the Right Size and Placement for T-shirt Decals 206
Gathering Everything You Need for HTV Projects. 207
Cutting and Applying HTV: A Step-by-Step Guide 207
Step 1: Designing your project 208
Step 2: Preparing the materials 209
Step 3: Loading and cutting the HTV 209
Step 4: Weeding and transferring your design 209
Following Washing and Care Instructions for HTV Projects 210

CHAPTER 16: Trying Infusible Ink 211
Exploring Infusible Project Ideas 212
Gathering Your Materials 212
Common materials for all Infusible Ink projects 213
Specific materials for projects using Infusible
Ink Transfer Sheets 213
Specific materials for projects using Infusible Ink Pens and
Markers 214
Choosing the right blanks for Infusible Ink 215
Working with Infusible Ink Transfer Sheets: A Step-
by-Step Guide 215
Step 1: Create your design 215
Step 2: Slice multilayer designs (if necessary) 216
Step 3: Adjust settings in Design Space 216
Step 4: Clean and prepare your materials 217
Step 5: Cut and weed your design 218
Step 6: Position and apply the design 218
Step 7: Cool and reveal your design 220
Drawing with Cricut Infusible Ink Pens and Markers 220
Step 1: Create and mirror your design 220
Step 2: Draw your design 223
Step 3: Prepare your blank 223
Step 4: Position and apply your design 224
Step 5: Cool and reveal 225
Caring for Your Infusible Ink Projects 225

viii   Cricut For Dummies

CHAPTER 17: Etching with Vinyl Stencils 227

  Exploring Glass Etching Projects 228
  Gathering Your Materials for Glass Etching Projects 229
  Creating Your Stencil in Cricut Design Space 231
  Etching Glass with Your Cricut: A Step-by-Step Guide 235
    Step 1: Preparing your design 235
    Step 2: Cleaning the glass. 235
    Step 3: Applying your transfer tape 235
    Step 4: Applying the etching cream 236
    Step 5: Rinsing off the etching cream. 237

PART 5: PROJECTS USING PRINTABLE MATERIALS 239

CHAPTER 18: Mastering Cricut Print Then Cut 241

  Knowing How Print Then Cut Works. 241
  Exploring Print Then Cut Project Ideas. 242
  Testing Different Print Then Cut Materials 243
  Preparing Your Cricut for Print Then Cut. 244
    Calibrating your Cricut 244
    Understanding Print Then Cut size limits 245
    Getting the best print quality. 246
    Distinguishing Bleed on from Bleed off 247
  Using Print Then Cut: A Step-by-Step Guide 248
    Gathering your materials 248
    Step 1: Setting up your design. 248
    Step 2: Printing your design. 250
    Step 3: Cutting your project 251

CHAPTER 19: Creating Custom Stickers 253

  Exploring Project Ideas Using Stickers 254
  Gathering Your Materials. 255
    Choosing your printable sticker paper. 256
    Making sure your sticker paper works with
    your Cricut model 256
  Designing Your Stickers in Cricut Design Space 257
    Using the Create Sticker tool with Cricut Access. 257
    Adding borders to your stickers without Cricut Access 258
  Printing Your Stickers 260
  Waterproofing Your Stickers 262
  Cutting Both Ways: Kiss-Cut Stickers versus Die-Cut Stickers. 262

CHAPTER 20: Crafting with Printable Heat Transfer Vinyl 265

  Understanding the Pros and Cons of Printable HTV 265
  Exploring Project Ideas with Printable HTV .266
  Gathering Your Materials for Printable HTV Projects. 266

Table of Contents   **ix**

Using Printable HTV: A Step-by-Step Guide. .268
    Step 1: Creating your design 268
    Step 2: Printing your design. 269
    Step 3: Cutting your design 270
    Step 4: Preparing your fabric. 270
    Step 5: Applying the design 271
    Step 6: Peeling the backing (if needed) 271
Following Proper Care Instructions 272

PART 6: THE PART OF TENS. 273

CHAPTER 21: Ten Beginner Cricut Projects 275

Making Birthday Banners. 276
Crafting Custom Bookmarks 277
Personalizing Water Bottles. 278
Assembling Acrylic Key Chains 280
Decorating Throw Pillows. 281
Designing Custom Hats 282
Monogramming Towels 284
Creating Infusible Ink Coasters 285
Organizing with Custom Labels. 287
Creating Custom Candle Labels 288

CHAPTER 22: Ten Advanced Cricut Projects 291

Engraving Pet ID Tags 291
"Etching" Coated Metal with Citristrip. 293
Fashioning Leather Earrings 295
Assembling Fabric Flowers. 297
Stenciling Wood Signs. 299
Creating Vibrant Coffee Mugs 301
Making Decorative Cake Toppers 303
Cutting Perfect Quilt Blocks. 304
Piecing Together Custom Puzzles. 306
Personalizing Elegant Envelopes. 309

INDEX. 313

Introduction

Imagine a tool that can bring any creative project to life — from designing custom clothing and home décor, to making personalized cards and more! Your Cricut machine is that tool, and this book is your guide to mastering it. I've spoken with many crafters who were so intimidated by their new Cricut that they left it in the box for months. If that sounds familiar, you're not alone. I understand the challenges of figuring out new technology, so in this book I've broken the process into simple, easy-to-understand steps to make crafting with your Cricut not only easy but also enjoyable. We'll start this creative journey together, and soon you'll be crafting on your own with confidence!

About This Book

Whether you're just starting out or ready to dive into more advanced projects, this book is your friendly guide to everything Cricut. Cricut machines are designed to do it all: cut, write, draw, score, and more, depending on the model you choose. Don't have a Cricut machine yet? No worries. Chapter 2 helps you find the best Cricut for your crafting needs.

After taking your Cricut out of the box, you can check out the chapters in Part 1 to find out how to turn it on and set it up. In Part 2, you can explore the ins and outs of Cricut Design Space — the software you'll use to create your designs and send them to your machine. Not sure what to make? This book is packed with lots of fun, easy-to-follow projects that will inspire you to Cricut everything in sight. You can also explore how to use a variety of materials — from paper and vinyl to leather and fabric — to truly maximize the potential of your machine. Each chapter offers practical tips and step-by-step instructions to make your crafting experience a breeze.

Whether you're looking to create beautiful home décor, personalized gifts, or even handcrafted items to sell, this book has you covered. It's organized to help you build your skills at your own pace, with plenty of projects so you can practice techniques that are new to you. So get ready to start crafting and turning your ideas into reality!

A quick note: Sidebars (shaded boxes of text) dig into the details of a given topic, but they aren't crucial to understanding it. Feel free to read them or skip them. You can pass over the text accompanied by the Technical Stuff icon, too. The text marked with this icon covers some interesting but nonessential information about Cricut crafting.

One last thing: You may note that some web addresses in this book break across two lines of text. If you're reading the print version of the book and want to visit one of these web pages, simply key in the web address exactly as it's noted in the text, pretending as though the line break doesn't exist. If you're reading this as an e-book, you've got it easy — just click the web address to be taken directly to the web page.

Foolish Assumptions

Here are some assumptions about you, dear reader, and why you're picking up this book:

- » You have a Cricut machine or are planning to purchase one.
- » You're interested in creating personalized projects, like custom T-shirts, home décor, or gifts.
- » You're willing to invest time to find out about Cricut's capabilities and experiment with new crafting techniques.
- » You're looking to join a community of like-minded crafters who share tips, tricks, and inspiration.

Icons Used in This Book

Like all *For Dummies* books, this book features icons to help you navigate the information it contains. Here's what they mean.

REMEMBER

If you take away anything from this book, it should be the information marked with this icon.

TECHNICAL STUFF

This icon flags information that delves a little deeper than usual into the world of Cricut.

TIP

This icon highlights especially helpful advice about how to make the most of your Cricut.

WARNING

This icon points out situations and actions to avoid to help you use your Cricut machine safely and effectively, and sidestep common mistakes.

Beyond the Book

In addition to the material in the print or e-book you're reading right now, this product comes with some access-anywhere goodies on the web. Check out the free Cheat Sheet for info on must-have supplies, vinyl decal sizing, and mat usage to enhance your Cricut projects. To get this Cheat Sheet, simply go to www.dummies.com and type "*Cricut For Dummies* Cheat Sheet" in the search box.

Where to Go from Here

You don't have to read this book from cover to cover, but if you're an especially thorough person, feel free to do so! If you just want to find specific information and then get back to work, take a look at the table of contents or the index, and then dive into the chapter or section that interests you.

If you're curious about the various tools you can use with your Cricut, Chapter 4 is a great place to start. Want to become a pro at Cricut Design Space? Head over to Part 2. If custom clothing is what you're interested in, Chapter 15 shows you how to craft beautiful wearable designs. And when you're ready to expand your horizons, Chapters 21 and 22 in the Part of Tens offer projects ranging from beginner to advanced skill levels.

With this book in hand, you're well on your way to becoming a Cricut expert. Every page you turn is a new chance to craft something extraordinary. Start with what excites you most, and create projects you're proud to share!

1

Getting Started with Your Cricut

IN THIS PART . . .

Kickstart your Cricut journey by exploring what this versatile crafting machine can do.

Decide which Cricut model is best for you based on what you want to create.

Get your Cricut set up quickly and start crafting right away.

Discover the essential tools and supplies you'll need for your projects.

Find out how to take care of your Cricut and fix common issues.

IN THIS CHAPTER

» **Understanding what Cricut is and how it works**

» **Creating cool projects with a Cricut**

» **Becoming part of the Cricut community**

Chapter **1**

Welcome to the World of Cricut

ver wished you could turn everyday items into unique, personalized creations? With Cricut, you can transform the ordinary into the extraordinary, all from the comfort of your home. Welcome to the world of Cricut, where your creative ideas come to life with the help of this incredible cutting machine. Whether you're dreaming of a one-of-a-kind T-shirt, a custom card, or a stunning piece of home décor, Cricut's precise cutting and versatile features make it easy to craft projects that show off your style and creativity.

In this chapter, I introduce you to what a Cricut machine is and how it works. You discover the endless possibilities for crafting, whether you're doing it for personal enjoyment, making thoughtful gifts, or even starting a small business. Additionally, I guide you on how to connect with the crafty Cricut community, where you can find inspiration, share your creations, and get advice from fellow craft enthusiasts. By the end of this chapter, you'll be ready to dive into the exciting world of Cricut and start turning your crafting ideas into reality.

Cricut 101: What It Is and What It Does

A Cricut is a versatile cutting machine that can precisely cut materials ranging from paper to wood. Think of it as your personal crafting assistant, transforming your ideas into beautiful creations.

Cricut machines use various blades for different materials. The Fine-Point Blade handles delicate paper, and the Deep-Point Blade cuts thicker materials like foam and chipboard. The Rotary Blade is perfect for fabric, and the Knife Blade tackles tougher materials like wood and acrylic.

REMEMBER

Different Cricut models offer unique capabilities. The Cricut Maker can cut through wood and acrylic with its specialized Knife Blade, but the Cricut Joy and Cricut Explore Air 2 are limited to lighter materials like paper and vinyl. For more details on each machine's capabilities, check out Chapter 2.

Cricut Design Space, the software that powers your Cricut machine, allows you to create custom projects or choose from premade designs. After your design is ready, Cricut Design Space sends it to the machine for precise cutting. You load your material onto a Cricut mat, which holds it in place during cutting. Mats come in different colors, each offering varying levels of stickiness to match your material. (I give you full details on Cricut Design Space in Part 2; find out more about mats in Chapter 4.)

After cutting, the next step is weeding — removing excess material to reveal your design. Then you transfer the design to your "blank" (T-shirt, tote bag, mug, and so on) using transfer tape for vinyl or the carrier sheet for heat transfer vinyl (HTV). For more on the differences between vinyl and HTV, check out Chapter 15.

Making Cool Stuff with a Cricut

Cricut's versatility lets you create nearly anything you can dream up. For example

- » You can design custom cards for any occasion using the Fine-Point Blade and Cricut Pens (see Chapter 12 for details).
- » For home décor, make personalized wall decals, pillows, and framed art that reflect your style.
- » Custom tees are a Cricut favorite — create wearable art for group outings, fundraisers, or family events using heat transfer vinyl (see Chapter 15 for guidance).

- » Beyond these, Cricut lets you explore projects like jewelry making, scrapbooking, and sign making (see Chapter 22), with endless possibilities limited only by your imagination.

Joining the Cricut Community

Joining the Cricut community is a wonderful way to connect with new friends who share your passion for Cricut crafting. By engaging with fellow crafters, you'll discover endless inspiration, pick up new techniques, get answers to your questions, and find plenty of encouragement. Whether you're just starting out or you're a seasoned pro, being a part of the vibrant Cricut community will make your crafting journey even more fun and rewarding.

Social media is a great way to connect with Cricut enthusiasts and stay inspired:

- » On Facebook, join Cricut-specific groups to share projects and exchange ideas; just be cautious of scammers.
- » YouTube offers detailed tutorials and project walk-throughs; use popular search terms like "Cricut project ideas" and "Beginner Cricut."
- » TikTok provides quick, bite-size tutorials and creative ideas.
- » Instagram gives daily inspiration and project ideas.
- » Pinterest is ideal for saving and organizing creative ideas.

To stay ahead, follow Cricut bloggers like me at www.kerricraftsit.com for in-depth articles and tutorials, and influencers on Instagram, TikTok, and YouTube, such as Jennifer Maker and myself, for fresh inspiration and new techniques.

TIP

Using hashtags on platforms like Instagram, TikTok, and Pinterest can help you connect with other crafters and discover new ideas. Try searching #Cricut, #CricutCrafts, or #CricutDesignSpace to find your next project inspiration.

TIP

Being part of the Cricut community means supporting each other. If you see a project you love, show your appreciation with a like or comment! Your compliments and encouragement can make a big difference in boosting another crafter's confidence. When someone asks a question on a post, try to provide a helpful answer. Remember, we all started as beginners. Above all, always be kind and supportive.

IN THIS CHAPTER

» **Exploring different models**

» **Discovering each machine's capabilities**

» **Shopping for a new Cricut**

Chapter **2**

Choosing the Right Cricut for You

You may be asking yourself, "Which Cricut machine is the best fit for me?" Choosing the perfect Cricut can feel a bit overwhelming with all the options out there, but don't worry — I've got you covered! The answer comes down to the types of projects you want to make, your budget, and what each machine can do.

Cricut currently offers four families of machines: the Maker series, the Explore series, the Joy series, and the Venture. Each family offers something a little different depending on the types of projects you're looking to make. This is the complete lineup of machines available at the time of writing:

» Cricut Maker 4

» Cricut Maker 3

» Cricut Maker

» Cricut Explore 4

» Cricut Explore 3

» Cricut Explore Air 2

» Cricut Joy Xtra

- Cricut Joy
- Cricut Venture

Older models like the Cricut Explore Air 2, the original Maker, and the Explore 3 and Maker 3 are still available in some places, but they're gradually being phased out. Although fully discontinued models aren't covered in detail, this chapter walks you through each of the machines currently offered by Cricut, their capabilities, and the types of projects they're best suited for. So dive in and find your perfect match!

TIP

Chapter 4 has details on tools and materials for your new Cricut machine. Parts 3, 4, and 5 are chock-full of project ideas.

The Cricut Maker Series

The Cricut Maker series is designed for crafters who want more power, precision, and versatility. With models including the Cricut Maker, Cricut Maker 3, and the newest Cricut Maker 4, these machines can handle everything from delicate fabrics to tough materials like leather and balsa wood. With a variety of interchangeable tools, these machines go beyond cutting — you can engrave, deboss, and even use the Rotary Blade for fabric projects. The Maker series gives you the flexibility to tackle just about any creative project you have in mind!

The Cricut Maker 4

The Cricut Maker 4, released in February 2025, is the latest addition to the Cricut Maker series. It does everything the Maker 3 does but can be up to two times faster, with speed varying by the material and use of a cutting mat. This model introduces two new colors, seashell and sage.

The Cricut Maker 3

The Cricut Maker 3, released in June 2021, is an upgraded version of the original Cricut Maker (which I cover later in this chapter) and is the most versatile Cricut machine for both hobbyists and pros.

The Cricut Maker 3 is loaded with features. It can cut, write, draw, foil, score, engrave, deboss, and perforate. Check out some of the new and improved features of the Cricut Maker 3:

- » Cuts 300+ materials, including Smart Materials
- » Works twice as fast as the original Cricut Maker
- » Uses the Adaptive Tool System for a wide range of tools
- » Has dual tool clamps for simultaneous cutting and writing
- » Supports Print Then Cut, allowing precise cuts around printed designs (see Chapter 18 for details)

The largest cut size for the Cricut Maker 3 is 11.7 inches wide by 12 feet long when you're using Smart Materials. Because Smart Materials don't need a mat, you're not limited by mat size for longer projects. If you're using other materials with a mat, the biggest mat size is 12 inches by 24 inches, so that's your limit.

WARNING

Although the Cricut Maker 3 is incredibly versatile, it does have some limits. It can only cut materials up to 12 inches wide, which may not be enough for large projects like oversize wall decals or banners. Also, although it can engrave aluminum and acrylic using the Engraving Tip, it can't cut these materials.

The Cricut Maker 3 works with all the same tools as the original Cricut Maker, giving you lots of project options. Here's a list of the QuickSwap tools and accessories you can use:

- » Premium Fine-Point Blade
- » Foil Transfer Tool
- » Pens and Markers
- » Deep-Point Blade
- » Scoring Stylus
- » Bonded-Fabric Blade
- » Scoring Wheel Tip (single and double)
- » Rotary Blade
- » Wavy Blade
- » Knife Blade
- » Engraving Tip
- » Debossing Tip
- » Perforation Blade

The Cricut Maker

Released in August 2017, the Cricut Maker was a big deal before the Maker 3 and 4 arrived. Although it doesn't support Smart Materials for matless cutting, it remains highly versatile with its Adaptive Tool System. You can use it for custom apparel, home décor, paper crafts, and personalized gifts like engraved items or custom mugs.

TECHNICAL STUFF

It's worth noting that the series doesn't include a "Cricut Maker 2" — it jumped right from the original Cricut Maker to the Cricut Maker 3.

The Maker can perform all the same functions as the Maker 3. It can cut, write, draw, foil, score, engrave, deboss, and perforate. Here's what you can expect from the original Cricut Maker:

- Cuts 300+ materials
- Uses the Adaptive Tool System, which supports 13+ tools
- Works faster than the Cricut Explore Air 2 (twice as fast, to be exact)
- Supports Print Then Cut, so you can cut out printed designs like stickers

With a cutting mat, the Cricut Maker can cut designs up to 11.7 inches by 24 inches. This works well for large projects like oversize wall decals or banners made in sections that you piece together. If you need continuous cuts for extra-long designs without seams, consider the Cricut Maker 3 or 4.

WARNING

The Maker can't use Smart Materials, meaning you'll need a cutting mat for every project. This limits your cuts to a maximum length of 24 inches, so you can't work with extra-long matless designs. And although it's fast, it doesn't quite hit the speed of the newest Maker 4, but it's still a solid machine.

Here's a list of the tools and accessories that work with the original Cricut Maker:

- Fine-Point Blade
- Deep-Point Blade
- Rotary Blade
- Knife Blade
- Scoring Wheel Tip (single and double)
- Bonded-Fabric Blade
- Engraving Tip

>> Debossing Tip

>> Perforation Blade

>> Wavy Blade

>> Foil Transfer Tool

The Cricut Explore Series

The Cricut Explore series is a great middle-ground option for crafters who want more versatility than the Cricut Joy offers but don't need all the advanced tools of the Cricut Maker series. These machines, which include the Explore Air 2, the Explore 3, and the newly released Explore 4, these machines can handle a variety of materials, making them great for projects like T-shirts, decals, and greeting cards. With features like a Fine-Point Blade for precision cuts and compatibility with Cricut Pens for writing and drawing, the Explore series is a solid choice for everyday crafters looking to bring their designs to life.

The Cricut Explore 4

Released alongside the Maker 4 in February 2025, the new Cricut Explore 4 doubles the cutting speed of its predecessor, the Explore 3. For more on what the Explore 4 can do, just look at the Explore 3's features — they're pretty much the same.

The Cricut Explore 3

Released in June 2021, the Cricut Explore 3 is an upgrade from the Explore Air 2, offering matless cutting with Smart Materials for longer and faster projects.

The Cricut Explore 3 can cut, write, draw, score, and foil. Check out some of the new and improved features of the Cricut Explore 3:

>> Cuts 100+ materials, including Smart Materials

>> Can cut designs up to 12 feet long

>> Cuts twice as fast as the Explore Air 2

>> Has a dual tool holder for simultaneous cutting and writing

>> Compatible with Print Then Cut, allowing for accurate cutting of printed designs

With Smart Materials, the Explore 3 can cut up to 12 inches wide and 12 feet long. If you're using a mat, the maximum size is 11.7 inches by 24 inches.

WARNING

Unlike the Maker series (which I cover earlier in this chapter), the Explore 3 doesn't support advanced tools like the Rotary Blade, Knife Blade, or Debossing Tip. It can't handle heavy materials like chipboard or thick leather, which are a breeze for the Maker machines.

The Explore 3 is compatible with the following tools:

- Premium Fine-Point Blade
- Foil Transfer Tool
- Pens and Markers
- Deep-Point Blade
- Scoring Stylus
- Bonded-Fabric Blade

The Cricut Explore Air 2

The Cricut Explore Air 2, released in August 2017, is an upgraded version of the original Cricut Explore, cutting and writing up to two times faster. Although not as fast as the Cricut Maker series, it can still handle a variety of projects, including vinyl decals, custom T-shirts, gift boxes, personalized signs, and full-color stickers using the Print Then Cut feature.

The Cricut Explore Air 2 can cut, write, draw, foil, and score. With a mat, the Explore Air 2 can cut materials up to 11.7 x 24 inches. Benefits of the Cricut Explore Air 2 include the following:

- Cuts 100+ materials
- Cuts and writes up to two times faster than previous Explore models
- Is compatible with the Fine-Point, Deep-Point, and Bonded-Fabric blades
- Has a dual tool holder for simultaneous cutting and writing
- Works with Print Then Cut, so you can cut out printed designs with precision

WARNING

Unlike the Explore 3 and 4, the Explore Air 2 can't cut Smart Materials, so it's not suited for extra-long projects. Plus, it doesn't have the Adaptive Tool System, so you can't use the more advanced QuickSwap tools that are available for the Maker series.

The Explore Air 2 works with

- Premium Fine-Point Blade
- Foil Transfer Tool
- Pens and Markers
- Deep-Point Blade
- Scoring Stylus
- Bonded-Fabric Blade

The Cricut Joy Series

The Cricut Joy series is perfect for crafters looking for a compact, easy-to-use cutting machine for quick projects. These machines are smaller than the Explore and Maker series but still pack a punch, handling a variety of materials like vinyl, heat transfer vinyl (HTV), and cardstock. Designed for convenience, the Joy series is great for making cards, labels, decals, and other small-scale projects without taking up much space.

The Cricut Joy Xtra

The Cricut Joy Xtra, released in September 2023, is the newest and slightly larger member of the Cricut Joy family, offering more space for bigger projects. It's perfect for printable projects like stickers and custom labels, thanks to its compatibility with Cricut Print Then Cut.

The Cricut Joy Xtra can cut, write, draw, and foil. The maximum cut size is 8.5 inches by 4 feet. Here's what the Cricut Joy Xtra brings to the table:

- Cuts 50+ materials, including Smart Materials
- Is compact and portable, like the original Cricut Joy

CHAPTER 2 Choosing the Right Cricut for You

- Has Print Then Cut capability for stickers and labels
- Features dual tool clamps for simultaneous cutting and writing

WARNING

The Cricut Joy Xtra has a few limitations to keep in mind:

- It cannot perform scoring, engraving, debossing, or perforating, which are functions available on more advanced machines like the Cricut Maker series.
- It's not compatible with a range of specialized tools, such as the Deep-Point Blade, Scoring Stylus, Bonded-Fabric Blade, Rotary Blade, or Engraving Tip. This means that you won't be able to work with thick materials or create intricate textures like you would on a more versatile machine.
- Although it allows for larger projects than the original Cricut Joy, its maximum cut width is still limited to 8.5 inches, making it less suitable for big designs or materials like large T-shirts.

The Cricut Joy Xtra works with

- Premium Fine-Point Blade
- Foil Transfer Tool
- Pens and Markers

The Cricut Joy

The Cricut Joy, released in February 2020, is Cricut's smallest and most portable machine, perfect for crafting in tight spaces or taking to craft fairs.

The Cricut Joy has the same functions as the Cricut Joy Xtra. It can cut, write, draw, and foil. The Cricut Joy's maximum cut size is 4.5 inches by 4 feet. Key features of the Cricut Joy include

- Cuts 50+ materials, including Smart Materials
- Is ultra-compact and easy to take with you
- Has a single tool clamp for cutting or writing

TIP

It's a great beginner's machine, but as you dive deeper into crafting, you may want a machine with more versatility, such as the Cricut Maker 3, which can tackle more advanced projects like intricate jewelry, large paper flowers, and more.

WARNING

The Cricut Joy does have quite a few limitations to keep in mind:

- » It can't do Print Then Cut projects, which means it can't precisely cut around printed designs. Although you can create greeting cards using Cricut's card-making features, like Insert Cards, predesigned templates, and writing with Cricut Pens, it isn't capable of cutting around printed invitations or stickers because it doesn't have a sensor to detect printed registration marks.
- » It isn't compatible with a lot of the tools you can use with other Cricut machines. This includes the Deep-Point Blade, Scoring Stylus, Bonded-Fabric Blade, Scoring Wheel Tip, Rotary Blade, Wavy Blade, Knife Blade, Engraving Tip, Debossing Tip, and Perforation Blade.
- » It only cuts materials up to 4.5 inches wide, so it's not ideal for large designs like custom shirts with HTV, because adult sizes typically need about 9 inches.
- » The Cricut Joy has only one tool clamp; other machines have two. This means you'll have to pause and switch tools if your project involves both cutting and writing.

The Cricut Joy works with

- » Premium Fine-Point Blade
- » Foil Transfer Tool
- » Pens and Markers

The Cricut Venture

The Cricut Venture, released in July 2023, is Cricut's largest cutting machine, designed for professional crafters and small businesses. It's perfect for large projects like wall decals, custom apparel, 3-D paper crafts, and stickers.

The Venture can cut, write, draw, score, and foil. Here are some of the features that make the Cricut Venture stand out:

- » Cuts 100+ materials, including Smart Materials
- » Has an adjustable wide-format design (13 inches and 25 inches)
- » Works at super-fast, commercial-grade cutting speeds

- » Features a space-saving 45 degree–angled design
- » Has dual tool clamps for simultaneous cutting and writing

The Venture can cut Smart Materials in both 13-inch and 25-inch widths, which makes it the only Cricut machine with adjustable widths. For comparison, the Maker and Explore machines (I cover both earlier in this chapter) can only cut materials up to 11.7 inches wide, so the Venture can handle designs that are twice as wide.

When it comes to length, the Venture can cut a single image up to 12 feet long. This means that you can create large, continuous designs — like a banner or a long decal — without having to break the design into sections. On top of that, the Venture can cut repeated images up to 75 feet long, making it perfect for bulk projects like creating a batch of shirts or decals for a business, team, or fundraiser without reloading material.

WARNING

The Cricut Venture has a few limitations compared to the Maker series. It doesn't work with QuickSwap tools, so you can't engrave, *deboss* (impress or imprint a design), or *perforate* (create a small series of cuts for easy folding or tearing) with it. It also can't cut thick materials like wood or fabric without a backing. For example, though the Maker can cut fabric directly using the Rotary Blade, the Venture needs the fabric to have a sticky backing and uses the Bonded-Fabric Blade instead. Another key difference is that the Venture doesn't have a Card Mat, which all other Cricut models offer. The Card Mat makes card-making much easier by holding pre-folded cards in place while cutting. If you're interested in card projects, check out Chapter 12 to see how other Cricut models handle card-making.

TIP

If you need more speed and cutting width, the Venture is a great option, but for more versatility, the Maker series may be a better choice.

The Venture is compatible with seven tools to write, score, *foil* (press metallic foil onto materials for a decorative effect), and more, including

- » Performance Fine-Point Blade
- » Foil Transfer Tool
- » Pens and Markers
- » Deep-Point Blade
- » Scoring Stylus
- » Bonded-Fabric Blade
- » Automatic Cutoff Blade

TIP

Keep in mind that the Cricut Venture isn't compatible with the Cricut Maker's QuickSwap tools — like the Scoring Wheel Tip, Debossing Tip, Engraving Tip, Perforation Blade, Knife Blade, and Wavy Blade — which means it's limited when it comes to handling different materials. However, some new accessories were made just for the Venture:

- » **Docking Stand:** The Docking Stand gives you a secure place to store your machine while keeping your workspace tidy. Now, you don't have to use the Docking Stand — it's optional — but it does come with some nice perks! It has easy-glide wheels with a safety lock, making it a breeze to move around and put away, plus it comes with built-in roll supports for Smart Materials. The antistatic catch baskets keep your cut projects from falling to the floor, and it even has handy hooks to store your mats. You can buy the Docking Stand on its own or as part of a bundle.

- » **Performance Machine Mats:** The Cricut Venture's Performance Machine Mats come in two sizes — 24 by 12 inches and 24 by 28 inches — and are available in LightGrip, StandardGrip, and StrongGrip varieties. However, no fabric or card mats are made specifically for the Venture, and mats from other Cricut machines won't work in it.

Where to Buy a Cricut

You can buy Cricut machines from various retailers, but shopping on Cricut's official website, www.cricut.com, offers several benefits. They provide better bundles, trusted sales, warranty protection, and often a free Cricut Access trial (see Chapter 6 for details). If you prefer to shop in person, check stores like Amazon, Best Buy, Costco, Hobby Lobby, Michaels, and Walmart.

Once you've got your new Cricut, flip to Chapter 3 to find out how to set it up. Happy crafting!

IN THIS CHAPTER

» **Powering up and connecting your Cricut**

» **Setting up your Cricut account and Design Space**

Chapter 3

Setting Up Your Cricut

Setting up your Cricut may seem a bit overwhelming at first, but don't worry — it's easier than it looks. Think of it like putting together a simple puzzle. With a little patience and the easy-to-follow steps in this chapter, you'll be crafting in no time. So, grab your machine, find a comfy spot, and get started on your crafting adventure!

Firing Up Your Cricut

Follow these steps to power up your Cricut:

1. Find the power adapter that came with your Cricut machine.

All Cricut machines use a two-part power adapter: a small white box with a cord and a second cord that connects to the wall plug. However, power adapters are model-specific, so be sure to use the one designed for your machine if you're purchasing a replacement.

2. Connect the two parts of the adapter.

The cords are designed to fit together in only one way, so you can't go wrong.

3. **Locate the power port on the back of your Cricut.**

   It's a small round hole that matches the end of the cord coming from the white box.

4. **Plug the cord into the power port on your Cricut (see Figure 3-1), and then plug the adapter into a wall outlet.**

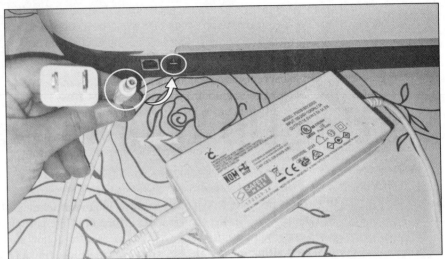

FIGURE 3-1: How to connect the power adapter to your Cricut.

Source: Kerri Adamczyk

Now your Cricut machine is powered up and ready to connect to your computer.

Syncing Your Cricut with Your Computer

You can connect your Cricut machine to your computer in two ways: with the included USB cable (for compatible models) or via Bluetooth for wireless convenience. The following sections cover how to set up each connection.

Connecting via USB cable

Follow these steps to connect your Cricut with a USB cable:

1. **Find the USB cable that came with your machine.**

   One end has a rectangular USB-A connector (for your computer), and the other has a square USB-B connector (for the Cricut).

2. **Plug the USB-A end into your computer and the USB-B end into the back of your Cricut (see Figure 3-2).**

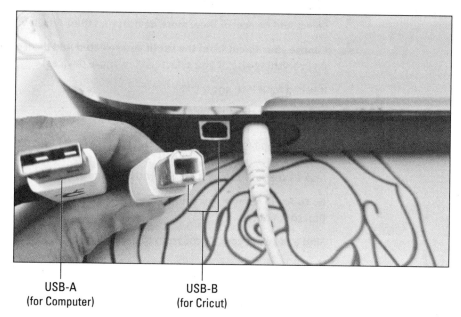

FIGURE 3-2: Where to plug in each end of the USB cable on your Cricut and computer.

USB-A (for Computer)   USB-B (for Cricut)

Source: Kerri Adamczyk

TIP

The plugs fit only one way, so if they don't go in, just flip them around. Once connected, your computer should recognize the Cricut.

Connecting via Bluetooth

For a clutter-free setup, you can connect your Cricut using Bluetooth.

REMEMBER

Cricut Joy and Cricut Joy Xtra both require Bluetooth, because they don't have a USB port.

Here's a quick guide to pairing on different devices. For more detailed instructions, visit Cricut's support website (https://help.cricut.com/hc/en-us).

For a Windows PC, follow these steps:

1. **Make sure your Cricut is powered on and within 10 to 15 feet of your computer.**

CHAPTER 3 **Setting Up Your Cricut** 25

2. **Go to Start > Settings > Bluetooth & devices on your computer and make sure Bluetooth is on.**

   If Bluetooth is off, toggle it on.

3. **Select Add device, or View more devices and then Add device.**

4. **Choose your Cricut from the list (if you selected Add device) or click on Everything else (if you selected View more devices).**

5. **If asked for a PIN, enter 0000.**

   This may apply to older models.

Follow these steps for a Mac:

1. **Make sure your Cricut is on and within range of your Mac.**

2. **Go to Apple Menu > System Preferences > Bluetooth and turn Bluetooth on.**

3. **Find and select your Cricut from the list.**

   If multiple devices appear, choose the one with your Cricut's Bluetooth device code, which is printed on the machine near the serial number.

4. **If asked for a PIN or pairing code, enter 0000.**

   This may apply to older models.

Follow these steps for iOS/Android:

1. **Be sure your Cricut is on and your mobile device is within range.**

2. **Open Settings > Bluetooth on your device.**

3. **Make sure Bluetooth is on and select your Cricut from the list.**

   If multiple devices appear, select the one with your Cricut's Bluetooth device code, which is printed on the machine near the serial number.

Once your desktop or mobile device is connected, head back to Design Space for the final setup, where your machine should now show up as connected. (Flip to Part 2 for details on Cricut Design Space.)

TIP Bluetooth may not work as well on metal surfaces, which can interfere with the signal. Place your Cricut and connected device on a nonmetal surface for a better connection.

Creating Your Cricut Account

Before diving into crafting, you'll need a Cricut account. This is your personal login for Cricut Design Space (see Part 2), where all the magic happens! Creating an account means you'll have access to thousands of designs, project ideas, and tools to make crafting easier and more fun. Plus, you can save your work and return to it later — perfect if you need a quick break. You can also access your account on the Cricut Design Space mobile app, allowing you to manage your projects from your phone or tablet anytime.

Consider the following benefits of your Cricut account:

- Track all your purchases on Cricut.com.
- Manage your Cricut Access subscription. (Flip to Chapter 6 to discover all the perks Cricut Access offers.)
- Store payment info for easy design purchases.
- Save purchased designs for quick access.

Create your account by following these steps:

1. **Open your web browser and go to Myaccount.Cricut.com.**
2. **Click on Create Cricut ID (see Figure 3-3).**
3. **Fill in your email, password, name, country, and phone number.**
4. **Read the Cricut Terms of Use and Privacy Policy, and then check the box to agree.**

   You can also opt in to emails and text messages from Cricut.
5. **Click Create Cricut ID.**

That's it! You're ready to explore Cricut Design Space and start bringing your creative ideas to life.

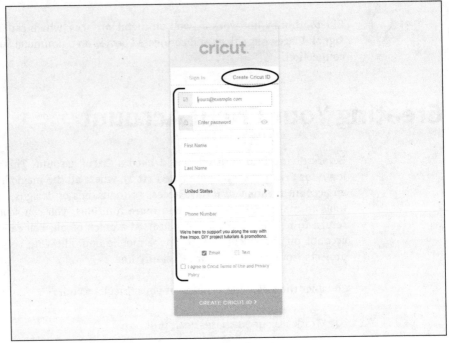

FIGURE 3-3: To create a new account, go to Myaccount.Cricut.com, click on Create Cricut ID, and fill in the form.

Source: myaccount.cricut.com

Getting Cricut Design Space Up and Running

With your Cricut account set up, it's time to install Cricut Design Space — your digital crafting playground. Here's where you'll design projects, choose materials, and send creations to your Cricut machine.

Design Space works with all current Cricut machines, including the Joy, Explore, Maker, and Venture series (see Chapter 2). If you're using one of these machines, you're good to go!

TECHNICAL STUFF

If you have an older Cricut machine released before the Explore series (such as the Cricut Expression or Cricut Cake), it won't work with Cricut Design Space. These models relied on Cricut Craft Room, which was discontinued in July 2018. Since then, they have had no official software support, meaning that they can only be used with physical cartridges unless modified with third-party solutions.

The following sections get you started; flip to Part 2 for full details on Cricut Design Space.

Meeting system and internet connection requirements

Before installing Design Space, make sure your device meets these requirements:

- » **Windows:** Windows 10 or later, Intel Dual-Core or equivalent AMD processor, 4 gigabytes (GB) RAM, 2GB free disk space
- » **Mac:** macOS 11 or later, 1.83 gigahertz (GHz) CPU, 4GB RAM, 2GB free disk space
- » **iOS:** iOS 14 or later (iPhone 6s or newer, iPad Air 2 or later)
- » **Android:** Android 8.0 or later, 2GB RAM, 2GB free disk space

Design Space is not compatible with Chromebook computers, because it requires a Windows or Mac operating system.

To utilize Cricut Design Space fully, you need a high-speed internet connection to sign in, download, install, and use certain functions. However, if you're using the desktop version or the iOS app, you can use the offline feature for designing projects without an internet connection. This option is currently not available on Android devices. Find out more about working off-line in Cricut Design Space later in this chapter.

Installing Design Space on different devices

For Windows and Mac, follow these steps:

1. **Go to** design.cricut.com.
2. **Click the Search bar and choose your Cricut model from the drop-down list.**
3. **To download Design Space for Windows or Mac, agree to the terms of use and click Download (see Figure 3-4).**
4. **Double-click the installer file and follow the instructions.**

   If you don't see the file to install, check your Downloads folder. After Design Space is installed, you'll see a shortcut on your desktop.

Follow these steps for iOS:

1. **Open the App Store and search for Cricut Design Space.**
2. **Download the app and log in to your Cricut account.**

FIGURE 3-4: Downloading Cricut Design Space from design.cricut.com.

Source: design.cricut.com

Follow these steps for Android:

1. **Open Google Play and search for Cricut Design Space (see Figure 3-5).**
2. **Install the app and log in to your Cricut account.**

FIGURE 3-5: Google Play with Cricut Design Space displayed.

Source: Cricut.com

30 PART 1 Getting Started with Your Cricut

Navigating the Home screen

Upon logging in to Design Space, you'll land on the Home screen, which offers inspiration and helpful tools, as shown in Figure 3-6. You can switch between the Home screen and your designs on the Canvas tab, much like using tabs in a browser.

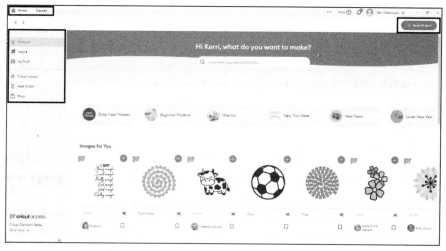

FIGURE 3-6:
The Home screen in Cricut Design Space.

Source: design.cricut.com

REMEMBER

On the left side of the Home screen, you'll find the following tabs:

- **Discover:** Explore new projects, images, fonts, and more.
- **Inspire:** Browse through tons of project ideas for all skill levels.
- **My Stuff:** Find your saved and bookmarked images and projects.
- **Cricut Access:** Manage your subscription for exclusive content. Flip to Chapter 6 to discover all the perks included in this optional paid subscription.
- **Heat Guide:** Use the Heat Guide shown in Figure 3-7 to quickly find the recommended time and temperature settings for your heat transfer projects. Select your heat press type, heat transfer material, and base material to get tailored instructions. For more details on working with heat transfer projects, check out Chapters 15 and 16.
- **Shop:** Go directly to cricut.com, where you can shop for all the latest tools and materials.

CHAPTER 3 **Setting Up Your Cricut** 31

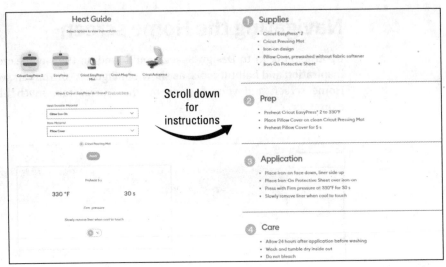

FIGURE 3-7: Using the Heat Guide in Cricut Design Space.

Source: design.cricut.com

Finding and adjusting your settings

After exploring the Home screen, you can tweak your settings to get the most out of Design Space. It's a good idea to adjust your settings right away because the software will remember your preferences, keeping your workspace just the way you like it every time you log in.

Follow these steps, shown in Figure 3-8, to find and adjust your settings in Design Space:

1. **Click on the drop-down menu next to your name in the upper-right corner of the screen.**
2. **Select Settings from the drop-down menu.**
3. **Click through the different tabs — General, Content, Machines, Canvas, Load Type, Notifications, and System — to adjust your preferences.**
4. **When you're finished, click Done to save your settings for future use.**

REMEMBER

Here are some important settings worth exploring:

» **Register a new machine:** Use the New Product Setup option under Machines to set up and register your Cricut machine.

» **Calibrate your machine for precise cuts:** Under Machines, select Machine Calibration and follow the prompts to calibrate your Cricut.

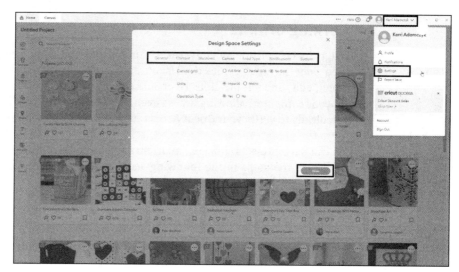

FIGURE 3-8: Finding and adjusting your Design Space settings.

Source: design.cricut.com

- » **Set your preferred units:** Change the unit type under Canvas to Imperial (inches) or Metric (centimeters) to match your preference.

- » **Hide grid lines for a cleaner Canvas:** If the grid lines on your Canvas drive you nuts, you can permanently hide them in the Canvas settings. Just select No Grid for a blank background.

TIP

You can also adjust the grid lines by clicking on the small square between the two zeros, found where the rulers intersect on the top and left side of the Canvas.

- » **Filter out mature content:** Don't want to see mature-themed designs? Head to the Content settings and uncheck categories like Strong Language, Alcohol, or Violence.

- » **Save projects off-line:** Want to work somewhere without internet access, such as a craft fair? Under General, select Cloud & Computer to save projects both online and to your device locally. That way, when you don't have an internet connection, you can work on any projects saved to your computer.

These small adjustments can make a big difference in your crafting experience.

Saving for online or offline use

TIP

Because Design Space is cloud-based, you can start a project on one device and pick it up on another. For example, you can begin designing on your tablet and complete the project on your desktop, with all your designs and projects accessible from any compatible computer or mobile device.

CHAPTER 3 **Setting Up Your Cricut** 33

Working off-line

Design Space's offline mode is perfect for crafting on the go, like at craft fairs, or when your internet connection is unreliable. Once you're signed in, you can design, edit, and cut off-line. To enable this, save your project to both the cloud and your computer, allowing access even without internet. You'll need to connect periodically to verify your Cricut Access subscription and keep the app up-to-date.

You can save projects, images, and fonts for offline use in Cricut Design Space. Just follow the steps in the following sections to keep them accessible anytime, even without an internet connection.

Saving projects for offline use

Here's how to save your projects for offline access so that you can work on them anytime:

1. Go to the My Stuff page (see Figure 3-9).

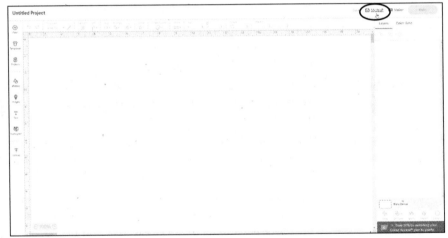

FIGURE 3-9: Finding the My Stuff page on the Design Space Canvas.

Source: design.cricut.com

2. Click on the three dots on the project tile you'd like to save (see Figure 3-10).

3. Switch the Save for Offline toggle on.

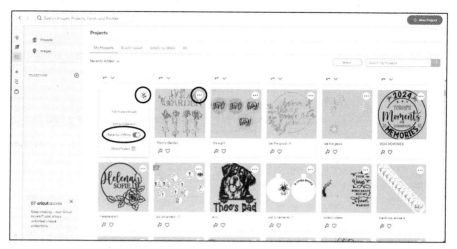

FIGURE 3-10: Click on the three dots on a project tile to enable the Save for Offline toggle.

Source: design.cricut.com

When you save your first project offline in Design Space for desktop, you'll see a settings dialog box asking where to save projects (see Figure 3-11).

» **Save to Cloud & Computer:** Projects are saved to both your computer and the cloud for offline use by default if you click on this setting.

» **Save to Cloud Only:** Projects are saved only to the cloud, so they won't be available when you're off-line.

You can update these settings anytime in the Design Space menu under Settings.

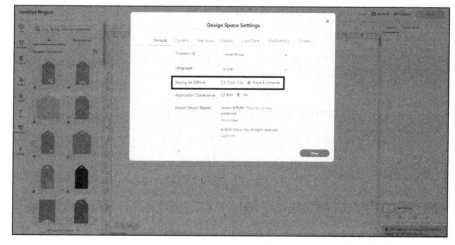

FIGURE 3-11: Locating the Save for Offline settings in Design Space under Settings.

Source: design.cricut.com

CHAPTER 3 **Setting Up Your Cricut** 35

Saving images for offline use

You can save images for offline use by bookmarking them in Design Space. This allows you to access them without an internet connection. Follow these steps to bookmark images for offline use:

1. Go to the Images tab and search for the image you'd like to save.
2. Hover over the image tile and click the bookmark icon that appears (a small ribbon); see Figure 3-12.

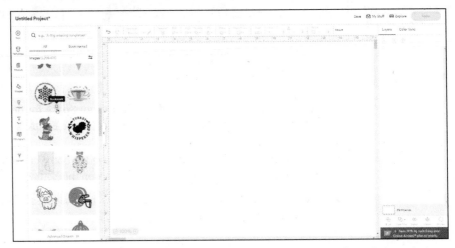

FIGURE 3-12: Bookmarking an image.

Source: design.cricut.com

3. To access your saved images off-line, go to My Stuff, select Images, and then choose Bookmarked (see Figure 3-13).

REMEMBER

You can view bookmarked images off-line, but specific image collections may not be accessible without an internet connection.

Saving fonts for offline use

Design Space offers two types of fonts: System fonts and Cricut fonts. System fonts are already installed on your computer, so no download is needed.

To find your bookmarked images, click on Images on the left, and then Bookmarked.

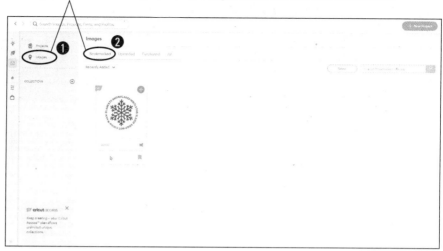

FIGURE 3-13:
Finding your bookmarked images under the My Stuff tab.

Source: design.cricut.com

To save Cricut fonts for offline use, follow these steps:

1. **Open the Fonts menu on the Design Space Canvas.**
2. **Find the font you'd like to save off-line.**

   Hover over it, and a download button will appear on the right side (see Figure 3-14).

3. **Click the download button to save the font for offline access.**

   Once a font is saved for offline use, a small computer icon will appear next to it to confirm it's downloaded (you can see the icon in Figure 3-14).

After your Cricut is set up and ready to go, you're all set to dive into Cricut Design Space and start creating. In Chapter 7, you'll pick up right where you left off by exploring the Design Space Canvas, where you'll find out how to start a project from scratch, navigate the Canvas, and discover new images and designs to bring your ideas to life.

CHAPTER 3 Setting Up Your Cricut   37

2. A small computer icon appears next to the font, confirming it's downloaded and ready for offline use.

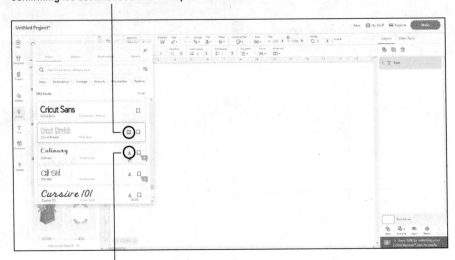

FIGURE 3-14: Finding the font download button, and the computer icon, which appears after a Cricut font is saved for offline use.

1. Click the download button to save the font for offline access.

Source: design.cricut.com

IN THIS CHAPTER

» Exploring essential Cricut tools

» Choosing the right mat for your needs

» Selecting Smart Materials and Cricut Maker tools

» Using Cricut blades, styluses, pens, markers, and foil transfer tools

» Picking a heat press and blanks

Chapter 4

Checking Out Cricut Tools and Materials

Crafting with Cricut becomes a breeze when you have the right tools at your fingertips. Whether you're cutting vinyl, scoring cards, or layering iron-on designs, using the right tools helps you work smarter and achieve cleaner, more professional results. In this chapter, you discover the essential tools every Cricut user needs, along with advanced options to level up your skills. Plus, you'll explore handy extras like heat presses and customizable surfaces (blanks), including mugs, shirts, totes, and more.

Looking at Tools and Accessories for All Cricut Machines

Buying your first Cricut machine is just the beginning. With so many tools and materials to choose from, it can be overwhelming to figure out what you really *need.* This section clears up the confusion by outlining the essential tools and explaining how to use them, no matter which Cricut model you have. Although some tools are specific to certain machines, these are the must-have basics that will get you started on any Cricut project. Curious about what to pick up alongside your new machine? Keep reading to find out.

Starting with the Cricut Essential Tool Set

First, grab the Cricut Essential Tool Set. This seven-piece set comes with almost every essential tool for using your Cricut, regardless of the model. The Cricut Essential Tool Set includes the following tools:

- **Hook Tweezers:** A fancy pair of tweezers for handling tiny vinyl pieces without messing up your design.
- **Hook Weeder:** Your new best friend for picking out those stubborn little bits of vinyl when weeding.
- **Portable Trimmer:** Also known as a paper cutter, a trimmer is used to measure and cut your materials. The Cricut brand trimmer has a swing-out arm with a ruler, making it easier to measure long pieces.
- **Scissors:** Great for cutting a variety of materials like vinyl, paper, and fabric.
- **Scoring Stylus:** A tool used to create fold lines in paper and other materials.
- **Scraper:** Perfect for smoothing out vinyl and removing it from the mat. Also handy for scraping mats clean.
- **Spatula:** A tiny pancake flipper–like tool that helps you lift delicate materials without tearing or bending them.

Don't overpay for tools! I found the Cricut Essential Tool Kit for as low as $27.49 on Cricut.com and as high as $54.99 at Michaels — for the exact same kit! You can also pick up individual tools like weeding hooks, scissors, and scrapers at Dollar Tree. Cricut makes its own tools, but many off-brand alternatives work just as well — often for far less money. Check reviews and make sure the tools are compatible with your Cricut model before buying.

Keep in mind that using non-Cricut branded tools may affect your machine's warranty, so it's wise to review those terms carefully before buying.

Considering other essentials

In addition to the Cricut Essential Tool Set, I recommend buying a few other essentials:

>> **Brayer:** Think of it as a mini rolling pin. It helps your material stick firmly to the mat and smooths out bubbles and wrinkles.

>> **Mats:** Mats are a must-have for any Cricut machine. They hold your material in place during cutting. Mats come in different sizes and stickiness levels, (see the section "Distinquishing types of mats" later in this chapter).

>> **Lint roller:** An invaluable tool for removing lint or fur from fabrics before applying heat transfer vinyl (HTV). It's also great for preventing round objects like wine glasses from rolling while applying vinyl decals, or for picking up small debris from your mats.

>> **Rubbing alcohol:** Perfect for cleaning hard surfaces like glass before applying vinyl. It cleans and degreases, ensuring that your vinyl has a clean surface to stick to.

>> **Lint-free wipes:** Clean surfaces with alcohol without leaving fuzz behind. Coffee filters are cheap, effective, and easy to find.

>> **Ruler:** Used for accurately measuring your materials so that you know how big to resize your design in Cricut Design Space.

>> **Painter's tape:** For materials that need a stronger hold on the mat, like balsa wood or engraving projects, use painter's or masking tape to hold down the edges. Just make sure not to tape over the area where your design will go.

Choosing the Right Cricut Mat

After you have your essential tools (see the preceding section), it's time for another crucial part of Cricut crafting: choosing the right mat. Cricut mats hold your material in place while your machine cuts it.

Distinguishing types of mats

Each mat has a different level of stickiness, designed to grip specific types of materials. Here's a quick guide to help you select the right mat for your project:

>> **LightGrip Mat (blue):** Best for light materials like printer paper, thin cardstock, vellum, and construction paper. The gentle stick keeps things in place without tearing.

>> **StandardGrip Mat (green):** Great for everyday use. Works with vinyl, iron-on vinyl (HTV), medium cardstock, and printable vinyl. It holds things well but still lets you peel them off easily.

CHAPTER 4 **Checking Out Cricut Tools and Materials** 41

- **StrongGrip Mat (purple):** Super sticky — perfect for heavier materials like chipboard, leather, magnetic sheets, and Glitter Iron-On.
- **FabricGrip Mat (pink):** Made for cutting fabric with the Rotary Blade or Bonded-Fabric Blade. It holds fabric like cotton or felt firmly but won't leave a sticky mess behind.

The FabricGrip Mat is compatible only with Cricut Maker and Cricut Explore machines.

- **Card Mat:** Made just for cards. Slide your card into the little pocket and let your Cricut cut or write on the front. Works with all Cricut Insert and Cutaway Cards. (Check out Chapter 12 for a step-by-step guide to making cards.)

Mats naturally lose their stickiness over time, but that doesn't mean you have to throw them out! A worn StrongGrip Mat can act more like a StandardGrip Mat, and an old StandardGrip Mat can work like a LightGrip Mat, which can still be perfect for projects requiring less tack. Simple cleaning methods can help bring your mats back to life. Visit Chapter 5 for guidance on how to clean and care for your mats.

Picking the right size mat for your machine

Cricut mats aren't a one-size-fits-all tool. You need to buy the right size mat for your machine. Check out this list to find out which size mats go with your machine:

- **12-x-12-inch mat:** For Maker/Explore series
- **12-x-24-inch mat:** For Maker/Explore series
- **2-x-2-inch Card Mat:** For Maker/Explore series
- **4.5-x-12-inch mat:** For Cricut Joy
- **4.5-x-6.25-inch Card Mat:** For Cricut Joy
- **8.5-x-12-inch mat:** For Cricut Joy Xtra
- **4.7-x-6.6-inch Card Mat:** For Cricut Joy Xtra
- **24-x-12-inch Performance Machine Mat:** For Cricut Venture
- **24-x-28-inch Performance Machine Mat:** For Cricut Venture

Surveying Smart Materials

Normally, Cricut machines need a mat to hold material in place while cutting, but Smart Materials are the exception. You can load these special materials directly into your machine and start cutting right away. Another great perk of Smart Materials is that they allow you to make longer continuous cuts, which is perfect for big projects like wall decals, banners, and signs.

Smart Materials are compatible only with the following Cricut machines:

- Cricut Maker 4
- Cricut Maker 3
- Cricut Explore 4
- Cricut Explore 3
- Cricut Joy Xtra
- Cricut Joy
- Cricut Venture

Smart Materials are designed to be cut without a mat on compatible Cricut machines, saving time and setup. Cricut's Smart Materials include Permanent and Removable Smart Vinyl for long-lasting or temporary projects, plus several Smart Iron-On types — like Everyday, Glitter, Glitter Mesh, and Holographic — for customizing fabric. You'll also find Smart Label Paper (dissolvable or writable), Smart Paper Sticker Cardstock for making easy stickers, and Smart Stencil for clean, reusable paint stencils.

Although Smart Materials offer the convenience of mat-free cutting, they typically come at a higher price than standard vinyl and HTV. Using these materials may be "Smart" because you don't need a mat, but is cutting without a mat really worth the extra cost? That's something to consider when deciding which materials to use for your projects.

Cutting with Basic Blades

When it comes to getting the perfect cut on your Cricut projects, the blade you use makes all the difference. Whether you're slicing through delicate paper or tough leather, there's a blade for every task. I cover the more advanced blades and machine-specific tools later in this chapter, but I start with the basics in this section. The two most common blades you'll use are the Deep-Point Blade and the Fine-Point Blade:

- » **Deep-Point Blade:** Great for thick materials like heavy cardstock, magnetic sheets, chipboard, and cardboard. It has a 60-degree angle for deeper cuts and works with all Cricut Maker, Explore, and Venture machines.

    You can't use a Deep-Point Blade in any of the Cricut Joy machines.

- » **Fine-Point Blade:** This blade with a 45-degree angle is your go-to blade for most projects. It's perfect for cutting through popular materials like paper, vinyl, and iron-on. Every Cricut machine comes with a Fine-Point Blade, although the name may change slightly depending on the machine. For example, the Cricut Explore/Maker series uses the Premium Fine-Point Blade, the Cricut Venture uses the Performance Fine-Point Blade, and the Cricut Joy and Joy Xtra use the Cricut Joy Blade. Although they perform similar functions, each is designed to fit its specific machine.

Each blade fits into a *blade housing*, which is a small piece that holds the blade securely in place. It's important to match the right blade with the right housing: Premium Fine-Point Blades must always be used in the Premium Fine-Point Housing, and the Deep-Point Blade has its own specialized housing. And note that all blades must be replaced over time. For more tips on when and how to replace your blades, flip to Chapter 5.

Cricut-branded blades and housings are available through various retailers, but you can often score big savings by purchasing off-brand blades. For example, `Cricut.com` charges $14.99 for a single Premium Fine-Point Replacement Blade, but a 20-pack of off-brand blades on Amazon costs just $7.49.

Although off-brand blades can be a great way to save money, the quality may vary, but at 20 blades for less than the price of one, it's an easy gamble. Even if only a few work as well as Cricut's, you're still saving a ton. Just check reviews before buying to make sure you're getting a decent batch.

Writing and Drawing with Pens and Markers

Every Cricut machine can write or draw using a variety of pens and markers, and Cricut offers its own brand of writing tools with several colors and types to choose from. Explore the versatility of these pens and markers through hands-on projects in Chapters 10 and 12.

Looking at Cricut Pens and Markers

Some popular types of Cricut Pens and Markers include

- » **Everyday Pens:** Great for everyday projects like cards and labels.
- » **Extra Fine and Fine Point Pens:** Best for detailed or general writing.
- » **Glitter Gel and Metallic Pens:** Add sparkle or shine to your designs.
- » **Infusible Ink Pens and Markers:** Draw custom designs that permanently transfer to compatible blanks with heat.

Let your child draw a picture on laser copy paper, then heat press it onto a mug for a meaningful gift. Just be sure to skip the handwriting or have Cricut write and mirror your text, as your design transfers in reverse. See Chapter 16 for full steps.

- » **Opaque Gel Pens:** Show up well on dark paper.
- » **Permanent Markers:** For long-lasting results.
- » **Washable Fabric Pen:** Useful for making fabric that needs cutting because the marks wash out easily.
- » **Watercolor Marker & Brush Set:** Creates watercolor effects with no paint needed.

Always test your pen on scrap paper first to avoid dry or clogged pens mid-project.

Cricut pens work well, but they can be pricey. I love the Craverland Universal Pen Adapter Set on Amazon — it lets you use almost any pen or marker with your Cricut. Want to see how it works? Check out my quick tutorial on YouTube (https://youtu.be/uzOVySRHDqw).

Just keep in mind that using non-Cricut tools may void your warranty, so proceed with caution if that's a concern.

How to use Cricut Pens and Markers

Follow these steps in Cricut Design Space (see Part 2) to put your pens and markers to good use:

1. **Select the type of pen or marker.**

   Pick a Cricut Pen type (like Fine Point, Glitter Gel, or Infusible Ink), or use a universal pen adapter to work with non-Cricut pens.

CHAPTER 4 **Checking Out Cricut Tools and Materials** 45

2. Prepare your design in Design Space.

Click on the parts you want drawn and change the operation from Basic Cut to Pen.

3. Select and adjust fonts.

Use a handwriting font for connected letters or a regular font for outlined text. Change the font's operation to Pen and adjust size and alignment.

TIP

Use the Attach tool to keep your text or drawings exactly where you want them in relation to other design elements. This is especially important for designs that involve both drawing and cutting. For detailed guidance on using the Attach feature, see Chapter 8.

4. Select your pen type and color in Design Space.

Click on the Color box next to the Operation drop-down menu to select your pen type. A large list of pen options will appear. First, select the type of pen, such as F-Fine Point (0.4mm), and then choose the color you want. Always match the pen type in Design Space to what you're using. This helps your Cricut apply the right pressure.

5. Click Make.

Choose your base material, such as Light Cardstock – 65lb. Design Space will guide you through loading instructions.

6. Load tools and materials.

Follow these steps depending on your Cricut machine.

- **For Cricut models with two clamps (A and B):** Open clamp A, which is typically used for pens and markers. Insert your chosen pen or marker until it clicks into place, then close the clamp.

- **For Cricut Joy:** Use the single clamp for both pens and blades. Open the clamp, insert the pen, and ensure that it's securely in place before closing the clamp.

Place your material on the mat, align it with the guides, and press the Load button.

TIP

Use smooth, flat materials for best results. Textured materials can cause uneven lines or make it difficult for the pen to transfer ink consistently.

7. Start drawing.

Press the Go button. Keep an eye on your Cricut machine to make sure that the pen doesn't run out of ink and that the material is held firmly in place on the mat.

46 PART 1 Getting Started with Your Cricut

8. **Unload and finish.**

   Press Unload and remove your project. Then proceed as follows depending on your Cricut machine.

   - **For Cricut models with two clamps (A and B):** If further steps such as cutting are required, your blade should already be in place in clamp B, so you can proceed directly with the next phase of your project without needing to swap tools.

   - **For Cricut Joy:** If your project requires cutting after drawing, replace the pen with the cutting blade and continue with your project.

TIP

Keep your Cricut pens stored tip-down in a cool, dry spot with their caps on. This helps the ink stay ready at the tip and stops the pens from drying out.

Adding Accents with a Foil Transfer Kit

The Foil Transfer Kit lets you add stunning foil accents to Cricut projects like cards, invitations, and gift boxes. The kit includes everything you need to get started:

» **1 Foil Transfer Tool Housing:** The main holder that attaches to your Cricut machine. It securely holds the foil transfer tips and applies pressure to transfer foil designs onto your material.

» **3 interchangeable Foil Transfer Tips:** These tips determine the thickness of the foil lines in your design. Each tip is marked with lines for easy identification:

   - **Fine Tip (one line):** Best for detailed designs and intricate text.
   - **Medium Tip (two lines):** Great for standard designs, offering a balance of detail and visibility.
   - **Bold Tip (three lines):** Ideal for thicker accents and bold foil effects.

» **12 Foil Transfer Sheets:** Special metallic sheets that react to pressure from the Foil Transfer Tool, leaving behind a shiny foil design. Available in various colors and can be purchased separately.

» **Tape:** Used to hold the foil sheet in place during the transfer process.

CHAPTER 4 Checking Out Cricut Tools and Materials   47

The Foil Transfer Tool is compatible with the following Cricut machines:

- Cricut Maker 4
- Cricut Maker 3
- Cricut Maker
- Cricut Explore 4
- Cricut Explore 3
- Cricut Explore Air 2
- Cricut Venture

If you have a Cricut Joy or Joy Xtra, you'll need the Cricut Joy Foil Transfer Kit, designed just for those machines.

Foiling is easy with Cricut when you follow these simple steps:

1. **Set up your design.**

   In Cricut Design Space, select the elements of your design that you want to foil.

   Foil doesn't work well for large filled-in designs — it's best used for lines, text, and outlines.

   Click on the Operation drop-down menu at the top and change it from Basic Cut to Foil. Choose the correct tip size (Fine, Medium, or Bold).

2. **Click Make and select your material.**

   Select your base material. Design Space will automatically hide materials that aren't compatible with the Foil Transfer Tool, so you can only select materials that work for foiling.

3. **Prepare your material.**

   Follow the on-screen instructions in Design Space for loading tools and materials. Place your base material (such as cardstock) onto a Cricut cutting mat.

   Cut a piece of foil slightly larger than your design area. Place the foil sheet shiny side up over your material. Secure all edges using the provided tape to keep it flat and prevent shifting.

   Dust or fingerprints can cause uneven transfers, so handle foil carefully by the edges.

4. **Insert the Foil Transfer Tool.**

   Insert the selected foil tip (Fine, Medium, or Bold) into the Foil Transfer Tool Housing. Place the housing into Clamp B of your Cricut machine.

5. **Load the mat and begin the foil transfer.**

   Load the mat into the machine and press Go when prompted in Design Space. The machine will apply precise pressure to transfer the foil onto your material.

6. **Reveal your design.**

   Don't unload the mat yet if additional cutting is required.

   If your work is complete, unload your mat and carefully remove the tape and foil sheet to reveal your design.

7. **Complete additional steps (if needed).**

   If your project includes cutting, Design Space will prompt you to replace the foil tool with a blade (only needed for Cricut Joy, as other machines have separate clamps).

   Once cutting is done, unload the mat and remove your project.

Store your foil sheets flat in a folder or protective sleeve to prevent creases.

TIP

Making Lines with the Scoring Stylus

The Scoring Stylus is a tool designed to add precise score lines to your projects, making it easy to create clean folds in materials like cardstock, paper, and poster board. It's a popular choice for crafting projects like greeting cards, envelopes, 3-D paper crafts, and boxes.

The Scoring Stylus is not to be confused with the Scoring Wheels. They both create fold lines, but they function differently:

» The Scoring Stylus fits into Clamp A and works with all machines from the Explore, Maker, and Venture series.

» The Scoring Wheels (see the later section "QuickSwap tools") are exclusive to Cricut Maker models. Unlike the Stylus, the wheels roll across the material, creating deeper, more defined score lines, especially on thick materials.

Use the Scoring Stylus if

- » You're working with thin paper or lightweight cardstock that may tear under too much pressure.
- » You want to avoid swapping tools, since the stylus fits in Clamp A, leaving your blade in place.
- » Your project needs only light score lines and doesn't require deep folds.
- » You don't have a Cricut Maker, so your machine isn't compatible with the Scoring Wheel.

Use the Single Scoring Wheel if

- » You're working with medium to heavy cardstock, kraft board, or coated materials that need deeper, more defined folds.
- » You need precise, crisp score lines that help prevent cracking on thick paper.

TIP

If Cricut Design Space suggests a Scoring Wheel on the Make screen but you prefer to use the Scoring Stylus, click Edit Tools and select Scoring Stylus before continuing. See Part 2 for details on working in Cricut Design Space.

The Scoring Stylus is compatible with the following Cricut machines:

- » Cricut Maker 4
- » Cricut Maker 3
- » Cricut Maker
- » Cricut Explore 4
- » Cricut Explore 3
- » Cricut Explore Air 2
- » Cricut Venture

Follow this step-by-step guide to using the Scoring Stylus for clean, precise fold lines:

1. **Add a score line to your design.**

    If you're using a Cricut Access Project, score lines are already built into the file — just insert the Scoring Stylus when prompted. Need help finding Cricut Access projects? Flip to Chapter 7 to discover new projects and images to work with.

If you're designing your own project, you'll need to add a score line manually:

- Click Shapes in the Design panel on the left.
- Select the score line to place it on your canvas. It looks like a vertical line in the upper-left corner of the Shapes menu.
- Place the score line where you want the fold to be and resize or rotate as needed.

2. **Align and attach the score line.**

To center the score line on a shape (like a card or box panel), select both the shape and the score line and click Align > Center in the top menu.

Once the score line is positioned correctly, highlight both the shape and the score line and click Attach to link them together.

3. **Click Make and select your material.**

Click Make to proceed to the Make Screen. Select your base material (such as Cardstock) from the list.

4. **Select the Scoring Stylus in Design Space (if needed).**

If Design Space prompts you to use the Scoring Wheel but you want to use the Scoring Stylus instead:

- Click Edit Tools next to the tool selection.
- Select Scoring Stylus instead of Single Scoring Wheel.
- Click Apply to confirm the change.

Design Space will now update the instructions to load the Scoring Stylus into Clamp A.

5. **Prepare your material.**

Place your material (such as cardstock, paper, or poster board) on a StandardGrip or LightGrip mat and press it down smoothly.

6. **Insert the Scoring Stylus.**

Open Clamp A on your Cricut machine. Hold the clamp open while inserting the Scoring Stylus, pushing down until you hear a click and the arrow on the stylus disappears. Close Clamp A securely.

Now your Scoring Stylus is ready to create fold lines for cards, envelopes, gift boxes, and 3-D paper crafts!

Staying Sharp with the Bonded-Fabric Blade

The Bonded-Fabric Blade is specially designed for cutting fabrics that have been prepped with an iron-on backing, known as *interfacing*. This preparation step is crucial as it stabilizes the fabric, helping you get clean, fray-free cuts. This tool is perfect for creating appliqués, sewing patterns, and fabric details. Although it works similarly to the Fine-Point Blade (see the earlier section "Cutting with Basic Blades"), the Bonded-Fabric Blade is specifically made for bonded fabrics.

Both the blade and the mat you'll use with it are pink. The Bonded-Fabric Blade pops into its own housing, just like other Cricut blades, so it's easy to switch out when needed.

The Bonded-Fabric Blade and the Rotary Blade are both fabric-cutting tools, but the Rotary Blade is designed for unbonded fabrics, and the Bonded-Fabric Blade is for bonded materials. The Rotary Blade, which I cover in the later section "Specialty blades" as part of the Maker series tools, is available only for the Cricut Maker, Cricut Maker 3, and Cricut Maker 4.

The Bonded-Fabric Blade and its housing are available for purchase directly from Cricut's official website or through third-party retailers like Amazon. It's important to note that though the housing for the blade is reusable, the blades themselves can dull over time and will eventually need to be replaced. You can purchase replacement blades separately.

Compatible machines for the Bonded-Fabric Blade include the following:

- Cricut Maker 4
- Cricut Maker 3
- Cricut Maker
- Cricut Explore 4
- Cricut Explore 3
- Cricut Explore Air 2
- Cricut Venture

For best results with your Bonded-Fabric Blade, follow these steps:

1. **Prepare your fabric.**

   Begin by ironing interfacing onto the back of your fabric. Place the rough side of the interfacing against the wrong side (back) of the fabric.

   Trim any excess interfacing around the edges of your fabric so that the interfacing fully covers the area to be cut but does not extend beyond the fabric edges.

2. **Prepare the cutting mat.**

   Place the fabric on the FabricGrip Mat with the interfaced side facing down and the fabric side facing up. This orientation ensures that the blade cuts the fabric and not the interfacing first.

   Use a brayer to firmly stick the fabric to the mat, ensuring that there are no wrinkles or bubbles.

3. **Set up the machine.**

   Insert the Bonded-Fabric Blade into Clamp B of your Cricut machine. Set the material type to Bonded Fabric in Cricut Design Space.

4. **Cut the fabric.**

   Load the mat into the Cricut machine by aligning it with the mat guides and pressing the Load button. Once the mat is loaded, press Go to begin the cut.

Trying Out Cricut Maker Series Tools

The Cricut Maker series is known for its versatility, thanks to the Adaptive Tool System. This system allows the Maker, Maker 3, and Maker 4 to use a variety of tools that can be easily switched out depending on your project needs.

REMEMBER

With these specialty tools and blades, the Cricut Maker series can handle anything from delicate paper crafts to tough, rugged materials, giving you the flexibility to create nearly any project.

QuickSwap tools

QuickSwap tools are a set of interchangeable tool tips that snap into one housing, called the QuickSwap Housing. This housing lets you quickly switch tools, making it easy to change up your projects without needing multiple blade housings.

You can purchase these tools individually or in bundled sets, either directly from Cricut.com or through third-party sellers. If you already own a QuickSwap Housing, you can buy just the individual tool tips to expand your collection.

Types of QuickSwap tools

The QuickSwap Tools Everything Bundle includes the following interchangeable tools:

>> **Debossing Tip:** The Debossing Tip presses intricate designs into materials, creating custom patterns and details on materials like foil cardstock and shimmer paper. It's great for making elegant wedding cards and personalized gift tags. To use the Debossing Tip, select Deboss from the Operation drop-down menu at the top of your Canvas in Cricut Design Space. Position the design where you want the debossing to appear on the mat preview in the Prepare screen after clicking Make. Then insert the Debossing Tip into Clamp B, and follow the prompts. Want to see this tool in action? Flip to Chapter 22 for a hands-on project.

>> **Engraving Tip:** The Engraving Tip engraves text, monograms, or designs on materials like aluminum sheets or anodized aluminum. It's perfect for crafting pet tags or personalized jewelry. To engrave text or images in Design Space, select Engrave in the Operation drop-down menu at the top of your Canvas. Position the design where you want the engraving to appear on the mat preview in the Prepare Screen after clicking Make. For best results, choose bold fonts and simple designs, as fine details may not engrave clearly. Turn to Chapter 22 for a full tutorial.

>> **Perforation Blade:** The Perforation Blade creates evenly spaced perforation lines, making it easy to produce clean tearaway designs like coupons or raffle tickets. You can also find ready-to-cut raffle ticket designs by searching "raffle tickets" in the Projects library in Design Space.

>> **Single Scoring Wheel and Double Scoring Wheel:** The Single Scoring Wheel makes deep single-line scores on light uncoated materials like crepe paper and light cardstock, perfect for greeting cards, paper flowers, and origami designs.

The Double Scoring Wheel creates two parallel score lines on heavier coated materials like cardboard and poster board, ideal for pop-up cards and custom boxes.

To create a score line in Design Space, add a Score Line from the Shapes panel, adjust its size, and attach it to your base shape before cutting. After selecting your base material, Design Space automatically recommends the correct scoring tool. For example, setting the material to Flat Cardboard prompts you to load the Double Scoring Wheel in Clamp B, but Light

54   PART 1 Getting Started with Your Cricut

Cardstock changes the prompt to load the Single Scoring Wheel instead. Depending on your material, you may be able to manually change the tool by clicking on Edit Tools and selecting either the Scoring Wheel or Scoring Stylus based on your preference.

To understand how the Scoring Wheels compare to the Scoring Stylus, see the earlier section "Making Lines with the Scoring Stylus."

» **Wavy Blade:** The Wavy Blade adds fun wavy edges to your projects, perfect for homemade cards, gift tags, and stylish borders on scrapbook pages or invitations. To create a wavy line in Design Space, add a Score Line from the Shapes panel and change its operation to Wave. Position the design where you want the cut to appear on the mat preview in the Prepare Screen after clicking Make. Although the line appears straight on-screen, it will cut with a wave pattern. You can also change the operation of shapes and images to Wave for wavy edges. Keep designs at least ¾ inch in radius to prevent distortion or the blade digging into the mat.

How to use QuickSwap tools

Using QuickSwap tools is simple — just swap out the tool tip, set up your design in Cricut Design Space, and let your machine do the rest. Follow these steps to get started:

1. **Attach the tool tip to the QuickSwap Housing.**

   Press the button on top of the QuickSwap Housing to release the current tip. Insert your chosen tool tip until it clicks into place. Load the housing into Clamp B of your Cricut machine.

2. **Set up your design in Cricut Design Space.**

   Select the part of your design that you want to modify. Click the Operation drop-down menu and select the function that matches your tool:

   - Debossing for the Debossing Tip

   - Engrave for the Engraving Tip

   - Perforate for the Perforation Blade

   - Score for the Scoring Wheels

   - Wavy for the Wavy Blade

   Adjust your design as needed, then click Make to proceed to the Make screen.

3. **Select your material and load your mat.**

   Choose your base material from the list in Design Space. Follow the on-screen prompts to load your mat into the machine.

CHAPTER 4 **Checking Out Cricut Tools and Materials** 55

4. **Start the project.**

Press Go and let your Cricut apply the selected effect.

Specialty blades

Unlike the QuickSwap tools, specialty blades such as the Rotary Blade and Knife Blade have their own dedicated housing and cannot be swapped out. These blades are designed for more heavy-duty tasks.

» **Knife Blade:** The Knife Blade is built to handle materials up to 2.4 millimeters thick, such as balsa wood, heavy leather, and chipboard. It's the go-to tool for heavy-duty projects that require deep, precise cuts. When you select a material in Cricut Design Space that requires the Knife Blade (such as Heavy Chipboard or Balsa Wood), the software will automatically prompt you to use this tool. The machine will ask you to insert the Knife Blade into Clamp B when you reach the Tool Setup screen. Use a StrongGrip Mat and secure your material with tape on all sides to prevent shifting. Expect long cut times, as the Knife Blade makes multiple slow passes to ensure a clean cut — some projects can take over an hour. Check between passes before unloading the mat to avoid cutting through your mat or leaving incomplete cuts. Avoid Fast Mode, as slower cuts help maintain accuracy.

» **Rotary Blade:** The Rotary Blade is designed for fabric crafters, gliding through hundreds of materials like fleece, denim, and cotton without needing any backing. When you select a material in Cricut Design Space that requires the Knife Blade (such as Heavy Chipboard or Balsa Wood), the software will automatically prompt you to use this tool. The machine will ask you to insert the Knife Blade into Clamp B when you reach the Tool Setup screen. It's perfect for sewing projects, quilts, and other fabric crafts, as well as delicate materials like tissue paper and crepe paper. For fabric, use a FabricGrip Mat and smooth it out with a brayer before cutting. For fragile materials like tissue or crepe paper, a LightGrip Mat works best to prevent tearing. If you notice fraying or incomplete cuts, it may be time to replace the blade.

Picking the Right Heat Press

If you want your heat transfer vinyl (HTV) projects to last, choosing the right heat press is a big deal. With the right heat press, you can transfer your designs using the even heat and proper pressure they need to stick well and hold up over time.

Without the right press, your designs may peel, crack, or just not turn out the way you want.

But don't worry — it's not hard to find the right one! The following sections take a look at the key features to consider, and break down the different types of heat presses so you can choose the one that works best for your projects. Flip to Chapter 15 for full details on working with HTV.

Features to look for

When selecting a heat press, matching its features to your crafting needs is essential. Here are the basics:

- » **Size:** The size of the heat press should match the typical size of your projects. Sizes range from small (9 x 12 inches) to large (24 x 36 inches), with the 15-x-15-inch model being a popular choice. It's a versatile option for most HTV projects, including T-shirts, tote bags, and pillows.

- » **Safety features:** When you're working with high heat, safety is key. Look for features like *auto shutoff,* which turns the machine off after a period of inactivity.

  Never leave your heat press unattended while it's in use. Always keep a fire extinguisher or fire blanket nearby just in case. True story: Years ago, I had a mug press wire catch fire. Luckily, I was standing right next to the machine and noticed it smoking before things got worse. If I had walked away while it was heating up, the situation could've ended in disaster.

- » **Adjustable settings:** Different materials and projects require specific temperature and pressure settings to stick properly. Look for a heat press with adjustable controls to handle different types of heat transfer projects easily.

  Be cautious with automatic heat presses, because many don't allow you to manually adjust the pressure. The automatic system often doesn't apply enough pressure, which can lead to designs not adhering well. Although auto presses are convenient, manual adjustment is often the key to making durable products.

- » **Even heat distribution:** Uneven heat can cause parts of your design to peel off. To ensure even heating, look for presses that mention features like *double-tube heating* or *cast-in heating elements,* because they tend to distribute heat better.

  A temperature gun (also called an infrared thermometer) is a helpful tool that allows you to check whether your press is delivering consistent heat across the *platen* (flat heating surface). Inexpensive options are available on Amazon, at home improvement stores, or at hardware stores.

- **Cost:** More expensive, high-end models usually come with extra features like digital controls, auto shutoff, and quicker heating. However, a midrange model that offers good heat distribution and adjustable settings is usually more than enough for most crafters.

TIP

Think about the features you truly need before overspending on bells and whistles you may never use.

- **Attachments:** Some heat presses come with attachments that allow you to work on different types of projects. Common attachments include
  - **Hat and cap attachments** for pressing designs onto curved surfaces like hats.
  - **Mug and tumbler attachments** for decorating mugs, tumblers, and other cylindrical items.
  - **Plate attachments** for specialty items like plates or other flat objects.

Types of heat presses

You can choose between several types of heat presses, each with its own benefits. Here's a quick overview of the most popular options:

- **Swing-away press:** The top swings out to the side so that you have more room to work and less chance of burning yourself. It gives even pressure, which is great for thicker materials. Some models even come with attachments for mugs, hats, and plates.
- **Clamshell press:** Opens and closes like a clam. It's compact, so it fits well in small spaces, but the top presses down from above, which can make burns more likely. It may not press thick materials as evenly as a swing-away.
- **Automatic press:** Just push a button and it applies pressure for you. Super convenient for long crafting sessions, but most don't let you adjust the pressure manually, which can be a downside with certain materials. If you can't adjust pressure, some designs may not stick as well.
- **Portable press (like Cricut EasyPress):** Lightweight, affordable, and great for small projects. You press down by hand, which works fine for small stuff but can be tricky for larger shirts since you'll need to press in sections.
- **Mini press:** Perfect for tiny or detailed work like baby clothes, hats, or patches. It's small and easy to use but not strong enough for big jobs.

TIP

REMEMBER

- » **Specialty presses:** Made just for mugs, hats, and tumblers. These are shaped to fit curved items and make pressing a lot easier.

  Choose a mug press that fits a wide range of cup sizes. This way, you'll have the flexibility to customize everything from small mugs to large tumblers.

  Cricut has its own presses, but you'll also find great ones from brands like HTVRont, Vevor, PowerPress, Fancierstudio, and Geo Knight. Think about size, pressure control, and the type of projects you want to do when choosing.

Heat press accessories

In addition to the heat press itself, several essential accessories can make your heat-transfer projects more successful and safer. Here are a few key items you'll want to have on hand:

- » **Butcher paper:** Perfect for Infusible Ink projects because it absorbs excess ink, preventing it from transferring to the heat press.
- » **Heat press mat:** Needed for the EasyPress to protect your table and get even pressure.
- » **Heat press pillows:** These foam pads help press over seams, zippers, or buttons by evening things out.
- » **Lint roller:** A quick way to remove lint and dust before pressing so your design sticks better.
- » **Parchment paper:** Similar to a Teflon sheet, this disposable paper protects your design from sticking to the heat press. You can use either parchment paper or a Teflon sheet, depending on your preference, but both serve the same purpose.
- » **Protective gloves:** These keep your hands safe when handling hot items.
- » **Teflon sheet:** A reusable nonstick sheet that you place between your HTV design and the heat press. It prevents both the design and the press from sticking, scorching, or getting damaged during the transfer process.
- » **Temperature gun:** An infrared thermometer that helps you check for even heat across your press. Just point and read.
- » **Thermal tape:** Heat-resistant tape that holds your design in place during pressing to keep it from shifting.
- » **T-shirt ruler guide:** Helps you quickly center and align your design on shirts before pressing — no more guessing!

Customizing Items with Blanks

When it comes to personalizing items with your Cricut, blanks are the foundation for all your Cricut projects. *Blanks* are undecorated items that you customize with materials like vinyl, HTV, or Infusible Ink.

Here are some of the best blanks to add adhesive vinyl decals to:

>> Acrylic keychains

>> Ceramic tiles

>> Mugs

>> Ornaments

>> Phone cases

>> Storage bins

>> Tumblers

>> Water bottles

>> Windows

>> Wine glasses

Popular HTV blanks include

>> Aprons

>> Can coolers (Koozies)

>> Coasters

>> Garden flags

>> Hats

>> Holiday stockings

>> Kitchen towels

>> Pillows and pillowcases

>> Tote bags

>> T-shirts

You can use the Cricut Maker's Engraving Tip with the following engraving blanks:

>> Acrylic key chains

>> Aluminum business cards

>> Aluminum dog tags and ID tags

>> Bracelets (metal cuffs)

>> Grill spatulas and pie/cake servers

>> Jewelry pendants and stamping blanks

Projects that use leather blanks include

>> Belts

>> Coasters

>> Earrings

>> Key chains

>> Leather patches

>> Wallets

>> Watch straps

IN THIS CHAPTER

» **Keeping your Cricut clean**

» **Taking care of blades and mats**

» **Updating software and firmware**

» **Calibrating your machine**

» **Dealing with typical issues**

Chapter **5**

Keeping Your Cricut in Top Shape

Keeping your Cricut running smoothly doesn't require a ton of work — just a little routine care. Regular maintenance helps keep your cuts clean and your machine working at its best. In this chapter, I walk you through a few easy steps to keep your Cricut in great shape and show you how to troubleshoot issues along the way.

Cleaning Your Cricut Regularly

Regular cleaning helps keep your Cricut dust-free and running smoothly. Be sure to keep the top and front panels of your machine closed when not in use to keep the interior dust-free. Aim to clean your machine at least once a month or as soon as you notice it's getting dirty.

WARNING

Always unplug your machine before cleaning it.

CHAPTER 5 **Keeping Your Cricut in Top Shape** 63

Here's how to clean both the outside and inside of your machine:

- **Exterior cleaning:** Wipe down the outside with a soft cloth or alcohol-free baby wipe. You don't need any harsh chemicals.

  Never spray cleaner directly onto your Cricut machine. Always spray onto a cloth first to avoid getting moisture inside the machine. Also, avoid using acetone-based products (like nail polish remover), which can permanently damage the machine's plastic surfaces.

- **Interior dusting:** Use compressed air to blow out any dust inside the machine. This keeps debris from building up and affecting the machine's performance. For models equipped with internal sensors, such as the Cricut Maker series, pay special attention to keeping these sensors clean. Dust on sensors can interfere with machine operations and cause errors in Cricut Design Space.

A dust cover can help keep your Cricut protected between crafting sessions. You can find covers on Amazon to prevent dust buildup when the machine's not in use. When searching for a dust cover online, make sure to specify your Cricut model to find one that fits properly.

Changing Your Cricut Blade

Even with regular cleaning, blades eventually wear out. There's no set time frame for replacing them — how quickly they become dull depends on how often you use your Cricut and the types of materials you're cutting. When your cuts aren't sharp despite regular cleaning, or if you notice that the blade begins to tear materials like cardstock instead of cleanly cutting through, it's probably time for a new blade.

Signs that it's time to replace the blade include jagged cuts, incomplete cuts, or difficulty cutting through materials it used to handle easily. Some materials, like glitter cardstock or thick vinyl, can wear down blades faster.

The blade you'll most likely need to replace most often is the Fine-Point Blade, as it's used for the majority of common projects involving materials like vinyl, heat transfer vinyl (HTV), paper, and cardstock. Over time, other blades may also need replacing depending on your project needs. For a complete guide blades, flip to Chapter 4.

For Cricut Explore, Maker, and Venture machines

Explore, Maker, and Venture models are equipped with two tool clamps, Clamp A and Clamp B, which allow you to switch easily between cutting and other functions such as writing or scoring without needing to change tools.

» Clamp A is located on the left side and is primarily used for holding accessories like pens and scoring styluses. This clamp allows you to add detailed writing or scoring lines to your projects without having to swap out the cutting blade.

» Clamp B is on the right side and is specifically designed for blades. This is where you change your cutting tools. If you're unsure about where to place your blade or accessory, don't worry — Cricut Design Space will guide you with clear instructions before each cut. (See Part 2 for details.)

Follow these steps to change your blade:

1. **Open Clamp B and carefully remove the blade housing.**
2. **Press the plunger at the top of the housing to release the blade, and then carefully pull it out from the bottom.**

    The process for changing Fine-Point and Deep-Point blades is the same, but be sure to use the correct housing for your blade. Figure 5-1 shows the Fine-Point Blade and Housing.

    REMEMBER

    Fine-Point Blades use the silver Fine-Point Housing, but Deep-Point Blades must be paired with the black Deep-Point Housing.

3. **Remove the protective cover from your new blade.**
4. **Pop the new blade into the housing with the sharp side facing out.**

    The magnet inside will keep it in place.

5. **Insert the blade housing into Clamp B.**

    Be sure the blade housing sits flat and snug against the top of Clamp B. If it's sitting too high, the blade won't cut right. To close Clamp B, start by securing the left arm. There's a small indentation that should fit around the blade housing. Hold the left arm steady, then swing the right arm over, and snap the plastic tab into place.

    TIP

    You may need to press down gently to get it to lock — that's totally normal. When both clamps are closed right, the tabs on Clamps A and B should line up evenly. Give it a quick check to make sure everything's secure, and you're good to go.

Figure 5-2 shows the basic process of replacing a blade.

The blade will pop out here   Press down on this plunger to release the blade

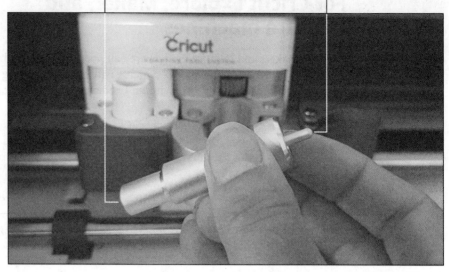

FIGURE 5-1: Removing the Fine-Point Blade from the Fine-Point Housing.

Source: Kerri Adamczyk

Cricut Maker: Blade Installation Tips

Installing your blades in the Cricut Maker is easy!

FIGURE 5-2: Removing and reinserting the Fine-Point Housing into Clamp B when replacing a blade.

1. Open Clamp B and remove blade housing.

2. Place blade housing in Clamp B, ensuring that housing is seated on the top surface of the clamp. For Rotary and Knife blades, make sure the gears fit together.

3. Close the clamp.

Adapted from Cricut.com

For the Cricut Joy series

The process for changing blades on a Cricut Joy and Joy Xtra is similar to the steps outlined in the previous section but with one key difference. Unlike other Cricut models that have two clamps — one for the blade and one for pens and accessories — the Cricut Joy series has only one clamp. This means that if you want to switch from cutting to writing, you need to take out the blade and put in the pen because there isn't a separate clamp for different tools. Also, note that the Cricut Joy uses its own specific blades and accessories. Always buy blades that are made just for the Cricut Joy to make sure they fit and work properly.

Cleaning Your Cricut Blade

Your blade does the hard work for all your cuts, so keeping it clean is key to achieving smooth, precise results. Here's how to check and clean your blade:

- » **Check for debris.** Inspect the blade regularly, especially after cutting thick materials like vinyl or cardstock. Remove any bits of material that are stuck on the blade.

- » **Clean the blade with aluminum foil.** Press the plunger to expose the blade and carefully poke it into a ball of aluminum foil several times (see Figure 5-3). This clears off debris and can improve your Cricut's cutting performance. It's a common misconception that foil sharpens the blade; it actually just helps keep it clean.

Although some suggest soaking blades in soapy water to clean them, this practice isn't recommended. Not only are the blades extremely sharp, which poses a risk of cuts, but soaking may also lead to rusting.

Instead of soaking blades, I recommend the aluminum foil trick. If your blade is still dull after that, it may be best to replace it (as I explain earlier in this chapter). Thankfully, Cricut blades are fairly inexpensive, so replacing them is an easy way to keep your cuts sharp and safe.

FIGURE 5-3: Press the blade tip into a ball of aluminum foil to remove debris.

Source: Kerri Adamczyk

Caring for Your Cricut Mats

Your cutting mats (see Chapter 4), which hold materials in place with light adhesive, also benefit from regular cleaning to extend their life. With regular use, mats naturally lose stickiness and need to be replaced. They typically last a few months with regular use, but this can vary depending on how often you craft and the materials you use. Here's how to keep your mats in good condition:

» **Cover them with the protective film.** After each use, cover your mats with the clear protective film they came with. This helps keep dust and dirt off the sticky surface.

TIP

Write "This Side Up" with a permanent marker on one side of the mat's protective film. This helps you put it back the same way each time. If you always flip the film onto the same surface when using your mat, any dust, pet hair, or debris that collects won't transfer to the sticky side when replacing the film. This keeps your mat cleaner for longer!

» **Store them flat or hang them on a wall.** Keep mats flat or hang them up to prevent bending or curling. This also helps maintain their stickiness.

» **Scrape away debris or use a lint roller.** After each project, gently scrape excess material off your mats, or use a lint roller to pick up tiny bits.

- » **Wipe them with alcohol-free baby wipes.** For a gentle cleaning, use alcohol-free baby wipes to wipe down your mats and restore some of their stickiness.
- » **Scrub them with Dawn dish soap.** If your mats are really dirty, give them a scrub with warm water and Dawn dish soap. Let them air-dry completely before using them again. Keep in mind that drying can take a while, so it's best not to wash your mats if you need to use them immediately.

WARNING

Avoid using adhesive sprays to restore your Cricut mats' stickiness. Glue buildup can jam your machine, damage materials, or void your warranty. Stick to Cricut-approved methods to keep your mats in top shape.

Maintaining the Software and Firmware

To keep your Cricut performing at its best, it's important to update its software and firmware regularly. Cricut Design Space (see Part 2) is the software you use to create your projects; *firmware* is the internal software that helps your machine communicate with your computer or mobile device. Both need occasional updates to keep everything running smoothly.

Updating Cricut Design Space software

Cricut Design Space releases regular updates to fix bugs and add new features. Make sure that you're using the latest version to avoid any issues. Here's how to ensure that you're using the latest version of Cricut Design Space.

On a Windows PC or Mac, follow these steps:

1. **Launch the Design Space application on your computer.**
2. **Check for update alerts.**

    If a new update is available, you'll usually see a prompt when you open the app. If not, the update may happen automatically in the background.

3. **If an update prompt appears, simply follow the on-screen instructions to download and install the latest version.**

    This usually takes only a few minutes.

4. **Once the update is complete, restart the app to ensure that the changes take effect.**

For mobile devices with iOS or Android, follow these steps:

1. **Go to the App Store (iOS) or Google Play (Android) on your mobile device.**

2. **Type "Cricut Design Space" into the search bar.**

3. **Tap Update to download the latest version.**

   If an update is available, you'll see an Update button next to the app.

4. **After the update finishes, open Cricut Design Space to enjoy the newest features.**

Cricut Design Space may also update automatically depending on your device settings. If you have automatic updates enabled on your device, Design Space will install updates without needing any action from you.

Updating your Cricut's firmware

Keeping your firmware up-to-date helps your machine working smoothly. Here's how to make sure your Cricut is always current:

>> **Automatic updates:** Cricut Design Space automatically notifies you when an update is needed. Simply follow the on-screen instructions to complete the update.

>> **Manual updates:** If you're having trouble with your machine's connection or it isn't working right, you may need to update the firmware yourself.

Here's how to manually update the firmware:

1. **Open Design Space and click on the drop-down menu next to your name in the top right corner.**

2. **Select Settings.**

3. **Go to the Machines tab.**

4. **Click Start next to Update Firmware.**

Design Space will guide you through the process. Just make sure your machine is powered on and connected to your device via USB or Bluetooth. Once the update begins, a progress bar will show the status, and your machine will automatically restart when the update is complete.

70   PART 1 Getting Started with Your Cricut

Calibrating Your Cricut

Calibrating your Cricut helps fine-tune the alignment of the blade and the machine's sensors, ensuring that your cuts are exactly as you expect. It's especially important to calibrate after you replace a blade or update the machine's firmware (as I describe earlier in this chapter). Here's how to calibrate your Cricut:

1. **Open Cricut Design Space and click on the drop-down menu next to your name in the upper-right corner.**

2. **Select Settings.**

3. **Go to the Machines tab.**

4. **Click on the drop-down menu next to Machine Calibration, select your model, and click Start.**

5. **Follow the on-screen instructions to calibrate your machine.**

Troubleshooting Common Issues

Sometimes things don't go as planned, but don't worry! Most issues can be solved with a little troubleshooting.

Identifying cutting problems

If your Cricut isn't cutting like it used to, there's no need to panic. Here are a few simple steps to help you get back on track:

>> **Check the blade.** Make sure it's sharp and free from sticky residue and debris. Clean it regularly or replace it if needed.

>> **Inspect the mat.** A worn or nonsticky mat can affect how well your material stays in place, which leads to cutting issues. Make sure your mat is sticky enough and replace it if necessary.

>> **Verify the settings.** Double-check your cut settings in Cricut Design Space. Sometimes the wrong setting can make cuts too shallow or too deep. Adjust the settings to match the material you're using.

>> **Perform a test cut.** Before diving into a big project, make a test cut with a simple shape like a circle or square. This will let you know whether the blade and settings are working correctly.

CHAPTER 5 Keeping Your Cricut in Top Shape 71

>> **Check the design.** Intricate, small designs or thin fonts can sometimes be too detailed for your Cricut to cut cleanly. Simplify parts of your design if you notice jagged or incomplete cuts.

Resolving Design Space connectivity issues

If you're having trouble with Cricut Design Space, you can take a few easy steps to fix any connectivity problems:

>> **Check your internet connection.** Make sure your Wi-Fi connection is stable and strong. A weak or intermittent connection can cause issues with loading designs or completing cuts.

>> **Restart your devices.** Sometimes, all your Cricut machine, computer, or mobile device needs is a quick restart to clear up any glitches.

>> **Update the software.** Ensure that you're running the latest version of Cricut Design Space. Outdated software can sometimes lead to connectivity problems, so keeping it updated can help prevent this.

Applying advanced troubleshooting tips

If the basic fixes for the preceding issues don't work, here are some additional steps you can try:

>> **Consult the user manual.** Your Cricut's user manual is packed with helpful information, including troubleshooting advice for specific issues.

>> **Visit Cricut support.** Cricut's official support site (https://help.cricut.com/hc/en-us) has a wide range of articles, videos, and tips that can help you solve more complicated problems.

>> **Contact customer service.** If you've tried everything and your Cricut still isn't working properly, reach out to Cricut's customer service. They can help troubleshoot more complex issues or arrange for repairs if necessary. Visit https://help.cricut.com/hc/en-us/articles/360020316674-Cricut-Contact-Information.

>> **Join Cricut community groups:** Sometimes, the best help comes from fellow crafters who have experienced similar issues. Join Cricut community groups on platforms like Facebook, where thousands of members are willing to share their insights and solutions. For more information on connecting with the Cricut community, flip to Chapter 1.

72   PART 1 **Getting Started with Your Cricut**

2
Mastering Cricut Design Space

IN THIS PART . . .

Consider the advantages of Cricut Access and how it expands your creative possibilities.

Navigate through Cricut Design Space and explore its main features.

Create your own designs using Design Space tools like Text, Shapes, and Offset.

Complete the final steps of turning your digital designs into physical projects.

IN THIS CHAPTER

» Accessing premium designs and features with a standard subscription

» Breaking down other Cricut Access subscription tiers

» Exploring alternatives to Cricut Access

Chapter 6
Joining Cricut Access

Cricut Access is like having an all-you-can-craft buffet at your fingertips. This paid subscription within Cricut Design Space (see Part 2) is packed with tons of images, fonts, project ideas, and exclusive features to make your crafting experience easier and more enjoyable.

In this chapter, I provide an overview of what a Cricut Access subscription offers, and point you in the direction of some other options if a subscription isn't what you're looking for.

TIP

Visit `https://cricut.com/en-us/join-cricut-access` for full details on Cricut Access.

Unlocking Exclusive Content with a Standard Cricut Access Subscription

You don't need Cricut Access to use your Cricut machine but it does have its perks. With a standard subscription, you get access to over 1 million images, 1,000+ fonts, and 100,000+ ready-to-make projects you can customize. You'll also get 10 percent off premium licensed images from brands like Star Wars, Disney, and Marvel, plus 10 percent off `Cricut.com` purchases to restock on vinyl, tools, and accessories.

REMEMBER

You can use Cricut Access fonts for commercial projects, but there are limits on how many items you can sell before needing a separate license. Be sure to check out the latest version of Cricut's Angel Policy (https://cricut.com/en/legal) and subscription terms to ensure that you're complying with their guidelines.

WARNING

When using licensed images from popular brands such as Disney, it's important to understand copyright and trademark laws. You can legally use these licensed images in your personal projects through Cricut Access, which has obtained the rights to these designs. Avoid using them for commercial purposes without permission. For detailed legal advice on using these and other designs, see Chapter 8 and explore Cricut's Angel Policy at https://cricut.com/en/legal.

Plus, all of these exclusive features in Design Space make your crafting experience easier, fun, and more enjoyable:

- **Automatic Background Remover:** This feature is a huge time-saver when you're uploading images that need a clean background. With just one click, you can remove backgrounds without having to manually erase or use other apps.
- **Warped Text:** Add a fun twist to your designs with the Warped Text feature. Whether you want your text to curve, arc, or bend, this tool helps you create custom designs with ease.
- **Create Sticker:** This Cricut Access–exclusive tool makes it super simple to create full-color Print Then Cut stickers. It comes with preset settings to ease the process, whether you're making one sticker or a full sheet. For detailed instructions on using this tool and tips on sticker making, see Chapter 18.
- **Multiple Layers:** This feature allows you to create up to nine separate layers from a multicolored image, each distinguished by color. This tool instantly converts your complex images into organized, editable layers.
- **Priority member support:** Need help? As a Cricut Access member, you'll get priority support. Jump to the front of the line and chat with a friendly Member Care representative during their support hours.

TIP

If you need only a few designs for your projects, it may be more cost-effective to purchase them a la carte rather than subscribing to Cricut Access. You can access hundreds of free images and fonts and purchase digital designs with a free subscription, which I describe in the next section.

There are two payment options for the standard subscription: $9.99 per month or $95.88 per year (saving you $24).

Checking Out Additional Cricut Access Subscription Types

Cricut Access offers three different subscription tiers: free, standard (see the previous section), and premium. Each tier has its own perks, so you can pick the one that best fits your crafting needs:

- **Free subscription:** The free subscription is included with your Cricut account, so even without upgrading, you get access to some great resources:
  - **3,000+ images:** A solid selection of images for free projects.
  - **100+ fonts:** A good variety of fonts to get you started.
  - **A la carte digital purchases:** You can buy images and fonts as you go.
  - **250+ ready-to-make projects:** Predesigned projects ready for you to make. Check out Chapter 7 to discover where to find these projects and images to work with in Design Space.
  - **Up to five collections:** Organize your projects into five collections to keep things tidy. Not sure what a collection is? Flip to Chapter 9 to find out.

TIP

Looking for free designs in Design Space? You can filter by "Free" under the Images, Projects, and Fonts tabs to quickly find options that don't require a Cricut Access subscription or additional purchase.

- **Premium subscription:** The premium subscription gives you everything in the standard plan (described earlier in this chapter), plus a few extra perks to make your crafting life even easier:
  - 20 percent off all materials
  - Free economy shipping on $50+ orders

The cost for a premium subscription is $119.88 per year, which breaks down to $9.99 a month and must be purchased annually in full.

Considering Other Options Besides Cricut Access

If Cricut Access doesn't work for you, there are many other websites where you can find fonts, images, and designs. Free resources are a good option if you're not looking to spend money, but many of these are only for personal use, meaning you can't sell projects made with them. Always check the licensing terms before selling anything you make. One popular free option is Dafont.com, which offers lots of fonts, but most are for personal use unless you pay for a commercial license. Facebook groups are another place where crafters share free designs, but be sure to check the licensing and avoid scams.

If you're planning to sell your crafts, third-party design websites are a better choice. These sites usually offer commercial licenses, so you can use their designs for business purposes. One of my favorites is CreativeFabrica.com, which has millions of designs and fonts. You can buy individual designs or subscribe for unlimited downloads at $3.99 a month or $47 a year. Although it's affordable and includes commercial use, it doesn't offer the Cricut-specific perks like discounts or special features in Design Space.

Etsy.com is another good option for where you can buy individual design files without a subscription, but it can get pricey if you need a lot of designs, and there are no bulk discounts. DesignBundles.net also offers bundles and sales, but their subscription costs more — $24.99 a month or $239 per year. They do provide commercial licenses, though.

For converting regular images into Cricut-ready files, you can use the free tool Picsvg.com. Other helpful sites for design files include FontBundles.net for fonts and TheHungryJPEG.com for bundles and individual purchases, plus occasional freebies.

IN THIS CHAPTER

» Launching a new project in Cricut Design Space

» Navigating the Design Space Canvas

» Discovering new projects and images to work with

Chapter 7
Exploring the Cricut Design Space Canvas

Ready to get crafty with your Cricut? Before you start, you'll need Cricut Design Space — the free software that powers your Cricut machine. Using Design Space doesn't cost anything, but many design elements like fonts, images, and ready-made projects may require a Cricut Access subscription.

TIP

For a deeper dive into the benefits and features of Cricut Access, check out Chapter 6, where I explore all the perks included in the subscription. If you're looking for just the freebies, you can easily filter your search to show only free content.

In this chapter, you find out how to start a brand-new project in Design Space. I take you on a tour of the software, making stops at the Home screen and Canvas so you can explore their helpful features. You also discover where to find ready-to-make projects, perfect for sparking your inspiration to start crafting right away. Check out Chapter 3 if you need guidance on signing up for a Cricut account and getting Design Space up and running.

Starting a New Project and Touring the Canvas

To start a new project in Cricut Design Space, click on the New Project button in the upper-right corner of the Home screen. This opens up a blank canvas where you can begin designing. You can also get to your Canvas by clicking on Canvas next to the Home tab in the upper-left corner.

The Canvas is where you'll create and edit all your designs. It's organized into several key areas, as shown in Figure 7-1:

» **Canvas:** This is your main workspace, located between the rulers, where you'll do all your designing.

» **Navigation bar:** Found at the very top of the screen, it includes options like Notifications, My Stuff, Save, and Make.

» **Design panel:** Located on the left, this is where you can add or upload images, text, and shapes to your design.

» **Edit bar:** The Edit bar consists of two rows of tools:

- The top row includes design tools like Flip, Offset, and Warp.

- The bottom row, known as the Text Edit bar, appears when you're working with text and allows you to change fonts, resize text, and adjust letter and line spacing. These tools are faded until you add text or images.

» **Layers panel:** Found on the right, this panel allows you to view and manage each layer of your design:

- **Top section:** Here's where you can group, ungroup, duplicate, or delete layers to organize your design.

- **Color Sync tab:** Located next to the Layers tab, this helps you organize and match colors across layers for better efficiency.

- **Bottom section:** This area includes the actions icons and Combine menu, where you'll find tools like Slice, Weld, and Attach.

» **Zoom controls:** Located in the bottom-left corner of the Canvas, these controls help you zoom in or out to get a better view of your design details or see the entire workspace. Use the + and – buttons to adjust the zoom level as needed.

Go to Chapter 8 for a closer look at these tools and how they help you make your designs.

80   PART 2 Mastering Cricut Design Space

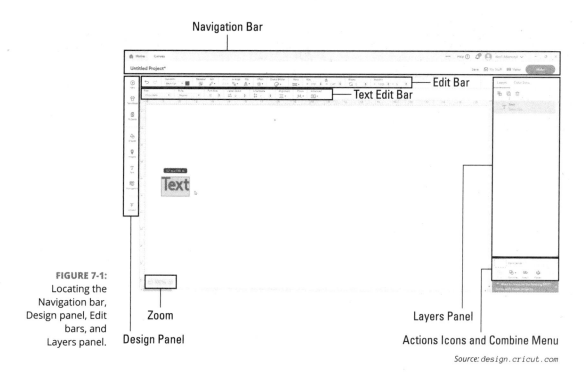

FIGURE 7-1: Locating the Navigation bar, Design panel, Edit bars, and Layers panel.

Source: design.cricut.com

Finding Inspiration: Projects and Images

After you've seen how the Canvas is organized, you may be wondering what kind of projects you should start making. If you're not sure where to start, Cricut Design Space has plenty of ready-made designs and ideas to spark your creativity. The following sections take a look at the Projects and Images tabs, which are perfect for finding inspiration or grabbing ready-to-use elements to help you plan your crafts.

Browsing the Projects library

Not sure what to make? Browse through Projects to discover hundreds of thousands of ready-to-make options! These projects in Cricut's library are beginner-friendly and provide you with all the essential information, such as a description of the project, the finished size, the materials you need, and step-by-step instructions on how to prep, cut, and assemble.

TIP

Keep in mind that the projects displayed in your search results may vary based on the machine you select.

CHAPTER 7 **Exploring the Cricut Design Space Canvas** 81

Follow these steps, corresponding to Figure 7-2, to see how to use the Projects tab:

1. **Click on Projects in the Design panel on the left.**
2. **Identify Cricut Access projects.**

   Use the scroll bar to browse through the projects. Any project with a green *a* icon is exclusive to Cricut Access subscribers (see Chapter 6 for details).
3. **Search for projects.**

   Use the search bar to find a specific type of project, like "birthday card" or "tote bag."
4. **Explore categories.**

   Click on the All Projects drop-down menu to explore different project categories, like Clothing, Free, Infusible Ink, and more.
5. **Show some love to the creator by clicking on the heart icon.**
6. **Bookmark projects.**

   Click on the Bookmark icon to save the project in your My Stuff folder.
7. **Share the project.**

   Click on the Share icon (the curved arrow) to copy a link for sharing outside Design Space, or share directly to Facebook or Pinterest.
8. **Click the three dots to Add to Collection.**

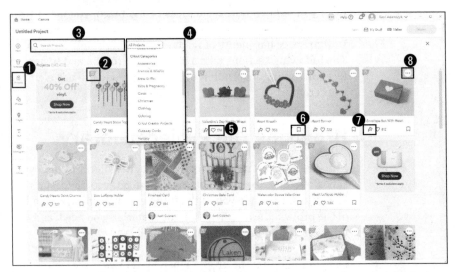

FIGURE 7-2: How to use the Projects tab.

Source: design.cricut.com

REMEMBER Wondering about the difference between bookmarking a project and adding it to a collection? Bookmarking lets you save individual projects for quick access later, much like bookmarking a page in your browser; adding a project to a collection allows you to organize related projects together. For instance, you can create collections for different themes or occasions like "Wedding Ideas" or "Halloween Decorations," which helps you keep your crafting space tidy and themed.

When you select a project, you can view the materials list, step-by-step instructions, and a preview of the finished design. Projects are an excellent way to get started when you're short on time or new to Cricut crafting.

TIP You can also find project ideas in the Discover and Inspire tabs on the Home screen.

Looking through Images

The Images tab is where you'll find tons of graphics, illustrations, and design elements to use in your projects. With thousands of images available, it's easy to find something for any craft.

Follow these steps that correspond to the steps in Figure 7-3 to see how to use the Images tab:

1. **Click on Images in the Design panel on the left.**

2. **Search for designs.**

   Use the search bar to find exactly what you're looking for.

3. **Apply filters.**

   Filter your results by type, such as free images, purchased designs, Print Then Cut images, designs you can edit, and more.

4. **Use Advanced Search.**

   Can't find what you're looking for? Click on the Advanced Search button at the bottom of the Images tab to search using more specific criteria, such as operation type, project type, language, or editable images.

5. **Bookmark your favorites.**

   Hover over an image to reveal the bookmark icon, allowing you to save the image for later in the My Stuff section.

6. **Add an image.**

   Click on the plus sign to add the selected image to your Canvas.

CHAPTER 7 **Exploring the Cricut Design Space Canvas** 83

7. **Close the Images tab.**

    Collapse the Images tab by clicking the arrow next to the Canvas ruler to free up more workspace.

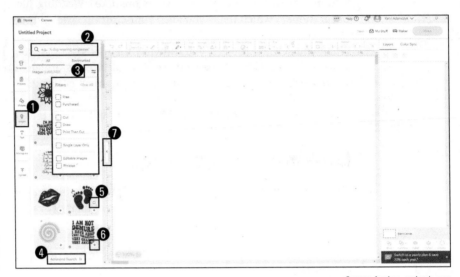

FIGURE 7-3:
Using the Images tab.

Source: design.cricut.com

TIP

If you're feeling inspired and ready to start creating unique projects but can't find exactly what you need, Cricut Design Space makes it easy to upload designs from third-party websites like Creative Fabrica (www.creativefabrica.com). In Chapter 8, you find out how to upload designs, work with text, use templates, manage layers, and handle various operations to help you turn your ideas into reality.

IN THIS CHAPTER

» **Following the basic steps for most Cricut projects**

» **Adhering to legal guidelines for fonts and designs**

» **Working with your own custom graphics**

» **Personalizing your projects with text and fonts**

» **Using templates to preview your projects**

» **Managing layers and operations**

Chapter **8**

Designing in Cricut Design Space

Now for the fun part — creating your project in Cricut Design Space! This free software has all the tools you need to turn your ideas into reality. In this chapter, you find out how to upload your favorite designs and customize them with Design Space tools like Offset, Text, and Shapes. You also figure out how to use templates to see what your design will look like on real items, like T-shirts or caps. Before you know it, you'll be a Design Space pro!

Creating Cricut Projects in Design Space: The Basics

REMEMBER

To begin, you can log into Design Space either via your web browser at https://design.cricut.com/ or through the Design Space desktop app. If you don't have the desktop app installed yet, the website will prompt you to download it. Once installed, you can easily find the app by searching for "Cricut Design Space" in the Start menu on Windows or in the Applications folder on a Mac. After you're logged in, click Start New Project to open the Canvas. This is the starting point for all your projects in Cricut Design Space, where all your design work will take place. For detailed guidance on installing Design Space on different devices, including system requirements and step-by-step instructions, see Chapter 3.

Before you dive into the advanced features, it's helpful to understand the basic workflow of creating a project in Design Space. These are the steps you'll follow for most projects:

1. **Create or upload your design.**

   Start from scratch using the Design Space tools and features that I cover in this chapter, or upload files like PNGs or SVGs.

   TECHNICAL STUFF

   PNGs are image files that can have transparent backgrounds, which is great when you don't want a white box around your design. Their quality can vary, but they usually look clearer and keep colors better than other image types. SVGs, on the other hand, are files that let you resize your design without making it blurry or losing any detail. They work best for Cricut projects because they help your machine cut clean, sharp lines, even for detailed designs.

2. **Measure your blank and resize your design.**

   Make sure your design fits on your *blank* (the material you're applying the design to) by measuring the blank and adjusting the size of your design in Design Space.

3. **Set the operation.**

   Use the drop-down menu under Operation at the top of your Canvas to choose the right operation for your project, like cutting, writing, or scoring, depending on your material and design. Double-check this setting in the Layers panel on the right side of the Canvas.

4. **Adjust your settings.**

   After clicking Make, fine-tune important settings like *mirroring* (flipping) your design for heat transfer vinyl (HTV) projects (see Chapter 15) and selecting your base material.

   TIP

   If you're using a new material, do a test cut with a small shape like a 1-inch (2.54-centimeter) star to check your settings before cutting your full design.

5. **Prepare the material and mat.**

   Make sure the surface you're transferring your design to is clean, and stick your material to the upper-left corner of your mat, aligning it with your design's location on the Prepare screen.

   TIP

   For cleaning, use rubbing alcohol and a lint-free wipe for most hard surfaces, and a lint roller for fabrics.

6. **Load the mat.**

   Load the mat into your Cricut by sliding it under the two guide tabs on the sides of the machine. Press the Load button to pull your mat into the machine. (With the machines in the Cricut Joy series, the mat automatically loads after you insert it.)

7. **Start the cutting/design process.**

   Press the Go button to begin the process, such as cutting, writing, or scoring, depending on the specifics of your project. (With the machines in the Cricut Joy series, you start the process through the software.)

8. **Weed your design (for cut projects).**

   Once cutting is complete, weed away the excess material using your fingers or a weeding tool to reveal your finished design.

9. **Apply your design.**

   Attach your design to your project using the appropriate method, such as heat transfer or transfer tape, depending on the material type.

Using Fonts and Designs Legally

As you're creating a project in Design Space, you may decide to personalize your designs even further by adding custom fonts or graphics. Before you upload any elements to Design Space, it's important to understand how to use them legally, especially if you plan to sell your projects.

Selling Cricut projects under the Cricut Angel Policy

If you plan to sell products made with Cricut designs, it's important to follow Cricut's Angel Policy, which outlines what you can and can't do with Cricut images, fonts, and materials:

» You can sell up to 10,000 finished items per year that use Cricut Access images and fonts, which are marked with the green *a* icon in Design Space. If an image or font doesn't have the green *a* icon, it's for personal use only and can't be used on products you plan to sell.

» You must include a copyright notice on any finished product that uses Cricut designs. This notice should read: "Includes Copyright Material of Cricut" and be placed in a reasonable size and location on the item, a tag, or a label.

» You can't mass-produce items — each finished product must be made by one person (no assembly lines or teams).

» Licensed images (Disney, Marvel, Hello Kitty, and so on) can't be used for commercial sales, even if they appear in Design Space. These designs are for personal use only.

» You can't sell individual die-cuts, sticker sheets, or unassembled pieces made with Cricut Designs. The Angel Policy allows only the sale of fully finished products with the designs permanently affixed.

» You can't sell digital files using Cricut designs. The Angel Policy applies only to physical products.

» Modifications don't change the rules — even if you modify or combine Cricut images, they are still covered by the Angel Policy.

» You can sell Cricut-made products online or in person with no restrictions on where you sell.

To read the full Cricut Angel Policy, visit `https://cricut.com/en-us/legal` and click on Angel Policy on the left-hand side.

Understanding personal versus commercial licenses

Licenses determine how you can use fonts and designs in your projects. Here's what each type allows:

- » **Personal license:** Allows you to use fonts and designs for your own projects or gifts, but not for selling.

- » **Commercial license:** Required if you want to sell items made with these fonts or designs. Some may have extra rules, like a limit on certain types of sales or an additional fee.

A Creative Fabrica subscription includes permission for personal and commercial use, allowing you to craft for yourself or sell finished products hassle-free. Visit www.creativefabrica.com for details.

Avoiding copyright and trademark issues

Even with a commercial license, you cannot legally use some designs for products you plan to sell. Keep these key points in mind:

- » **Copyrighted material:** Includes artwork, characters, and original designs that belong to someone else. Just because an image is online doesn't mean it's free to use.

- » **Trademarked material:** Includes brand names, logos, and recognizable phrases (such as Disney characters, sports team logos, or famous quotes). Selling items with trademarked content can lead to legal trouble.

Selling your Cricut creations safely

If you plan to sell your projects, follow these guidelines to stay compliant:

- » Check the license terms for every font or design you use to make sure they allow commercial use.

- » Read the details carefully — some licenses limit how many products you can sell or where you can sell them.

- » Avoid using copyrighted or trademarked material unless you have written permission from the owner.

By understanding these guidelines, you can confidently create and sell your designs while staying within legal boundaries.

Uploading Your Own Designs

Want to use your own artwork or download designs from the internet? Cricut Design Space makes it easy to upload and work with your custom files. Follow these steps to get started:

1. **Upload your design.**

   Click on the Upload button at the bottom of the left-hand toolbar. This opens the section where you can add your images or designs.

2. **Check the file type.**

   Make sure your file is one of the compatible file types: JPG, PNG, GIF, SVG, DXF, HEIC, or BMP.

   SVG files are best for resizing without losing image quality. They also let you adjust parts of your design separately, which is perfect for precise cuts.

3. **Add your file.**

   Click on Upload Image to browse and select your design file from your computer, and then click Continue.

4. **Remove the background.**

   The background removal process depends on the file format you upload.

   - If you upload an SVG or PNG with a transparent background, you're all set — Design Space does the work for you.

   - For other file types like JPGs, you'll need to manually clear the background. Use the Automatic Background Remover (for Cricut Access subscribers; see Chapter 6) or manual editing tools (Select, Erase, Restore) on the left side of the screen. Click on any background areas you want to remove until they show a checkered pattern, meaning that they're now transparent. Use the Zoom tool if you need a closer look.

5. **Preview your cut.**

   Select the Preview Single Layer option on the right side of the screen. This allows you to see the cut outline of your image so that you can make sure the background and any unwanted elements have been completely removed. Here are a few examples:

   - **Before background removal:** Figure 8-1 shows a solid white box around and inside the dice, indicating areas that need to be made transparent.

   - **Incorrect cut preview:** Figure 8-2 shows what happens if you don't remove the white spaces — the design would be cut as a solid square, not as the intended dice.

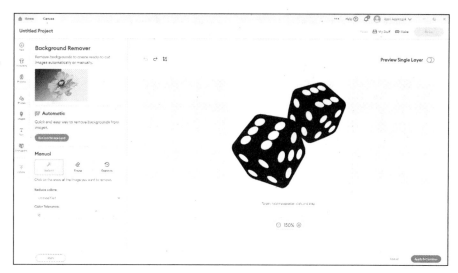

FIGURE 8-1: Before background removal.

Source: design.cricut.com

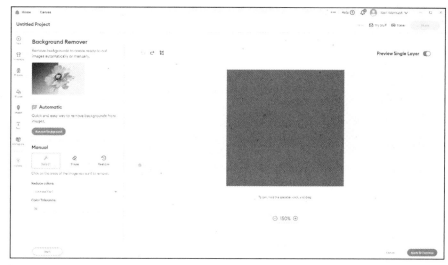

FIGURE 8-2: Incorrect cut preview.

Source: design.cricut.com

- **Correct cut preview:** Figure 8-3 displays the dice with all white spaces removed, showing the design against a transparent checkerboard background, indicating the design is now ready for cutting. This background pattern helps visually confirm that all unwanted areas have been successfully cleared.

CHAPTER 8 Designing in Cricut Design Space   91

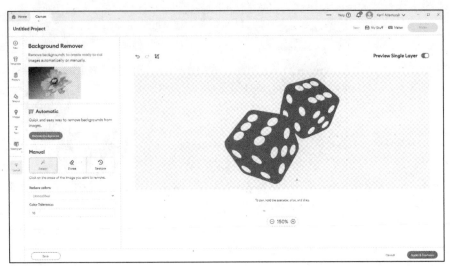

FIGURE 8-3: Correct cut preview.

Source: `design.cricut.com`

6. **Apply changes and continue.**

   Once you're happy with how your designs looks, click Apply & Continue to proceed with your project. (You can see this button in the bottom-right corner of Figure 8-3.)

7. **Choose how to process the upload.**

   On the Convert Upload To screen, you can choose from the following options:

   - **Multiple Layers:** This option creates up to nine color-separated layers, transforming your PNG into an SVG-style file. It's perfect for projects where you need to adjust each color separately. (*Note:* This feature requires a Cricut Access subscription. See Chapter 6 for details.)

   - **Single Layer:** This option converts your upload into a one-color silhouette, ideal for cutting designs out of vinyl or similar materials.

   - **Flat Graphic:** Best for Print Then Cut projects, this option keeps your upload in one full-color layer. (Flip to Chapter 18 for more info on Print Then Cut.)

8. **Finalize your upload.**

   Enter an image name and tags (if you want), and decide whether you want to add your upload to a collection. (Not sure what a collection is? Flip to Chapter 9.) Click Upload to finish. Now your design is ready to be brought to life with your Cricut!

Filling Your Designs with Patterns

Want to add a unique pop of color to your designs? Patterns are a fun way to bring your designs to life, especially for Print Then Cut projects (see Chapter 18). You can easily apply pattern fills to shapes, text, or other design elements in Cricut Design Space.

Applying pattern fills

Follow these steps to add a pattern fill to your design, and see Figure 8-4 for a visual guide. Each step in the figure corresponds to the numbered instructions here:

1. **Select the shape or layer you want to change.**

2. **Go to the top toolbar and open the Operation drop-down menu; change the setting to Print Then Cut.**

3. **Click the color square (next to the Operation drop-down menu, where you normally change colors).**

4. **Find the Print Type drop-down menu at the top of this new window.**

   Click on it and select Pattern instead of Color.

5. **Browse through the available patterns and select one to see a preview inside your shape.**

   This will fill your selected element with a vibrant pattern, perfect for stickers, labels, and other printed designs.

6. **Click anywhere on the Canvas to finalize the pattern selection.**

Uploading your own patterns

Don't see a pattern you like? No worries — you can upload custom patterns to Cricut Design Space! Here's how to upload a pattern:

1. **Click on Upload in the left-hand toolbar.**

2. **Select Pattern Fill near the top, and then click Upload Pattern.**

3. **Click Browse, then choose your file from your computer and click Open.**

   Compatible file types include JPG, GIF, PNG, and BMP.

4. **Preview your image, then click Continue.**

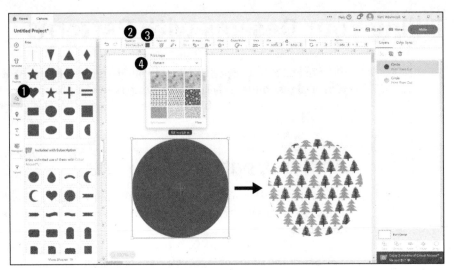

FIGURE 8-4: Applying a pattern fill to a circle shape in Cricut Design Space.

Source: design.cricut.com

5. **Skip the Background Remover screen — you don't need to remove the background for patterns.**

   Simply click Apply & Continue.

6. **On the Convert Upload To screen, select Flat Graphic and click Continue.**

7. **Name and tag your pattern and click Upload to finish.**

   Once uploaded, Design Space may automatically place the pattern on your Canvas — you can simply delete it if this happens. Your custom pattern will now appear in your pattern library, ready for use in any Print Then Cut project. To access your custom patterns, follow the steps in the earlier section "Applying pattern fills." When you get to Step 5, your newly uploaded pattern should appear at the top of the pattern library.

TIP

Patterns work best when you're using high-resolution images. This ensures that your patterned designs stay crisp and clear when printed.

Working with Text

Adding text to your designs is one of the easiest ways to make them uniquely yours. From picking the perfect font to adjusting the size and spacing, you'll find the tools you need to personalize your project in Cricut Design Space. Whether you're customizing a water bottle with a name, creating a personalized label for a wine glass, or designing a unique message for a gift, text can totally transform your crafts. The following sections explain how you can get started adding and customizing text for your designs.

Finding and adding text

Follow these steps (shown in Figure 8-5) to add text and search for the perfect font:

1. **Add text.**

   Click the Text button in the Design panel on the left, place a text box on the canvas, and start typing.

   REMEMBER

   After adding text to your Canvas, the operation automatically gets set to Basic Cut. If you want the text to be written, switch the operation to Pen after choosing a writing font.

2. **Find fonts.**

   Use the Font drop-down menu to explore a variety of fonts and find the perfect style for your design.

3. **Identify Cricut Access fonts.**

   Fonts with a green *a* icon require a Cricut Access subscription, which you can read about in Chapter 6. Be sure to use the filter option to sort for free fonts.

4. **Browse font categories.**

   Choose from the following categories:

   - **Cricut:** These free and Cricut Access–only fonts are exclusive to Design Space.
   - **System:** These are fonts installed on your computer, including ones you've downloaded (see the next section). If you can't find a font, check the System tab.
   - **Recent:** Quickly access fonts you've used recently.
   - **Bookmarked:** Save fonts you love by bookmarking them so you can easily find them later.

5. **Search for fonts.**

   Enter the font name, category, or style to quickly find what you need.

6. **Filter fonts.**

   Narrow down fonts by characteristics like free options or Cricut Access exclusives.

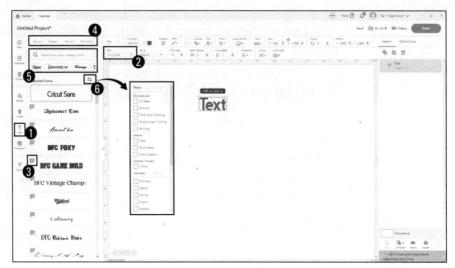

FIGURE 8-5: Finding and adding text.

Source: design.cricut.com

Installing your own fonts

When working on custom Cricut projects, you may want more font options than what's available in Design Space. Fortunately, it's super easy to install fonts into Design Space from other websites. Here's how:

1. **Find fonts.**

   Begin by searching for fonts online. Websites like Google Fonts (https://fonts.google.com/), DaFont (https://www.dafont.com/), and Creative Fabrica (www.creativefabrica.com/) offer a wide range of free and paid fonts.

   REMEMBER

   Check whether the font license allows for personal or commercial use, depending on your project needs. See the earlier section "Understanding personal versus commercial licenses".

2. **Download fonts.**

   Once you've selected a font, download the font file to your computer.

3. **Open the downloaded file.**

   Go to your Downloads folder and double-click the ZIP file to open it. Fonts typically come in ZIP files containing OpenType font (OTF) and/or TrueType font (TTF) files.

TECHNICAL STUFF

OTFs offer advanced features like *ligatures* (combined or attached letters), alternates, fractions, and *swashes* (letters with flourishes). For more design flexibility, choose OTFs over TTFs.

4. **Install the font on your computer.**

   - **Windows:** Double-click the OTF or TTF file, then click Install in the Font Preview window that opens.
   - **Mac:** Double-click the font file, then click Install Font in the Font Book app that appears.

5. **Restart Cricut Design Space.**

   If Design Space was open when you installed the font, close and reopen the program to ensure that the new font appears under the System tab in the Font menu.

Finding hidden font characters

Many fonts include decorative elements like swashes, alternate letters, or special *glyphs* (symbols) that don't appear when you simply type. To find these hidden characters, open Character Map on Windows or Font Book on Mac.

On Windows:

1. **Open Character Map in the Start menu.**
2. **Select your font from the drop-down menu at the top.**
3. **Set Character set to Unicode for the best results.**

   If you don't see Character set, make sure you've clicked the box for Advanced view.

4. **In the Group by menu, choose Unicode Subrange and then select Private Use Characters to find hidden alternates.**
5. **Click on the special character you want, and then press Select and Copy to paste it into Design Space.**

On Mac:

1. **Open Font Book in Applications.**
2. **Select your font and then switch to Repertoire view to see all available characters.**

CHAPTER 8 Designing in Cricut Design Space

3. **Click on the special character you want and copy it for use in Design Space.**

By using Character Map or Font Book, you can find special font characters like swashes and alternates to make your Cricut projects look unique and professional.

Customizing fonts

Once you select a font, you can customize it using the tools found in the Text Edit bar at the top of the Canvas. For a visual guide to identify these tools and see some of them in action, see Figure 8-6. Here are some text-editing tools you may find useful:

1. **Style:** Choose regular, bold, italic, or writing styles.

2. **Font Size:** Adjust the font size by dragging the bounding box corners or using the Font Size tool in the toolbar.

3. **Letter Space:** Change the spacing between letters to improve the design's flow.

4. **Line Space:** Adjust the space between lines of text for better readability.

5. **Alignment:** Align text left, center, or right to position it perfectly within your design.

6. **Curve:** Bend text into a gentle arc to match your design's layout.

7. **Warp:** Transform text into unique shapes for more creative designs.

8. **Ungroup to Letters:** Break your text into individual letters for advanced customization, like adjusting letter placement or changing colors. You can do this by selecting your text and using the Ungroup button in the Layers panel on the right side of the Canvas, or by clicking on Advanced in the Text Edit bar at the top of the Canvas and selecting Ungroup to Letters. After making changes, weld or unite the letters to ensure smooth cutting. (I cover welding and uniting in the later section "Mastering key tools in the Layers panel.")

9. **Offset:** To make your text or design stand out, use the Offset tool to add a border around it. You can adjust the thickness and color of the border to match your project's needs.

10. **Create Sticker:** This Cricut Access–exclusive feature allows you to easily convert text into print-ready stickers by applying an offset and grouping the elements into a single layer. (See Chapter 6 for details on Cricut Access.)

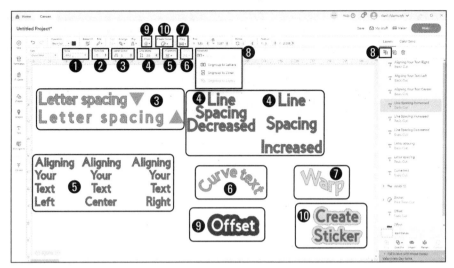

FIGURE 8-6: Tools used for customizing fonts.

Source: design.cricut.com

Creating monograms

Creating monograms is a fantastic way to personalize gifts and home décor. To get started with Monogram Maker in Cricut Design Space, ensure that you have a Cricut Access subscription (see Chapter 6). This tool artfully combines initials to create a custom design. Here's how to create your monogram, illustrated in Figure 8-7:

1. **Open Monogram Maker.**

   Click on the Monogram tool in the toolbar on the left.

2. **Enter your initials.**

   Start by typing the initials you want to include in the monogram.

3. **Choose a style.**

   Navigate between the Classic and Thematic tabs to explore various monogram styles. Click on different frames to see how each design looks with your initials.

4. **Select the operation type.**

   Decide how you want to create your monogram by choosing from Any, Cut, or Cut + Draw in the Operation Type drop-down menu:

   - **Any:** Displays designs that can be made using any operation type, such as Print Then Cut, Basic Cut, and Pen.
   - **Cut:** Filters designs that are meant to be cut from material using a blade. These designs work well with vinyl, cardstock, iron-on, and other cuttable materials.

CHAPTER 8 **Designing in Cricut Design Space** 99

- **Cut + Draw:** Filters monogram designs that include both drawn and cut elements. The Cricut will first draw the monogram with a pen or marker, then cut around it. This is useful for decorative monograms on cards, labels, and paper crafts.

5. **Click on Add to Canvas.**

    Once you're satisfied with the design, add it to your canvas to continue editing or to prepare for cutting.

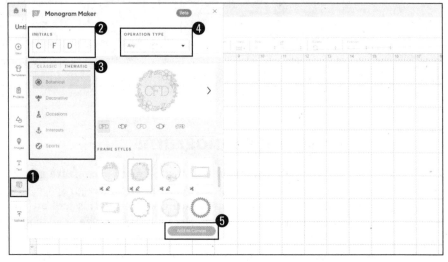

FIGURE 8-7:
The steps to use the Monogram Maker tool in Cricut Design Space.

Source: design.cricut.com

Visualizing Your Design with Templates and Guides

Templates are a great place to start in Cricut Design Space, because they help you visualize your design on real-world items like T-shirts, mugs, or cards. When you click the Templates button in the Design panel on the left side of the screen, you'll find a variety of guides (see Figure 8-8) that include precise measurements and markers for alignment. For example

>> The 15oz mug layout guide in Figure 8-8 includes dashed lines that indicate the handle, front, and back of the mug so that you know exactly where to place your design.

TIP

Infusible Ink is a great option for customizing mugs with vibrant, long-lasting results. For more on using Infusible Ink, see Chapter 16.

» A T-shirt layout guide marks important areas like the pocket and the recommended decal size for the front and back of the shirt. The guide on your Canvas should match the size of your shirt, making it easier to position your design correctly. You can also find helpful T-shirt sizing guides in Chapter 15.

» A Cutaway Card layout guide lets you choose the specific type of card you're using. The guide includes dashed lines to show where to place your images and text within the design area. It also provides instructions to help you design your cutaway card. For more details on creating cards, see Chapter 12.

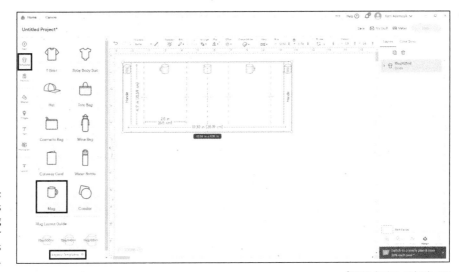

FIGURE 8-8: The Templates screen showing layout guides for items like mugs and T-shirts.

Source: design.cricut.com

REMEMBER

Guides and templates are strictly visual aids — they won't be cut or drawn, or appear on the mat.

Legacy Templates

At the bottom of the Templates screen is the Legacy Templates option (refer to Figure 8-8). These Legacy Templates, illustrated in Figure 8-9, allow for more customizable previews of your design on actual items. Unlike guides, Legacy Templates don't feature dashed lines for precise alignment, but they're still useful for visualizing the final appearance of your project.

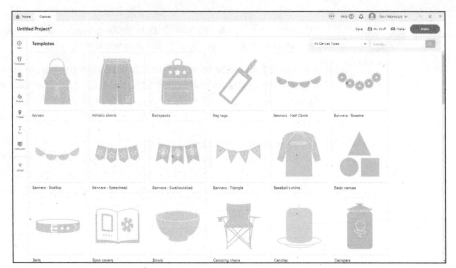

FIGURE 8-9: Legacy Templates options.

Source: design.cricut.com

For example, if you're designing a T-shirt or tote bag, a Legacy Template provides an outline of the item on your Canvas. Unlike guides, Legacy Templates allow you to adjust the type, size, and color of a specific template to better match your blank.

Follow these steps (see Figure 8-10) to customize a Legacy Template:

1. **Click Templates in the left-hand toolbar.**
2. **Scroll down and click Legacy Templates at the bottom of the Templates screen.**
3. **Select a Legacy Template from the list, such as Classic t-shirts.**
4. **Use the Edit Bar at the top of the Canvas to change the type, size, or color of the template:**
   - **Type:** Choose from options like Men Short sleeve, Women Short sleeve, Kid Short sleeve, Toddler, or Baby.
   - **Size:** Select Custom, Small, Medium, Large, X-large, or XX-large. Choosing Custom lets you enter specific width and height dimensions.
   - **Color:** Pick a color that matches your actual blank (shirt).

   TIP

   Editing options for Type and Size vary by template. For example, the Goblet template includes options for Water goblet, Sparkling wine, Champagne, or Cocktail under the Type drop-down menu.
5. **Add a design to your template to preview how your finished project will look.**

102 PART 2 Mastering Cricut Design Space

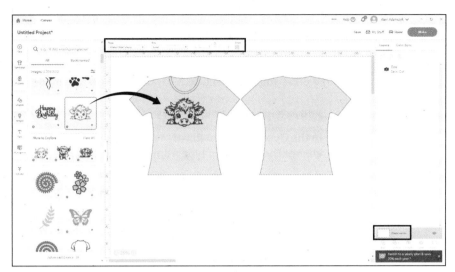

FIGURE 8-10:
Customizing a Legacy Template.

Source: design.cricut.com

When you add text, images, or other elements to your Canvas, the Edit Bar switches to editing those elements instead of the template. To bring the Template Edit Bar back, follow these steps:

1. **Click the template name at the bottom of the Layers panel on the right side of the screen.**

   The name will match the Legacy Template you chose (for example, Classic t-shirts).

2. **The Template Edit Bar will reappear, allowing you to make further adjustments.**

3. **Use the Eye icon in the Layers panel to hide or show the template on the Canvas as needed.**

Guides

Guides are a versatile Design Space feature that help you accurately size and position your designs. Although several different guides are included in Templates, you can also create custom guides with any shape, text, or image directly on your canvas.

TIP

You can add text to the Canvas as notes or instructions and then change the text's operation to Guide so it doesn't interfere with your design or appear on the mat. For example, if you're creating a multilayered vinyl decal, you may add a reminder note on the Canvas like "Layer the white vinyl first" or "Mirror this design for

CHAPTER 8 **Designing in Cricut Design Space**   103

HTV." Since Guide text doesn't cut, draw, or print, it stays visible for reference without affecting your final project.

Follow these steps (see Figure 8-11) to create custom guides:

1. **Add a shape, text, or image to your Canvas.**
2. **In the Operation drop-down menu in the Edit Bar at the top of the screen, change the operation type from Basic Cut to Guide.**
3. **Custom guides appear as a red outline and won't prompt your Cricut to cut, draw, or perform any other operation.**

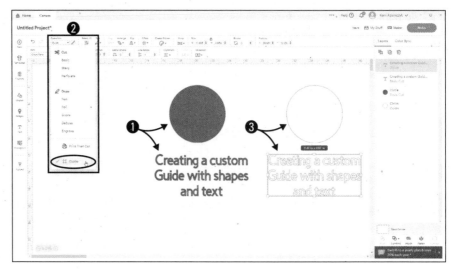

FIGURE 8-11: Custom guides created from text and shapes on the Canvas.

Source: design.cricut.com

Working with Layers

In Cricut Design Space, each piece of your design is assigned to a layer, much like stacking papers. Each layer can contain text, images, or shapes, and you can manipulate each layer without affecting others. All the layers in your design are located in the Layers panel on the right side of the Canvas.

Figure 8-12 shows the breakdown of a Christmas tree design into five layers within the Layers panel. You can also see the eye tool, which is used to temporarily hide layers. Hidden layers won't be included when you click Make, meaning they won't cut, draw, or print in the final project.

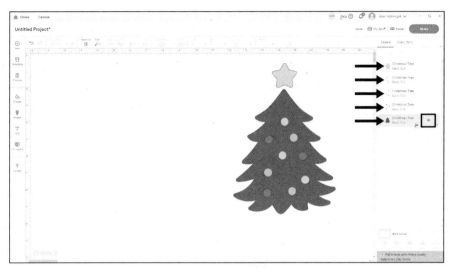

FIGURE 8-12: Identifying layers of a Christmas tree design in the Layers panel.

Source: design.cricut.com

Discovering how to use layers

Here's a guide to help you master working with layers:

>> **Creating new layers:** Every time you add a new piece of text, shape, or image to your Canvas, a new layer is automatically created. This keeps each element separate and editable. If you want to duplicate an existing layer, simply right-click on the layer in the Layers panel and select Duplicate. Alternatively, you can click the Duplicate button located at the top of the Layers panel, to the left of the trash icon. This is particularly handy for creating repeated elements in your design without having to recreate them from scratch.

>> **Ungrouping layers:** Often, designs imported to the Canvas are grouped, meaning the layers are combined into one manageable unit. To edit individual layers, you'll need to ungroup them first. Select the grouped layers and then click Ungroup in the Layers panel or right-click and select Ungroup.

REMEMBER

The Group and Ungroup functions share the same button, located at the top left in the Layers panel. This button is represented by two overlapping squares. Be careful not to confuse it with the Duplicate button, which is depicted by two overlapping squares with a plus sign inside, positioned to the right of the Group/Ungroup button.

>> **Grouping layers:** To move or edit multiple layers as one unit, select them by holding down the shift key and clicking on each layer you want to include. Then, click Group in the Layers panel or right-click and select Group. Grouping is helpful for keeping elements in their place relative to each other while you make changes.

CHAPTER 8 **Designing in Cricut Design Space** 105

TIP

» **Selecting layers:** Click on an element on your Canvas, and it will be highlighted in the Layers panel. You can also select layers directly from the panel to adjust their properties.

» **Moving layers:** Drag and drop layers within the Layers panel to rearrange the stacking order of your design elements. This is useful for placing one design element in front of or behind another. You can also right-click on a layer and choose Bring Forward to move it up one position, or Send Backward to move it down one position.

» **Hiding/showing layers:** Each layer has an eye icon beside it in the Layers panel. Click this icon to hide a layer, making it invisible on the Canvas. Click again to make the layer visible. This feature is useful for focusing on specific parts of your design without deleting any elements. Note that any layer you hide from view by clicking the eye icon next to it in the Layers panel won't appear in your project when you proceed to click Make. This allows you to control which elements are included in the final cut or print.

» **Deleting layers:** If you need to remove an element from your project, select the layer and either press the delete key on your keyboard or click the trash can icon in the Layers panel.

To find out more about how to work with multilayered designs, particularly with materials like vinyl, flip to Chapter 14.

Mastering key tools in the Layers Panel

The Layers Panel in Design Space is full of tools to help you manage and edit all the parts of your design. These tools help you cut, combine, and customize your designs to fit your project. See Figure 8-13 for a quick overview of many of these essential tools.

Group

Group keeps selected design elements together on the Canvas, allowing you to move, resize, or edit them as a single unit. Use Group to

» Move multiple elements together without changing their arrangement on the Canvas

» Resize or rotate a set of items as one unit

» Keep design pieces organized while working on multilayered or complex projects

PART 2 **Mastering Cricut Design Space**

FIGURE 8-13: A quick reference guide to key tools in Design Space.

Source: Kerri Adamczyk

How to use it:

1. **Select the items you want to group.**
2. **At the top of the Layers panel, click the Group button (represented by two overlapping squares), or right-click and select Group from the pop-up menu.**

Ungroup

Ungroup separates grouped elements, allowing you to edit or move them individually. Use Ungroup to

- Edit individual pieces of a grouped design separately.
- Adjust spacing or positioning of specific elements without affecting the whole group.
- Customize text designs by moving letters independently or changing their colors.

CHAPTER 8 Designing in Cricut Design Space 107

How to use it:

1. **Select the grouped items you want to separate.**
2. **At the top of the Layers panel, click the Ungroup button (represented by two overlapping squares), or right-click and choose Ungroup from the pop-up menu.**

Slice

Slice cuts one shape out of another, creating separate layers. Use Slice when you need to

TIP

- » Remove parts of your design.

    Because Design Space doesn't have an eraser, Slice is the best way to cut out unwanted sections of a design. For example, in Figure 8-13, I used Slice to customize a heart design by cutting out a rectangle, where I then added a name.

- » Create text cutouts by slicing a name or word into a shape, like a circle or rectangle — perfect for custom photo frames where you can place photos behind the letters.

- » Add colorful effects by slicing letters or shapes into photos or patterns, perfect for unique Print Then Cut projects (see Chapter 18).

- » Make custom shapes by slicing one image from another to create new designs.

- » Split images into pieces to rearrange or layer differently.

How to use it:

1. **Select two overlapping shapes.**
2. **Click Slice at the bottom of the Layers panel.**
3. **Drag apart the sliced pieces and delete any unwanted parts.**

REMEMBER

You can slice only two elements at a time.

Weld

Weld merges multiple shapes into one design, removing any overlapping lines. Use Weld when you want to

- » Combine shapes or text into a single, solid piece for cutting.
- » Keep script letters connected to prevent Cricut from cutting them individually.

» Create a new, unified design by joining overlapping shapes. For example, in Figure 8-13, Weld was used to permanently attach the name to the heart, ensuring they're cut as one piece.

TIP

For script fonts, welding is important to ensure that the Cricut machine cuts the text as one connected word rather than separate letters. Although cursive letters often weld automatically in Design Space, some fonts don't. To avoid unexpected cuts between letters, it's a good habit to always weld your script fonts before cutting. If needed, ungroup and adjust the letter spacing — also referred to as *kerning* — before welding for the best results.

Sometimes when you're welding script fonts, the inner parts of the letters may fill in with black, which isn't what you want. If this happens, click Undo, adjust the letter spacing to give them a bit more room, and then try welding again.

REMEMBER

Welding is permanent unless it's undone immediately. If you think you may need to make changes later, consider using Unite instead, which I discuss next.

How to use it:

1. **Select the shapes or text you want to combine.**
2. **At the bottom of the Layers panel, click the Combine button, which opens up a drop-down menu.**

   From this menu, select Weld.

After welding, your images will blend into a single color, and a new single merged layer will show up in the Layers panel.

TIP

The Font drop-down menu disappears after you weld text, so you can't see the font you used anymore. To find it, right-click on the welded shape in the Layers panel and select Image Info at the bottom. This will display the name of the font you used.

Unite

Unite works like Weld by merging shapes into one design, but it allows you to undo or adjust later. Use Unite when you want to

» Combine shapes or text but keep the option to separate them later.

» Create personalized designs where you may need to swap out names or text. For example, if you're making multiple custom heart designs with names,

CHAPTER 8 **Designing in Cricut Design Space** 109

Unite lets you easily change the names without starting from scratch. This makes it perfect for projects that may need tweaks or updates later.

» Experiment with different layouts without making permanent changes.

How to use it:

1. **Select the shapes or text you want to combine.**
2. **At the bottom of the Layers panel, click on the Combine button, which opens up a drop-down menu.**

    From this menu, select Unite.

Subtract

Subtract removes the top shape from the one underneath, leaving a cutout. Use Subtract to

» Quickly remove one shape from another without keeping the cutout piece

» Create custom cutouts, like making a hole in a tag for ribbon

» Design layered cutouts for cards, decorations, or stencils

How to use it:

1. **Select two overlapping shapes.**
2. **At the bottom of the Layers panel, click on the Combine button, which opens up a drop-down menu.**

    From this menu, select Subtract.

TIP

Subtract works like Slice but automatically deletes the removed pieces.

Intersect

Intersect keeps only the overlapping area of selected shapes and removes everything else. Use Intersect to

» Create unique patterns within shapes

» Add decorative elements to your designs by combining patterns with shapes

» Design custom cutouts for projects like cards or stencils

110 PART 2 Mastering Cricut Design Space

How to use it:

1. **Select overlapping shapes or a shape and a pattern.**
2. **At the bottom of the Layers panel, click on the Combine button, which opens up a drop-down menu.**

   From this menu, select Intersect.

Exclude

Exclude removes the overlapping parts of shapes, leaving only the nonoverlapping sections. Use Exclude to

- » Create frames or outlines by removing the center of a shape
- » Design hollow shapes for layered projects
- » Add decorative borders to your designs

TIP Place a small heart inside a large heart and click Exclude to create a heart-shaped frame.

How to use it:

1. **Select overlapping shapes on the Canvas.**
2. **At the bottom of the Layers Panel, click on the Combine button, which opens up a drop-down menu.**

   From this menu, select Exclude.

Attach

Attach keeps your design elements in place so they stay in the exact arrangement you see on the Canvas when Design Space sends them to the Cricut for cutting or other operations. It also connects operations like writing, scoring, or foiling to a cut layer. Use Attach to

- » Ensure that text, shapes, or images are in the same position on the mat as they are on the Canvas
- » Maintain spacing between letters or objects so they don't shift
- » Attach writing, drawing, scoring, or foiling to a cut layer to ensure everything stays aligned
- » Fasten multiple layers together for cutting in the correct arrangement

How to use it:

1. **Select the layers or elements you want to keep aligned.**
2. **Click Attach at the bottom of the Layers panel.**

REMEMBER

Group keeps items together on the canvas, while Attach locks their position on the mat for cutting or other operations.

REMEMBER

To better understand the importance of the Attach function, consider a practical example involving card-making. Suppose you want to create a card with text drawn on top of a rectangle. If you place text over a rectangle but don't use the Attach function, Design Space won't understand that you want them to be processed as a single project. Instead, it will treat the text and rectangle as separate elements to be cut on different mats. To ensure that your text is drawn onto the rectangle, you must change the operation from Basic Cut to Pen in the Operation drop-down menu, and then use the Attach button to link the text to the rectangle. This tells your Cricut to draw the text and then cut the rectangle as one integrated design, keeping them on the same mat in their correct positions relative to each other.

Flatten

Flatten combines multiple layers into one for Print Then Cut designs. Use Flatten to

- Create custom stickers, gift tags, or labels by combining text and shapes into one printable layer
- Prepare images for Print Then Cut so your Cricut knows to print the design instead of cutting separate pieces
- Make custom party invitations by combining text and images into one printable layer

How to use it:

1. **Select all layers you want to combine.**
2. **Click Flatten at the bottom of the Layers panel.**

Contour

Contour hides or removes certain parts of a shape or design. Use Contour to

- Simplify detailed designs by hiding small or intricate parts.
- Customize shapes by removing unwanted sections.

>> Make cutting and weeding easier by removing fine details. For example, if your project includes detailed snowflakes like the ones in Figure 8-13, Contour can remove the inner sections, leaving only the outline to make cutting and weeding faster.

How to use it:

1. **Select the design or shape you want to edit.**

2. **Click Contour in the bottom of the Layers panel.**

3. **In the Contour window, click on the parts of the design you want to hide.**

    Hidden sections will appear grayed out.

4. **Close the Contour window to apply your changes.**

Color Sync

Color Sync shows all the colors in your design and lets you combine them to save materials. Use Color Sync to

>> Simplify multicolored designs by reducing the number of colors.

>> Change elements to the same color when you don't have specific materials. For example, in the flower design in Figure 8-13, I didn't have purple or blue vinyl, so I used Color Sync to make all the flowers pink.

>> Organize colors for easier cutting and material preparation.

How to use it:

1. **Open the Color Sync panel, located at the top of the Layers panel, directly beneath the Make button.**

2. **Drag the layer you want to change onto the color you want to match.**

Setting the Correct Operations

Your Cricut machine is capable of handling a variety of tasks, from cutting and writing, to scoring and engraving. The Operation menu in Cricut Design Space helps you assign the correct function to each element of your design. For example, if you're making a card, you may need your machine to write the text and cut out the shapes.

CHAPTER 8 Designing in Cricut Design Space   113

You'll find the Operation drop-down menu in the Edit Bar at the top of your canvas once you've selected a design element. The following steps, shown in Figure 8-14, walk you through how to assign the correct operation to each part of your design:

1. **Select the element.**

   Click on a specific element in your design, such as text or a shape.

2. **Choose the operation.**

   Open the Operation drop-down menu in the Edit Bar to select from the following options:

   - **Basic Cut:** Cuts through a variety of materials and works for most of your cutting needs.
   - **Wavy Cut:** Adds a decorative wavy edge to cuts.
   - **Perforate:** Creates a dotted line for easy tearing, perfect for tickets or coupons.
   - **Pen:** Uses a pen to draw or write instead of cutting.
   - **Foil:** Applies metallic foil to your design for shiny accents.
   - **Score:** Adds a fold line to your material, perfect for making cards or boxes.
   - **Deboss:** Presses designs into the material, creating a recessed effect.
   - **Engrave:** Engraves designs into hard materials like metal or leather.
   - **Print Then Cut:** Sends your design to a printer and then cuts around the print.
   - **Guide:** Adds nonprinting lines to help you position and organize design elements.

TIP

Some operations, like Wavy Cut, Perforate, Engrave, and Deboss, are exclusive to the Cricut Maker series. For more on which tools and operations work with your machine, see Chapter 2.

3. **Confirm your settings.**

   Before starting your project, look at the Layers panel to double-check that each element of your design is set with the correct operation.

4. **Use the eye tool (optional).**

   Use the eye tool (which appears when you highlight a layer) to temporarily hide elements for a clearer view of your layout.

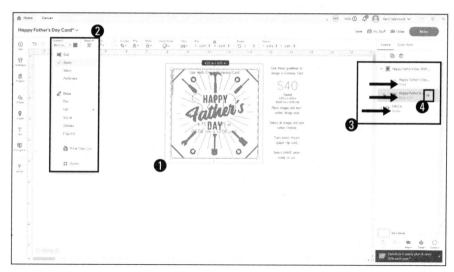

FIGURE 8-14: The Operation drop-down menu and Layers panel in Design Space.

Source: `design.cricut.com`

In Figure 8-14, I uploaded a Cutaway Card layout guide from the Templates section to help me figure out the perfect size and placement for my design. In the Layers panel on the right, you can see the different operation settings for each element:

» **Happy Father's Day design:** Set to Basic Cut, meaning these elements will be cut out on the front of the card, revealing the colorful backing underneath. This creates a visually striking effect by cutting through the cardstock.

» **Lines around text:** Set to Draw, indicating that these lines will be drawn on the card using a pen or marker, adding detailed decorations around the cutouts.

» **Cutaway Card guide:** Marked as Guide for layout visualization only and will not be cut or drawn.

Once you've assigned the correct operation to each part of your design, you're ready to send it to your Cricut machine. In Chapter 9, I guide you through preparing your project for cutting, drawing, or other tasks.

> **IN THIS CHAPTER**
>
> » Saving your projects for future edits
>
> » Sharing your projects with the Cricut community
>
> » Preparing your mat and materials in Design Space

Chapter 9
Bringing Your Designs to Life

In Chapter 8, you explore the ins and outs of Cricut Design Space so that you can begin to create, upload, and edit your designs. When you're finished editing, it's time to bring your designs to life! In this chapter, you find out how to prepare your materials and mat, send your design to the Cricut, and save and share your creations with the Cricut community.

Saving and Sharing Projects

REMEMBER

When you're satisfied with your project in Design Space, click Make in the upper-right corner of the screen. You'll be prompted to save your project.

REMEMBER

Always save your project by clicking the Save button in the upper-right corner of the Design Space screen. When saving, you have two main options:

» **Save:** Saves your current progress.

» **Save As:** Creates a new copy of the project, useful for variations.

Projects start as Untitled Project*. Once you add an element to the Canvas and hit Save, you can name your project.

Saving for offline use

TIP

To ensure that your projects are always accessible, even off-line, adjust your default save settings as follows:

1. **Navigate to Settings.**

   Click on the profile drop-down menu in the top-right corner of the screen, where you see your name. Select Settings from the options listed.

2. **Adjust your saving options.**

   Under the General tab, set your saving preference to Cloud & Computer to save projects both online and on your own device. This allows for offline access and editing, which is perfect for crafting on the go at craft fairs or wherever internet access may be unreliable.

Creating and managing Collections

You can organize your projects and images in Collections, similar to Pinterest boards, for easier access. Here are the details:

- **Creating a Collection:** Navigate to the My Stuff tab, which you can find directly under your name in the upper-right corner of the screen. Once you're there, look to the left side of the screen and you'll see the word COLLECTIONS in all capital letters with a plus sign next to it. Click on this plus sign to create a new Collection and give it a name. Whenever you come across projects or images you like, you can add them to your Collection by selecting the Bookmark icon.

- **Saving to Collections:** When saving a project, use the Save As option and select your desired Collection from the drop-down menu.

- **Reaching member limits:** All members can create up to five Collections. If you subscribe to Cricut Access, you enjoy the benefit of creating unlimited collections. (Flip to Chapter 6 for details on Cricut Access.)

Sharing your projects

You can boost your presence in the Design Space community by making sure your projects are set up for sharing. Follow these steps to share a project:

1. **Access your projects.**

   After saving your project, navigate to My Stuff, then click on My Projects to view all of your saved projects.

2. **Edit the project details.**

   Select the project you want to share, and click on the white circle with three black dots in the upper-right corner of the project thumbnail. From the drop-down menu, select Edit Project Details. Add a name, description, and tags to your project. Be sure to upload a photo if you want it to be visible in Design Space.

3. **Save your changes.**

   After entering all the details, hit Save at the bottom-right corner to update your project information.

4. **Choose your sharing options.**

   Click the Share icon (the curved arrow pointing to the right) in the lower-left corner of the project tile. Clicking on this icon opens a menu with two options: Share to Design Space or Copy Private Link.

   - **Share to Design Space:** Selecting Share to Design Space will make your project public within the Cricut community, allowing others to view, like, and comment on your work.

   - **Copy a private link:** If you prefer more control over who sees your work or want to share it outside Design Space, click the Share icon after saving your project and select Copy Private Link. You can use this link for private sharing via email or text message, or you can post it on social media platforms like Facebook or Pinterest to broaden your project's reach and engagement.

Sending Your Design to Your Cricut

After clicking Make and saving your design, you'll be taken to the Prepare screen, where you'll get your design ready to be sent to the Cricut. Simply follow the prompts highlighted by the green button, which guide you through the setup process step by step.

CHAPTER 9 Bringing Your Designs to Life 119

Introducing the Prepare screen

Before you start cutting or drawing your design, make sure that you set up the Prepare screen correctly so everything lines up just right. Figure 9-1 illustrates the steps you should follow to get everything set up perfectly:

1. **Project copies:** Decide how many copies of your project you want to make and enter the number at the top left. Click Apply to update the preview with your specified quantity.

2. **Material load type:** Choose how you want to load your material into your Cricut — either directly (if you're using Smart Materials) or on a mat.

REMEMBER

3. **Material size:** Select the size of your material to ensure that your design aligns correctly on the mat in the preview. This step is crucial, especially when you're using a specialized mat like the Card Mat.

4. **Mirror:** If you're working with heat transfer vinyl (HTV) or Infusible Ink materials (see Chapters 15 and 16), be sure to toggle on the Mirror option, which flips your design so it prints or cuts correctly. Always place the shiny side of these materials face down on the mat.

5. **Adjust the design placement:** Design Space automatically positions your design in the upper-left corner of your mat. However, you have the flexibility to move it around the mat as needed. This feature is particularly useful if you're cutting multiple colors on one mat.

TIP

For easy alignment, consider using the four corners of the mat. Just match up the grid lines on your screen with the grid on your mat to place your design precisely where you want it.

6. **Move objects between mats:** In Design Space, your designs are automatically sorted by color, with each color on its own mat on the Prepare screen. If you want to cut multiple colors on a single mat to save time and material, you can easily move objects between mats. Simply click on the three dots next to your design to find the Move Object option. From there, select the mat you want to move that layer of your design to.

7. **Hide selected layers on the mat:** Temporarily hide layers on the mat if you decide not to cut them right away. This can be done by selecting the layer and choosing the Hide Selected option.

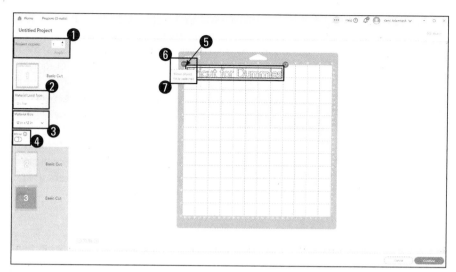

FIGURE 9-1:
The Prepare screen showing the initial setup options.

Source: design.cricut.com

Setting up your mat

Loading your materials onto your mat the right way is crucial for ensuring that your designs get made properly. It's important to match what you see on your computer screen with what's physically on your mat. The Prepare screen in Design Space shows you a preview of your mat, and you should place your material on the mat exactly where your design shows on the screen. Here are a few simple steps to ensure that your mat is set up properly:

1. **Choose the right mat.**

   Select the appropriate mat based on the material you're using. Cricut offers different mats for materials such as paper, vinyl, and fabric. Each mat has a specific level of adhesive strength to hold your material firmly during the cutting process. Check out Chapter 4 for details.

2. **Preview and adjust the material placement in Design Space.**

   Look at the Prepare screen in Design Space to see a preview of your mat. This helps you place your design exactly where you want it on the mat. Although the default placement is the upper-left corner, you can move your design anywhere on the mat. This is beneficial for

   - **Even wear and tear:** Regularly cutting in one area can wear out that part of the mat faster. By moving your designs around, you can evenly distribute the wear and extend your mat's life.

CHAPTER 9 **Bringing Your Designs to Life** 121

- **Organization and efficiency:** If you're using multiple colors, Design Space automatically assigns each color to a separate mat on the Prepare screen. To save time and material and keep your project organized, try placing different colors in different corners on the same mat. See the previous section for instructions on how to move objects between mats.

3. **Secure the material.**

   TIP

   After placing your material on the mat, press it down firmly with a brayer or scraper tool, paying extra attention to the edges. For thicker materials, consider using painter's tape along the edges to prevent them from lifting during the cut.

USING SNAPMAT FOR PERFECT PLACEMENT (IOS ONLY)

If you're using Cricut Design Space on an iPhone or iPad, SnapMat is a handy tool that helps you place your designs on your mat with pinpoint accuracy. It uses your device's camera to take a photo of your already loaded mat, showing exactly where your material is positioned. You can then drag and drop your design right on top of the material in the photo, making SnapMat perfect for using scraps, patterned materials, or precut items like tags and labels. Here's how to use SnapMat:

1. **Load your material onto the mat.**
2. **Click Make It and select SnapMat from the options.**
3. **Take a photo of your mat using your device's camera.**

   Make sure you have good lighting and place something white, like a sheet of paper, under the mat for contrast. Hold your camera parallel to the mat to avoid distortion and get the clearest view of your materials.

4. **Drag and position your design exactly where you want it on the material.**
5. **Click Continue to choose your material and send your design to your Cricut.**

   Before loading your mat into the machine, you'll have to move to the Make screen to tell your Cricut what type of material you're using. Click Continue to move to the Make screen, where you'll finalize your settings and start your project.

SnapMat is available only on iPhone and iPad. If you're using a desktop or Android device, this feature won't appear in Design Space.

Checking out the Make screen

The Make screen is your final checkpoint before your Cricut starts cutting or drawing. Follow these steps to make sure everything is set up right:

1. **Connect your machine.**

   Ensure that your Cricut machine is powered on and connected to your computer or mobile device, either via USB or Bluetooth. (You can see the Connect machine field at the top of the Make screen in Figure 9-2.) If you need detailed instructions on connecting your machine, go to Chapter 3.

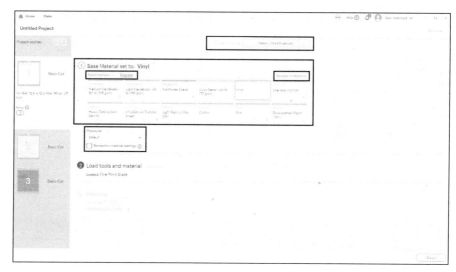

FIGURE 9-2: Make screen setup illustrating how to connect your machine, set materials, and adjust pressure.

Source: `design.cricut.com`

2. **Set your base material.**

   Click Browse All Materials to find and select the material you're using. You can bookmark up to 12 of your favorite materials for quick access.

   TIP If you're using the Cricut Explore Air 2, you can adjust the material settings quickly using the Smart Set dial on the machine.

3. **Adjust the cutting pressure.**

   After selecting your material, you'll see the Pressure drop-down menu, where you can adjust the cutting pressure. Choose More, Default, or Less depending on the thickness of your material.

   TIP If you're worried your Cricut won't cut through a thick material completely, try setting the pressure to More.

CHAPTER 9 **Bringing Your Designs to Life**   123

4. **Load the necessary tools into the correct clamp on your Cricut.**

   Design Space makes it easy, guiding you on which tool to use and where to insert it (that is, the correct clamp for your Cricut machine). It also tells you when to switch tools if your project includes different operations, like cutting and writing. See Figure 9-3.

5. **Load your mat and start your project.**

   Once everything's set, align your mat with the guides on your machine and press the Load button. (With the machines in the Cricut Joy series, the mat automatically loads after you insert it.)

   After loading your mat, press the Go button to begin cutting or drawing your design. (With the machines in the Cricut Joy series, you start the process through the software.)

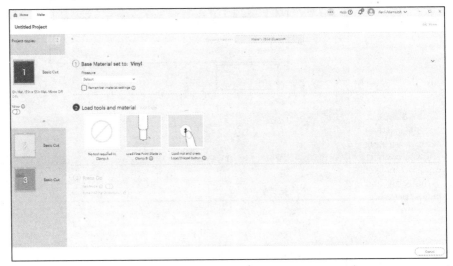

FIGURE 9-3: How to load tools and materials into your Cricut.

Source: design.cricut.com

3
Projects Using Paper and Cardstock

IN THIS PART . . .

Discover how to cut unique gift tags to personalize your presents and projects.

Create long-lasting rolled paper flowers to decorate your home or special events.

Have fun making personalized cards for friends and family.

IN THIS CHAPTER

» Discovering project ideas using gift tags

» Selecting the right tools and materials

» Deciding how to create your gift tags

» Designing and cutting your gift tags

Chapter **10**

Cutting Gift Tags

Creating custom gift tags with your Cricut is an easy way to add a personal touch to any gift. For holidays or special occasions, cutting themed tags shaped like snowmen, baby bottles, or balloons can make your gifts stand out.

This chapter not only focuses on gift tags but also serves as an introduction to mastering the art of paper cutting — a fundamental skill in the world of Cricut crafting. The techniques you read about here can be applied to a variety of projects, such as creating decorative paper banners for parties, designing scrapbook pages, or crafting cardstock bookmarks. You'll also explore multistep methods such as cutting combined with writing on tags, which you can use for other creative projects like writing on cards and making labels. (See a tag project in the color section.)

Checking Out Project Ideas Using Gift Tags

TIP

Gift tags don't have to be simple rectangle shapes. Cut them to match any theme or occasion! Here are a few fun ways to use them:

» **Baby showers:** Create tags shaped like rattles, baby bottles, or onesies to attach to prizes or party favors.

CHAPTER 10 **Cutting Gift Tags** 127

- » **Birthday parties:** Make tags shaped like balloons, cupcakes, or party hats for your favors.

- » **Pet-themed gift tags:** Create bone- or paw-shaped tags to attach to gifts for pet lovers, perfect for packaging treats or accessories. (This paper idea is not to be confused with engraved pet tags, which you can find out how to make in Chapter 22.)

- » **Price tags:** If you're selling at craft fairs or shops, use custom price tags to add a professional touch.

- » **Teacher gifts:** Make tags shaped like pencils or apples, perfect for organizing classroom supplies or as a fun add-on to teacher appreciation gifts.

- » **Thank-you tags:** Design thank-you tags that are perfect for party favors or custom orders in your small business.

- » **Wedding favors**: Add personalized tags with the couple's names and the date to wedding favors.

When I sold funny reusable egg cartons at a local shop, I made chicken-shaped price tags using my Cricut, proving how versatile it can be for any project (see Figure 10-1). They were a hit!

FIGURE 10-1: Chicken-shaped price tags made using white cardstock and Print Then Cut.

Source: design.cricut.com

128   PART 3 Projects Using Paper and Cardstock

Picking the Right Tools and Materials for Gift Tags

To start cutting your gift tags, make sure that you have these essential materials (see Chapter 4 for an introduction to tools and materials):

- **Brayer:** For securing your cardstock to the mat.
- **Cardstock:** This basic gift tag material is sturdy and available in a variety of colors and patterns. Glitter cardstock adds sparkle. If you're looking for something even sturdier, Cricut Kraft Board is an excellent option. It's thicker and holds up well, especially for packaged items that require a more durable tag.
- **Cricut Pens:** You can choose from a variety of pens to add text, drawings, or decorative details to your gift tags.
- **Inkjet printer:** Required only for Print Then Cut-style tags. Print your design on cardstock or printable sticker paper, and then have your Cricut precisely cut out the shapes. (See Chapter 18 for details on Print Then Cut.)
- **Premium Fine-Point Blade:** This blade cuts clean lines on cardstock and other basic materials.
- **Printable sticker paper:** Optional, but useful if you want to turn your gift tags into stickers using the Print Then Cut method.
- **Ribbon or string:** You'll need this for tying your finished tags to gifts.
- **StandardGrip Mat:** This is the best mat for holding your cardstock in place while cutting.
- **Weeding tools (hook, spatula, tweezers):** Use these tools to carefully remove and handle delicate pieces without damaging your gift tags.

TIP

Need to attach a bunch of tags quickly? Consider using 3-inch plastic hang tag fasteners — they're affordable and work like mini zip ties.

Want to add some extra flair? Here are more tools and materials to consider:

- **Cricut Rotary Blade (for Maker users):** This blade is handy for cutting fabric tags.
- **Double-sided adhesive tape or foam dots:** These are handy for layering or adding 3-D effects to your gift tags.

- » **Foil Transfer Kit:** For an elegant touch, you can add shiny foil accents to your gift tags.
- » **Iron-on vinyl (also known as heat transfer vinyl, or HTV):** You'll need this to add designs to fabric tags.
- » **Printable vinyl or sticker paper:** This is your go-to material for making sticker-style tags.
- » **Scoring Stylus or Scoring Wheel Tip:** For folded or tent-style tags, you can switch out your blade for one of these tools.

Choosing Your Gift Tag Method

You can create gift tags with your Cricut in a few different ways. Choose the method that works best for your project.

Method 1: Simple cut

Using a simple cut is the fastest and easiest way to make gift tags. If all you need are basic shapes like circles, rectangles, and triangles for standard holiday-themed tags (think snowmen or Christmas trees), the simple cut is your go-to method. You're just cutting out shapes — no text or extra details. Try searching for "gift tag shape" in Images to explore a wide range of options, just like the ones shown in Figure 10-2.

FIGURE 10-2: Use a simple cut for designs like these.

Source: design.cricut.com

Why pick this method?

- » You're in a hurry and want a quick way to make basic tags.
- » You're using decorative cardstock and don't need to add any extra design details.
- » You need to make a lot of tags quickly.

Method 2: Drawing and cutting

Think of the drawing and cutting method as having a calligraphy machine at your fingertips! Your Cricut can draw names, messages, or designs right onto your tags with pens or markers, and then cut them out. It's perfect if you love the look of handwritten tags but don't have the penmanship for it. Check out the cute birthday gift tags in Figure 10-3 made by drawing and cutting.

FIGURE 10-3: These birthday gift tags are made using the drawing and cutting method.

Source: design.cricut.com

Why pick this method?

- » You want to add names, messages, or designs to your tags.
- » You love the idea of using different ink colors to make your tags pop.
- » You want a uniform, professional finish without doing the handwriting yourself.

CHAPTER 10 **Cutting Gift Tags** 131

Method 3: Print Then Cut

Want colorful, detailed tags or tags with photos? With the Print Then Cut method, you can print customized, vibrant designs using your home printer and then have your Cricut cut them out. This technique is supported by all Cricut models except the Cricut Joy; find out more in Chapter 18.

The gift tags in Figure 10-4 are perfect examples of Print Then Cut tags that can be made with either cardstock or printable sticker paper.

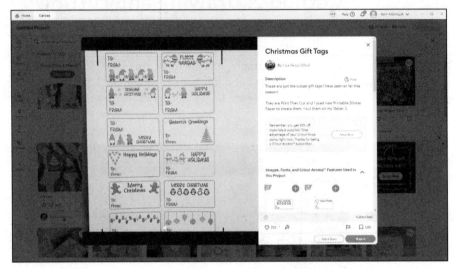

FIGURE 10-4: Designs like these are made using the Print Then Cut method.

Source: design.cricut.com

You can use white cardstock to create gift tags that tie to your presents by slicing a hole into your design (see the next section). Alternatively, if you're making tags to stick directly on gifts, you can print your design on a home printer and your Cricut will cut it out on sticker paper. Head to Chapter 19 to find out more about creating stickers with your Cricut.

Why pick this method?

>> You want customized, colorful, and detailed designs that are too hard to draw.

>> You need professional-looking tags with text, patterns, or images.

>> You're making sticker-style tags.

Creating Gift Tags: A Step-by-Step Guide

Ready to make your own gift tags? This guide can help you navigate making gift tags using any method you prefer: simple cuts, drawing and cutting, or print then cut:

1. **Start your project.**

   Open Cricut Design Space and click New Project to get started.

2. **Design your tag.**

   Choose how you want to create your tag:

   - **Use a template.** Search "gift tag" in Images or Projects, and select a design.
   - **Upload your own design.** Go to Upload, then Upload Image, and follow the prompts to add your custom design.
   - **Create from scratch.** Use Shapes to design your tag. For a hanging tag, add a circle at the desired spot for the string. In Figure 10-5, I used these two shapes to create a versatile tag design.

   Ensure that your tag is the right size for your project by clicking on the corner of the design and dragging to resize as needed.

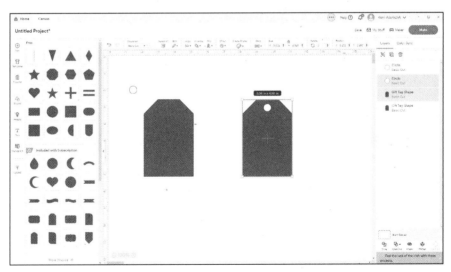

FIGURE 10-5: How to make a custom tag using shapes.

Source: `design.cricut.com`

3. **Customize your tag.**

   These customizations are optional, varying based on your method:

   - **Add a hole for hanging.** Position a circle shape where you want the hole, align it using Align and Center Horizontally, then use Slice to create the hole. Delete any unnecessary pieces.

   - **Insert text.** Click Text to add a text box, select a font, and adjust the size and color using the Edit bar at the top of the Canvas. The default operation is Basic Cut, which cuts the letters with a blade. For drawing: Change the operation to Draw using the Operation drop-down menu. Select a Writing font to automatically switch to Draw. Choose your pen type and color by clicking the color square next to the Operation drop-down menu, matching it with the type of pens you're using.

   - **Add images.** Use the Images tool to find the perfect image by using the Image filter to search for Cut, Draw, or Print Then Cut options. After uploading your own image or choosing one from the library, double-check the Layers panel to ensure that the operation settings are correct for your project.

4. **Prepare for cutting.**

   Set operations for each element. Use the Operation drop-down menu to specify how each design element should be processed (such as Basic Cut, Draw, or Print then Cut). Look in the Layers panel to see what each element of your design is set to. See Figure 10-6.

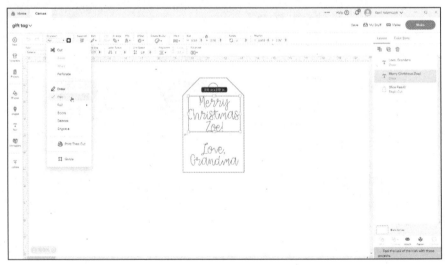

FIGURE 10-6: Change the operation to Draw for text and Basic Cut for the tag shape.

Source: design.cricut.com

134 PART 3 Projects Using Paper and Cardstock

TIP

To make sure that all parts of your design stay together during cutting, select the whole design and click Attach. This crucial step ensures that elements like text and shapes are cut in the correct positions on the same mat.

Highlight your entire design and select Flatten if you're preparing tags with the Print Then Cut method. The Flatten function combines multiple layers of a design into a single layer that's ready for printing.

5. **Save and advance.**

   Click Save in the upper-right corner, name your project, and confirm by clicking Save again. If you forget, Design Space will automatically prompt you to save your project after clicking Make.

   Click Make to move to the Prepare screen, where you can adjust material settings, align the design on the mat, and confirm other settings like project copies and mirror (if needed for heat transfer projects).

6. **Prepare your mat.**

   Place your material on the StandardGrip mat as shown in the Prepare screen. Use a brayer to secure it in place.

7. **Start the cutting process.**

   Follow these prompts:

   - **Go the Make screen.** Click Continue to move to the Make screen, where you'll prepare your machine for cutting.
   - **Connect your machine.** Make sure your Cricut machine is powered on and connected via USB or Bluetooth.
   - **Set your base material.** Select the correct material type (such as Cardstock) from Design Space to match your project's needs.
   - **Load your tools and materials.** Follow the instructions on the screen to load the correct blade or pen. For a detailed guide on tools, see Chapter 4.

   For projects using the Print Then Cut feature, click Send to Printer and follow the on-screen prompts to print your designs. Once printed, place the sheet on the mat and load it into your Cricut. The machine will read the registration marks and cut out your tags.

8. **Make your tags.**

Slide the mat under the guide tabs and press the Load button. (With the machines in the Cricut Joy series, the mat automatically loads after you insert it.)

Press the Go button to begin the drawing or cutting process. (With the machines in the Cricut Joy series, you start the process through the software.)

9. **Assemble your gift tags.**

Once done, unload the mat and gently peel off the tags. Use a spatula or tweezers for delicate pieces.

Thread ribbon through the holes and decorate with stickers, handwritten messages, or other embellishments before attaching them to your gifts.

IN THIS CHAPTER

» Discovering fun and creative ways to use paper flowers

» Picking the perfect paper for your flowers

» Exploring beginner-friendly templates for flower-making

» Getting the hang of quilling tools to roll and shape flowers

» Following a simple step-by-step guide for crafting flowers

Chapter **11**

Crafting Rolled Paper Flowers

magine transforming an ordinary sheet of paper into a stunning flower that lasts forever — this chapter shows you how! Rolled paper flowers are versatile, durable, and perfect for a variety of projects, from elegant decorations and personalized cards to eye-catching shadow boxes.

Your Cricut machine makes crafting paper flowers a breeze. It handles the intricate cutting, leaving you free to roll, shape, and assemble your blooms with ease. Whether you're making a tiny, delicate flower for a greeting card or a large, detailed floral arrangement for home décor, Cricut simplifies the process.

In this chapter, you discover everything you need to know to create beautiful, long-lasting paper flowers. I walk you through the process from start to finish — whether you're picking out the perfect materials, choosing the right templates, or perfecting your rolling techniques. Before you know it, you'll be able to craft stunning flowers that rival any blooms you find in nature. So, grab your Cricut and get started!

Exploring Project Ideas for Paper Flowers

Want to make your paper flowers the star of your next project? From eye-catching centerpieces to custom party décor, these creative project ideas will inspire you to get crafting. Here are some exciting ways to incorporate paper flowers into your next project:

- **Bouquets:** Craft everlasting bouquets for weddings, gifts, or table displays — no watering needed!

  Mix soft, rounded flowers with bold, spiky blooms to create a more visually interesting arrangement.

- **Cake toppers:** Make weddings, birthdays, or anniversaries even more special with a floral cake topper that's as unique as the occasion. Add paper flowers to enhance these cake toppers, giving them a beautiful personal touch. For details on making the actual cake toppers, flip to Chapter 22.

- **Decorations for special events:** Add a floral touch to weddings, baby showers, or birthday parties.

  For easy-to-reposition décor, use adhesive dots instead of hot glue, especially for temporary displays like backdrops or walls.

- **Gift accents:** Ditch the traditional bows and add paper flowers to your wrapped gifts for a unique touch.

- **Headbands or hair accessories:** Attach flowers to headbands, hair clips, or combs for a fun floral accessory.

- **Party backdrops:** Combine flowers of different sizes and colors to craft the perfect backdrop for photo ops at any party.

- **Shadow boxes:** Fill a shadow box with flowers of various sizes to create a beautiful display (see the color section).

  Flip to the color section to see a beautiful example of a shadow box with rolled paper flowers positioned in the shape of a heart. If you're more of a visual learner, watch the tutorial on my YouTube channel (www.youtube.com/@kerricraftsit), where I demonstrate exactly how to roll these paper flowers for this specific project.

- **Table centerpieces:** Combine paper flowers with candles or greenery to create stunning centerpieces.

  Choose colors based on the season or event. Think warm hues for autumn, soft pastels for spring, and bold metallics for festive occasions to make your flowers pop.

- **Wall décor:** Arrange flowers on canvases, wreath frames, or directly on walls.

Choosing the Right Paper for Rolled Flowers

Choosing the right paper is key to creating beautiful, long-lasting rolled flowers. The paper you use affects not only the sturdiness of your flowers but also their overall appearance. In this section, I walk you through how to pick the perfect paper for your next project, whether you're aiming for bold hardly blossoms or soft and delicate petals.

Exploring recommended paper types

You can use all kinds of paper to make flowers, but these are favored for their durability and great results:

- **Cardstock (65–80 lb):** This sturdy paper is easy to roll and holds its shape well. Matte finishes keep the look natural, and glossy and glitter options add some flair. Cardstock works well for flowers like roses.

- **Double-sided paper:** This paper has two colors or patterns, adding extra dimension and depth to your flowers. It works especially well where both sides of the petals are visible.

- **Patterned paper:** This option adds texture and flair to your flowers. It's perfect for creating projects with a theme.

- **Solid-core cardstock:** For a clean, polished finish, choose solid-core cardstock. It's colored all the way through, so you won't have unsightly white edges.

- **Metallic or glitter cardstock:** For flowers that truly sparkle, metallic or glitter cardstock is your best bet.

If you want to see what these rolled paper flowers look like, go to the Projects section in Cricut Design Space and search for specific flower types like "roses" or by paper type such as "crepe paper" to find a variety of designs and inspirations. See Part 2 for an introduction to Design Space.

Avoiding papers that don't work

Not all papers are ideal for crafting flowers, so it's best to avoid a few types that may lead to frustration and less-than-perfect results. Stay away from the following paper:

- **Thin paper:** Thin papers like regular printer paper are too flimsy to hold the shape of rolled petals. They're also more likely to tear during the rolling process, leaving you with weak, messy flowers. Go for sturdier paper for better results.

» **White-core cardstock:** This paper has a white core, which can create unsightly edges after cutting and make your flowers look unfinished, especially on intricate designs. Stick to solid-core cardstock for a clean, polished finish.

» **Crepe paper and tissue paper:** These materials are best for layered flowers rather than rolled flowers. Their softness and flexibility make them great for delicate, ruffled petals in designs like carnations, poppies, and peonies, but they don't hold their shape well when rolled.

Discovering Paper Flower Templates

Paper flower templates are predesigned patterns that guide your Cricut in cutting out all the pieces needed for your flowers: petals, leaves, and more. Floral templates come in an incredible variety of shapes and sizes, from simple spirals to complex layered designs.

At first glance, these templates may look like funky corkscrews or winding paths. But once rolled and assembled, they transform into stunning, lifelike flowers. With so many options available, you'll easily find the perfect template to match your creative vision and project needs.

For beginners, it's a good idea to start with medium-sized templates. They're easier to handle and assemble than very small or large flower designs, allowing you to get comfortable with the process before moving on to more intricate or oversize creations.

Although any Cricut machine can make paper flowers, the size of your designs depends on the machine you're using. For instance, the Cricut Joy can handle templates up to 4.5 inches (11 centimeters) wide, which is perfect for creating smaller flowers around 1.5 inches (4 cm) in diameter. The exact size may vary depending on how tightly you roll your flowers. For larger or intricate designs, the Cricut Maker or Explore models are your best bet.

Searching Cricut Design Space for templates

Cricut Design Space is a fantastic resource for finding paper flower templates. Whether you're new to paper crafting or a seasoned pro, you'll find a range of ready-to-use designs that fit all skill levels, from simple rolled flowers to complex 3-D blooms.

You can find templates in Cricut Design Space with these tools:

» **Images:** This option is perfect for quick and simple templates without any instructions. Just type "rolled flowers" in the search bar to bring up various designs (see Figure 11-1).

FIGURE 11-1: The Images area in Cricut Design Space showing template options.

Source: design.cricut.com

» **Projects:** If you're looking for more guidance, use the Projects tool to search for "rolled flowers" or "3D" for classic spiral flower designs. This is a great choice for beginners looking for step-by-step instructions along with the template (see Figure 11-2).

Browsing third-party websites for templates

Third-party websites such as Creative Fabrica (www.creativefabrica.com), Etsy (www.etsy.com), and Design Bundles (https://designbundles.net/) are fantastic resources for finding a wide variety of designs, from intricate rolled flowers to fun and quirky blooms.

CHAPTER 11 Crafting Rolled Paper Flowers   141

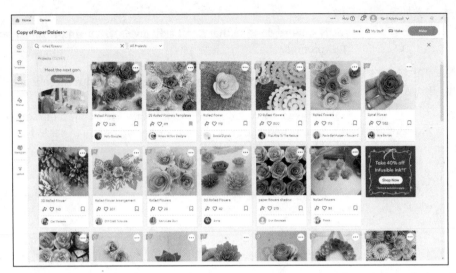

FIGURE 11-2:
The Projects area in Cricut Design Space showing complete project options.

Source: design.cricut.com

TIP

Look for templates that include previews of the finished flower to make sure that you love the design before you purchase it.

Choosing the Right Cut Size for Your Flowers

The size of your paper flowers depends on the cut size of the template you choose. Smaller cuts give you compact flowers, perfect for accents; larger cuts make bold blooms, ideal for statement pieces like bouquets and wall décor.

REMEMBER

The key to picking the right size is thinking about your project and how big or small you want your finished flowers to be. Here's a quick guide to help you decide:

» **Tiny flowers (0.5 inch to 1 inch [1.25 cm to 2.5 cm]):** Perfect for filling gaps or adding subtle accents on things like gift tags or bookmarks.

» **Medium flowers (1.25 inches to 2 inches [3 cm to 5 cm]):** Great for garlands, headbands, or centerpieces.

» **Large flowers (2.25 inches to 3 inches [6 cm to 8 cm]):** Best for dramatic displays like bouquets, wreaths, or shadow boxes.

For a detailed breakdown of how the cut size translates into the finished flower size, see Table 11-1.

142 PART 3 **Projects Using Paper and Cardstock**

TABLE 11-1 **Cut Sizes and Finished Flower Dimensions**

Paper Cut Size	Final Flower Size
1 inch (2.5 cm)	0.5 inch (1.25 cm)
2 inches (5 cm)	0.75 inch (2 cm)
3 inches (8 cm)	1 inch (2.5 cm)
4 inches (10 cm)	1.25 inches (3 cm)
5 inches (13 cm)	1.5 inches (4 cm)
6 inches (15 cm)	1.75 inches (4.5 cm)
7 inches (18 cm)	2 inches (5 cm)
8 inches (20 cm)	2.25 inches (6 cm)
9 inches (23 cm)	2.5 inches (6.5 cm)
10 inches (25 cm)	2.75 inches (7 cm)
11 inches (28 cm)	3 inches (8 cm)

TIP

When working on larger flowers, you want to use a 12-x-12-inch (30.5-x-30.5-cm) sheet of paper to accommodate bigger templates. For smaller, more detailed flowers, you can stick to an 8.5-x-11-inch (22-x-28-cm) sheet. The size of your paper affects both your cutting ability and the overall look of your flower, so pick the right paper size for your project!

Mastering Quilling Tools

A quilling tool may look simple, but it's an essential part of the process when you're crafting perfect rolled flowers. This tool has a small slotted tip that securely holds the end of your paper, making it easy to roll tight, even spirals. Whether you go for a manual or electric version, or even make your own with household items like bobby pins, a quilling tool helps you create flawless flowers every time.

Using manual quilling tools

Manual quilling tools typically come in a variety pack, with different tip sizes for various projects. You'll find that some tools have wider slots for thicker paper and others have fine tips perfect for delicate, detailed designs.

TIP

Take your time with manual tools — slow and steady wins the race! Many crafters find manual tools easier to manage than the other types, especially for working with delicate materials or intricate designs.

Trying electric quilling tools

If you're looking to speed up the rolling process, electric quilling tools are a great option. They're especially useful for large projects or when you need to make a lot of flowers quickly.

WARNING

Although electric tools are convenient, they can be harder to control for beginners and may not give you the same precision as manual tools when you're working with thick, delicate, or specialty papers.

Testing out alternatives to quilling tools

TIP

Don't have a quilling tool? Don't worry! You can find plenty of alternatives around the house that help you achieve the same beautiful, tightly rolled petals. Here are a few items you can easily repurpose:

- **Bobby pin:** Slide the paper into the opening of the bobby pin and use it to roll the paper tightly, just like you would with a quilling tool.
- **Thin paintbrush handle:** Wrap the paper around the handle for an easy, controlled roll.
- **Tweezers:** Secure the paper onto the tweezers with a binder clip to provide extra grip and control.

Although these DIY tools may not create rolls as tight as a specialized quilling tool, they can still do the job just fine with a little practice — and they're perfect for when you're in a pinch and need to save a little money.

Rolling Paper Flowers: A Step-by-Step Guide

Creating rolled paper flowers is easy and fun. Each flower takes about five minutes to roll for beginners, so plan your time if you're making multiples. Don't worry if your first few flowers aren't perfect — mistakes are part of the process, and it gets easier with practice.

Follow the step-by-step guide in this section to roll and assemble your paper flowers.

Gathering your materials

Start by collecting everything you'll need:

TIP

» **Adhesive:** Use quick-drying glue or a hot glue gun for a strong hold.

Bearly Art Precision Craft Glue works great for paper crafts. It sets quickly, dries clear, and has a strong hold.

» **Basic tools:** A spatula, scraper, and tweezers help with handling delicate pieces and lifting them off the mat without damage.

» **Cricut machine:** Any model works, but the Maker, Explore, or Venture machines are best for large designs.

» **StandardGrip Mat:** This mat holds paper securely but allows you to remove it without tearing.

» **Paper:** See the earlier section "Choosing the Right Paper for Rolled Flowers" to find the best option for your project.

» **Quilling tool:** This tool is a must-have for rolling paper evenly (see the earlier section "Mastering Quilling Tools").

» **Templates:** The earlier section "Discovering Paper Flower Templates" gives you the full scoop on finding predesigned files for making handmade flowers.

Step 1: Designing your flower

Prepare your design in Cricut Design Space (see Part 2) by following these steps:

1. **Import or open your template.**

   Open Design Space and search for a template in the Images or Projects libraries, or upload your flower design from another website.

2. **Customize the design.**

   After you've loaded your design, you may find that the elements (like petals and leaves) are grouped together. To work on them individually, you need to ungroup them first. Click on the design to select it, then find and click the Ungroup button in the Layers panel at the top right of the screen. This allows you to select and adjust each element separately. You may need to ungroup elements more than once to get them to fully break apart.

To resize individual elements, click on the one you want to adjust. Drag the Arrow icon at the corner of the selected element to resize it freely. If you want to maintain the proportion (keeping it to scale), make sure the Lock icon in the corner is closed (locked). If the Lock icon is open (unlocked), the element can be stretched or compressed horizontally or vertically.

Once you have resized the design to your liking, you can duplicate it if you need more of the same size. Right-click on the element and select Duplicate from the Context menu, or use the Duplicate button in the top of the Layers Panel. You can also press Ctrl + D (Cmd + D on a Mac) on your keyboard to quickly duplicate it.

TIP

Change the colors of the different parts of your flower so that you can picture it better while you're designing. To do this, select the part you want to change, click on the Color box in the top toolbar, and choose a new color from the palette. Color changes in Design Space are for visualization only and won't affect the cutting process.

3. **Adjust settings on the Prepare screen.**

   When you're finished editing your design, click Make to advance to the Prepare screen, where you can adjust several settings before cutting. Here, you can increase or decrease the number of project copies, set your material load type to On Mat, select your material size, and choose whether to mirror your image or not (don't mirror for rolled paper flowers).

   The screen will display a preview of your design on the mat, automatically placed in the upper-left corner. You can move your design to a different spot on the mat preview; just make sure that the placement on the screen matches how you position your paper on the actual sticky mat.

4. **Select your material.**

   Click Continue to move to the Make screen, where you can select Browse All Materials and choose your paper type.

Step 2: Cutting the flower

Transform your design into reality as follows:

1. **Place your paper on a StandardGrip Mat and align it properly.**

   Roll a brayer or smooth a scraper over the paper to secure it to the mat.

TIP

   Consider using two cutting mats to streamline your workflow. While one mat is in the machine, you can prep the other, keeping your project moving smoothly.

146   PART 3 Projects Using Paper and Cardstock

2. **Load the mat into the Cricut machine.**

   Press Load on your Cricut to load the mat and then press Go to start the cut.

3. **Carefully remove the flowers from the mat.**

   Bend the mat away from the paper instead of pulling the flowers directly off the mat. For delicate pieces, a spatula can help you lift the edges without damaging the paper.

TIP

Step 3: Rolling the flower

Follow these steps to create the shape of your bloom:

1. **Insert the paper into the quilling tool.**

   Starting at the outer edge of the spiral, slide the paper into the slot at the tip of the quilling tool, or use an alternative quilling tool like tweezers and a binder clip (see Figure 11-3).

FIGURE 11-3: Attaching the paper to the quilling tool.

Source: Kerri Adamczyk

2. **Begin rolling.**

   Begin rolling by twisting the quilling tool toward you, keeping the roll tight to form the base of the flower. Keep your hand in a horizontal position and continuously twist the tool as you work your way toward the center.

CHAPTER 11 **Crafting Rolled Paper Flowers** 147

3. **Allow the rolled flower to loosen.**

   After you finish rolling the flower, it may appear too tightly coiled. To give it a more natural, open appearance, carefully flip the flower upside down, placing the top of the rolled flower directly on the table. Gently release your hold on the roll, allowing it to expand slightly on its own. This process helps the petals to spread out slightly, mimicking the natural bloom of a flower.

Step 4: Gluing the flower

While your flower is still upside down, fold back the round flap at the base to expose the bottom, coiled part of the flower. Apply a generous amount of quick-drying glue to both the round flap and the exposed coiled base (see Figure 11-4). Press these parts firmly together and hold briefly to allow the glue to set.

FIGURE 11-4: Applying glue to the round flap and the bottom, coiled part of the flower.

Source: Kerri Adamczyk

Adding stems, leaves, and pistils

If you'd like, finish your flower with the following decorative details:

» **Attaching stems:** Use floral wire, green pipe cleaners, or green wooden dowels as stems. Wrap the base of the flower around the stem and secure it with floral tape or glue.

- » **Adding leaves:** Cut leaves from cardstock using your Cricut machine. To add realistic veins to the leaves, you can add a score line to your leaf design where you want the veins to appear. Use the Cricut Scoring Stylus or Scoring Wheel to precisely score these lines on your leaves. (For details on these scoring tools, see Chapter 4.) Once scored, fold and attach the leaves to the stem or the base of the flower with glue.

- » **Including pistils:** Use fringed templates to create *pistils* (the reproductive stalks that grow from the center of some flowers), glue them into the flower center, and decorate them with glitter or metallic paint if you want to add some sparkle.

TIP

After mastering paper flowers, try experimenting with fabric flowers. Turn to Chapter 22 for the steps!

This "Paws Off My Wine" wine glass was made with permanent vinyl and a stemless wine glass from Dollar Tree. For tips on making vinyl decals, check out Chapter 13.

Keep your bathroom organized with this "Hello Sweet Cheeks" wooden organizer, made with a vinyl stencil and paint. For details on painting stenciled wood signs, check out Chapter 22.

These personalized Easter baskets are made with canvas baskets from Five Below, and the secret is in the flock HTV. Its soft, fuzzy texture pairs perfectly with plush bunnies. To discover other types of HTV, see Chapter 15.

Featuring heartfelt messages, these hammers make perfect Father's Day gifts and are made with black glossy permanent vinyl for a clean, lasting design. Discover more vinyl tips in Chapter 13, and follow the tutorial on my YouTube channel (www.youtube.com/@kerricraftsit).

Here's my daughter wearing the K–12 shirt I made for her the day she started kindergarten. Every year, we take a photo of her in the shirt, seeing how she gradually grows into it until her graduation. The design was created using HTV. Check out Chapter 15 for more on working with HTV, and watch me create this project on my YouTube channel (www.youtube.com/@kerricraftsit).

A fun April Fools' prank: My kids thought they were getting a plate of brownies, but they really got a plate of Brown Es (cardstock cut letters). For more fun projects with paper and cardstock, check out Part 3.

This memorial lantern is beautifully personalized with permanent vinyl, creating a heartfelt tribute. See Chapter 13 for more on working with vinyl, and follow along with the tutorial on my YouTube channel (www.youtube.com/@kerricraftsit).

This "Dad's Spot" pocket pillow, made with heat transfer vinyl, is the perfect addition to any man cave. For more tips on using HTV, check out Chapter 15. You can also follow along with the custom pillow tutorials on my YouTube channel (www.youtube.com/@kerricraftsit).

A beautiful Happy Mother's Day card made with Cricut Insert Cards, featuring a striking holographic background that really makes it stand out! For more card-making tips, check out Chapter 12.

Craft pumpkins from Michael's, personalized with gloss layered permanent vinyl for stylish fall or Halloween décor. Check out Chapter 13 for vinyl tips, and watch me create this project on my YouTube channel (www.youtube.com/@kerricraftsit).

A candy apple with a cardstock cut gift tag that says "...and they lived appley ever after," featuring the couple's name and wedding date, used as a sweet wedding guest favor. See Chapter 10 for tips on making your own gift tags.

Personalized flower pots make the perfect gift! I create these custom pots with monograms and sweet sayings. The flower pots came from Dollar Tree, and after adding permanent vinyl, my kids filled them with their favorite flowers for their teacher. For more tips on working with vinyl, check out Chapter 13. You can also watch me make this project on my YouTube channel (www.youtube.com/@kerricraftsit).

This adorable stuffed unicorn says "Flower Girl" in gold glitter HTV, making it the perfect keepsake for a special flower girl. See Chapter 15 for more on personalizing with HTV, and watch me personalize stuffed animals on my YouTube channel (www.youtube.com/@kerricraftsit).

Not only does this magical cup change colors, but the color-changing vinyl used to personalize the name also transforms. How cool is that? Check out Chapter 13 to discover more exciting types of vinyl. You can also watch me make this project on my YouTube channel (www.youtube.com/@kerricraftsit).

A funny reverse canvas picture for the kitchen that says "Alexa, clean the kitchen." I removed the canvas from the frame, used heat transfer vinyl to press the saying onto the material, then placed the canvas back behind the frame and secured it with a staple gun. For more tips on using HTV, check out Chapter 15.

Welcome guests into your home with a custom outdoor sign, featuring your family name at the top. The black-stained wood board is personalized with permanent vinyl for a mess-free, long-lasting design that will hold up to the elements. See Chapter 13 for vinyl application tips.

Show appreciation to a bus driver with this oven mitt that says "Thanks for the Sweet Ride," packed with a bag of chocolate chip cookie mix and a rubber spatula. Everything in the photo is from Dollar Tree, and the design is made with yellow heat transfer vinyl. Check out Chapter 15 for more tips on working with HTV.

Start your day with a laugh! The labels on these reusable egg cartons are made with permanent vinyl, perfect for eggs from my chickens. Check out Chapter 13 for helpful techniques on working with vinyl.

For these Santa Cam and Elf Cam ornaments, I used white glossy permanent vinyl for the text and crafted a realistic-looking lens with bonded sealing washers. See Chapter 13 for more vinyl tips, and follow along with the tutorial on my YouTube channel (www.youtube.com/@kerricraftsit).

This shadowbox, featuring rolled paper flowers in shades of purple arranged into a heart shape, greets guests right when they walk through my front door. Check out Chapter 11 for details and follow along on my YouTube channel (www.youtube.com/@kerricraftsit).

For under $2 each, I discovered ceramic floor tiles at Home Depot that look just like wood, saving me tons of time on cutting and staining. I personalized them with permanent vinyl and low-tack transfer tape, turning them into art display signs. Check out Chapter 13 for tips on working with vinyl, and watch me make this project on my YouTube channel (www.youtube.com/@kerricraftsit).

Create a fun tradition with this plate, made with a Dollar Tree charger plate and white glossy permanent vinyl. Be sure to use low-tack transfer tape to avoid lifting the paint off the plate. Check out Chapter 13 for more on working with vinyl, and watch the tutorial on my YouTube channel (www.youtube.com/@kerricraftsit).

Each year, I design custom birthday shirts for my kids, making their special day even more fun with a one-of-a-kind shirt just for them. See Chapter 15 for more on using HTV to create custom designs.

Before and after: A glass beer mug transformed with a vinyl stencil and Armour Etch cream for a custom design. For more details, see Chapter 17.

Before and after: I used a vinyl stencil and Citristrip to remove the coating from a coated metal wine tumbler, revealing a finish so flawless that it looks like it was professionally laser engraved. For more details, see Chapter 22.

IN THIS CHAPTER

» **Creating a unique alternative to mass-produced cards**

» **Discovering the tools and materials you need for card-making**

» **Designing Insert and Cutaway Cards in Cricut Design Space**

» **Crafting your own cards from scratch with cardstock**

Chapter **12**

Making Cards

Handmade cards are the perfect way to show someone you care, whether it's for a birthday, holiday, or just because. Using your Cricut to make custom cards adds a personal touch that store-bought cards can't match.

With Cricut, card-making becomes not only easy but also a lot of fun. Here's how you can take your card-making skills to the next level:

» Cut intricate designs with precision.

» Write or draw custom messages using pens or markers.

» Layer materials like glitter and metallic cardstock for a professional finish.

In this chapter, I guide you through the materials, tools, and step-by-step instructions needed to create beautiful cards. Whether you're using Cricut's Insert and Cutaway Cards or making custom designs with cardstock, you have everything you need to craft something special.

Starting Your Card-Making Journey

Card-making can be as simple or as intricate as you like, and with Cricut, the possibilities are limited only by your imagination. Whether you're designing a card for a birthday, a wedding, or a baby shower, your Cricut machine will make the process quick and easy.

Celebrating all occasions

Handmade cards are great for any occasion, and with Cricut, you can make cards that feel special and unique. Here are some ideas to spark your creativity:

- **Everyday cards:** Birthday, thank-you, get well, and congratulations cards
- **Seasonal favorites:** Holiday, Valentine's Day, Mother's/Father's Day cards, and more
- **Special events:** Wedding invitations, baby announcements, and graduation cards

Building your skills

With Cricut, you can start with simple designs and gradually progress to more intricate, multistep projects as you build your confidence. Whether you're creating your first card or looking to tackle more advanced techniques, there's a project that will match your skill level and help you grow as a crafter.

Here's a breakdown of how you can take your card-making to the next level:

- **Beginner:** Start with basic designs, like cutting simple shapes or adding a colorful insert to your card.

TIP

For an easy project, choose a ready-made card design from the Projects library in Cricut Design Space. No editing is needed — just select a design, load your materials, and let your Cricut do the cutting!

- **Intermediate:** Use Cricut pens to write custom messages and pair them with cutout designs to create something more detailed.
- **Advanced:** Master Print Then Cut for complex designs or photos (see Chapter 18 for details), incorporate layered die cuts, experiment with interactive pop-up cards, and embellish your creations with glitter, foil, or other eye-catching materials for a professional, glamorous finish.

Choosing between Insert Cards and Cutaway Cards

Insert Cards and Cutaway Cards are both fantastic options for creating personalized cards with your Cricut, designed to be easy to use and beginner-friendly. Each has its own unique style and creative possibilities, allowing you to choose the best one for your project. Insert Cards offer a layered look, with decorative paper tucked behind cutouts for added dimension; Cutaway Cards keep all design elements securely in place with adhesive backers, making them a smoother and more polished option. For a quick side-by-side comparison of their features, check out Table 12-1.

TABLE 12-1 Insert Cards versus Cutaway Cards

Feature	Insert Cards	Cutaway Cards
Design style	Requires corner slots for inserts	Adhesive-backed; no slots needed
Image/font freedom	Stencil images or fonts needed for floating shapes	Any image or font works (floating shapes supported)
Customization	Layers a decorative insert behind cutouts	Decorative backer shows through intricate cuts
Sizes available	R10, R20, R30, R40, S40*	R10, R20, R40, S40*
Special effects	Provides a 3-D layered effect	Creates smooth, adhesive-backed designs

*See the later section "Picking the right size card."

TIP In addition to Insert Cards and Cutaway Cards, Cricut also offers Foil Transfer Insert Cards, which let you add shiny foil details to your designs. Instead of sliding a decorative paper insert behind cutouts like with standard Insert Cards, these use Cricut's Foil Transfer Tool and Foil Transfer Sheets. The foil is taped to the front of the card, and the Foil Transfer Tool presses the foil into the cardstock. When the process is complete, you peel away the foil sheet to reveal the shiny, impressed design. In Design Space, be sure to change the Operation setting of any elements you want foiled to Foil, and choose Fine, Medium, or Bold, depending on how thick you want the foil lines to appear.

Crafting Insert Cards

Insert Cards make it super easy to create cards with a three-dimensional effect. These cards come with pre-scored bases and precut slots so you can slide in decorative inserts, creating vibrant textured backdrops for your designs. (See one for yourself in the color section.)

Here's what's included in every Cricut Insert Card kit:

» **Pre-scored card bases:** These sturdy bases are ready to fold and serve as the foundation of your card. You can think of them as the main structure of your creation.

» **Decorative inserts:** You can choose from solid colors, glitter, holographic, or patterned designs to add texture and vibrancy behind your card's cut-out design.

» **Matching envelopes:** These are perfect for gifting or mailing your custom cards.

Insert Cards let you add a layered effect to your designs, like a wedding card with a bride and groom silhouette placed over a colored background (see Figure 12-1).

FIGURE 12-1: A wedding Insert Card design featuring a bride and groom silhouette over a colored background.

Source: design.cricut.com

WARNING

Although Insert Cards are fantastic for both simple and intricate projects, keep one thing in mind: Because these cards don't use adhesive backing, some parts of your design may fall out. For example, in Figure 12-2, the *HAPPY NEW YEAR* design shows missing elements in the *A*s, *P*s, and *R*. This happens because there's nothing to keep those pieces attached to the card. A design like this would work better as a Cutaway Card, which has an adhesive backer to hold all the elements in place.

FIGURE 12-2:
An Insert Card with missing design elements due to the lack of adhesive backing.

Source: design.cricut.com

To prevent pieces of your design from falling out of Insert Cards, try using stencil-style fonts, which have small slice marks that help keep the inner parts of letters securely attached to the card. Figure 12-3 shows a *HAPPY NEW YEAR* design using a stencil font.

FIGURE 12-3:
A stencil font design where the letter elements stay connected to the card base.

Source: design.cricut.com

CHAPTER 12 **Making Cards** 155

Creating Cutaway Cards

Cutaway Cards provide a cleaner finish by using an adhesive backing that holds everything in place. This feature allows you to create detailed, intricate designs without worrying about any loose pieces. In Figure 12-4, you can see how the adhesive backing holds elements like the centers of letters in place, keeping everything aligned.

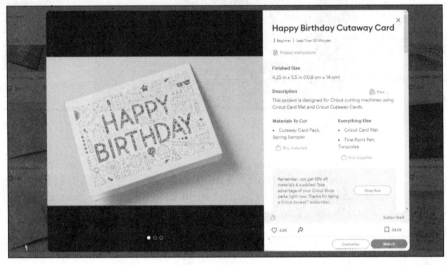

FIGURE 12-4: A Cutaway Card with adhesive backing that keeps the message intact.

Source: design.cricut.com

Here's what's included in every Cricut Cutaway Card kit:

» **Adhesive-backed card bases:** These pre-scored card bases have an adhesive layer that keeps all your design elements secure.

» **Decorative backers:** You can choose from holographic, foil, or patterned backers to add an extra pop to your cutouts.

» **Matching envelopes:** Envelopes are included for easy gifting or mailing.

Cutaway Cards are best for intricate designs where you need all the elements, including the centers of letters or detailed patterns, to stay attached.

Picking the right size card

Cricut cards come in five sizes, making it easy to find the perfect fit for your designs. You can choose from the following options:

- **R10:** 3.5 x 4.9 inches (8.9 x 12.4 cm)
- **R20:** 4.25 x 5.5 inches (10.8 x 14 cm)
- **R30:** 4.5 x 6.25 inches (11.4 x 15.9 cm)
- **R40:** 4.75 x 6.6 inches (12.1 x 16.8 cm)
- **S40:** 4.75 x 4.75 inches (12.1 x 12.1 cm)

Insert Cards are available in all five sizes; Cutaway Cards come in R10, R20, R40, and S40.

TECHNICAL STUFF

R stands for rectangular, and *S* stands for square. The numbers indicate size, with R10 being the smallest and R40 the largest.

Gathering Materials for Card-Making

The tools and materials you use will depend on how simple or intricate your card design is. Start with the basics and add optional extras as you gain confidence. (Flip to Chapters 2 and 4 for an introduction to Cricut machines, tools, and materials.)

Starting with the basics

Here's what you'll need to create your first card:

- **Blade:** The Fine-Point Blade is ideal for cutting cards and cardstock.
- **Cards:** You can use Insert Cards, Cutaway Cards, or custom-cut cardstock. (I explain the differences between Insert Cards and Cutaway Cards in the earlier section "Choosing between Insert Cards and Cutaway Cards.")
- **Cardstock:** Medium-weight cardstock (about 65–80 lb) is great for making custom cards or die-cut designs. It comes in a variety of colors, patterns, and textures, perfect for any type of creation.
- **Cricut Card Mat:** This mat is required for Insert and Cutaway Cards. Be sure to choose the correct size based on your machine model.
- **Cricut machine:** Any model will work for card-making.
- **Scraper, brayer, or weeding tool:** These tools help you lift delicate designs off the mat and keep your mats clean.
- **StandardGrip Mat:** This is used for custom card projects using cardstock instead of Insert or Cutaway Cards.

CHAPTER 12 **Making Cards** 157

Enhancing with optional materials

For more detailed designs, consider some additional tools and embellishments. You may find the following tools helpful:

>> **Adhesives:** Have double-sided tape, glue sticks, or liquid glue on hand for assembling layers.

>> **Debossing Tip:** Adds pressed-in designs to your card for a textured, elegant effect. Unlike scoring, which creates fold lines, debossing pushes patterns or text into the cardstock for a raised look on the reverse side. This is great for adding decorative accents to wedding invitations, holiday cards, or personalized stationery.

>> **Pens or markers:** Use these to write heartfelt messages or draw decorative designs directly on your card.

>> **Scoring Stylus:** Compatible with Cricut Explore, Maker, and Venture machines, this tool creates exact folds on thin cardstock by applying pressure.

>> **Scoring Wheel:** Exclusively for Cricut Maker models, it produces deep, precise score lines for thick or specialty materials, such as glitter cardstock.

With the following fun embellishment ideas in your crafting tool kit, you'll be able to take your cards from basic to beautiful, adding texture, color, and shine:

>> **Cricut Foil Transfer Sheets and Tool:** Foil Transfer Sheets are perfect for creating shiny, eye-catching details using the Foil Transfer Tool.

>> **Die cuts:** These precut shapes made from cardstock or other materials are ideal for layering and adding dimension to your cards. They can be store-bought or custom-made with your Cricut.

>> **Glitter accents:** Add sparkle to your designs for a glamorous touch.

>> **Photos with Print Then Cut:** Personalize cards with family photos or custom graphics.

>> **Specialty cardstock:** Experiment with solid-core, patterned, glitter, or metallic cardstock to create standout designs.

>> **Stickers:** Add store-bought stickers to your cards or create your own with Cricut's Print Then Cut feature and printable vinyl. (Check out Chapter 19 to discover how.)

>> **Washi tape:** This repositionable tape comes in a variety of colors and patterns, perfect for borders, accents, or creative details.

158 PART 3 Projects Using Paper and Cardstock

Using Cricut Card Mats

Cricut Card Mats are specially designed for holding folded cards in place, making the card-crafting process even easier. These mats feature a sticky surface and a divider that protects the back of folded cards while the blade cuts the design on the front.

REMEMBER

All Cricut Card Mats come with protective covers that are shiny on one side and matte on the other. The Cricut Card Mat – 2x2 comes with two protective covers on each half of the mat. Always remove all of the protective covers before starting your project, regardless of how many cards you plan to make. This prevents the cover from getting caught in the machine during cutting. When replacing the covers after use, place the shiny side facing down and the matte side up.

Cricut Card Mats are compatible with Cricut Insert Cards, Cricut Cutaway Cards, and Cricut Foil Transfer Insert Cards, as well as any cardstock you've precut and folded yourself.

Cricut makes three different types of card mats:

- **Cricut Joy Card Mat:** Fits smaller cards up to size R30 (4.5 x 6.25 inches [11.4 x 15.9 cm]).
- **Cricut Joy Xtra Card Mat:** Supports larger cards up to R40 (4.75 x 6.6 inches [12.1 x 16.8 cm]).
- **Card Mat – 2x2:** Designed for the Maker and Explore series, this mat can hold up to four cards at once, making it perfect for creating holiday cards or invitations in batches. It fits 5 Cricut Card sizes: R10, R20, R30, R40, and S40. Any Cricut Joy card will also work on this mat.

At this time, the Cricut Venture doesn't have a dedicated card mat. If you're making cards with this machine, you'll need to use a StandardGrip Performance Machine Mat.

TIP

If you don't have a Card Mat, use a StandardGrip Mat with painter's tape to hold your card securely.

WARNING

Unlike other machine mats, Card Mats must always be loaded top-first into your Cricut. If you load it bottom-first, your designs won't be properly aligned on the cards.

If your material isn't sticking well to the mat, use a brayer to create a firm bond. Over time, Card Mats will lose their stickiness with repeated use and will eventually need to be replaced.

CHAPTER 12 **Making Cards** 159

Making Cards with Your Cricut: A Step-by-Step Guide

Whether you're starting with a predesigned project or creating a unique card from scratch, Cricut Design Space has all the tools you need. The following sections help you find, customize, and complete your card project, step by step.

Step 1: Finding a project

Cricut Design Space (see Part 2) features thousands of ready-to-make card projects. Note that projects marked with a green *a* symbol require a Cricut Access paid subscription. For more details on whether a Cricut Access subscription is right for you, check out Chapter 6. If you can't find what you're looking for, you can always use the tools in Design Space to create your own card.

TIP

Another way to find card-friendly designs is by browsing the Images section. Click on Images, then select Advanced Search at the bottom. On the left side of the screen, you'll see a list of filter options. Under the Best For category, check off Cards to instantly pull up thousands of graphics perfect for custom card-making.

Follow these steps to find and select your next card project in Design Space:

1. **Open Cricut Design Space and click on Projects in the toolbar on the left side of the Canvas.**
2. **Click on the All Projects drop-down menu and choose from the available card-related options (see Figure 12-5).**

   Choices include

   - **Cards:** Browse general card projects.
   - **Insert Cards:** These cards often feature stencil-style designs that require a decorative insert behind the cutout areas for a layered effect.
   - **Cutaway Cards:** Best for designs that feature free-floating shapes and intricate cutouts that reveal a contrasting layer beneath.
   - **Free:** To find no-cost card projects, select Free from the drop-down menu, then use the Search bar to type "card" to show only free card projects.
   - **Square Cards:** Look for projects specifically designed with a square shape.

FIGURE 12-5:
Finding Insert and Cutaway Card projects in Cricut Design Space.

Source: design.cricut.com

3. **Browse through the results and select the card project that fits your needs to see a more detailed preview of the project.**

    Here you'll find important information such as the time it will take to complete, finished size, descriptions, materials, and detailed instructions.

    For some projects, you may find a drop-down menu that lists the card sizes as specified on the package you bought (see Figure 12-6). You must select the correct size from this menu if it appears to ensure that your project dimensions are correct. If the drop-down menu isn't there, you'll set the size on the Prepare screen that appears after you click Make It on the Canvas.

4. **Choose Customize or Make It (see Figure 12-6).**

    Here's what each option means:

    - **Customize:** Selecting this option adds your project to the Canvas in Cricut Design Space, where you can make changes such as altering fonts, phrases, cut shapes, and other elements to create a unique project.
    - **Make It:** This takes you directly to the Prepare screen, as it does when you click Make on the Canvas. Some projects may only offer the Make It option, which bypasses the customization stage and takes you straight to preparing to cut.

CHAPTER 12 **Making Cards** 161

FIGURE 12-6: Options for customizing or making a card project in Cricut Design Space.

Source: design.cricut.com

Step 2: Creating a template

If you choose to customize your card or even start totally from scratch, you'll need to add a template to your Canvas to help you plan out your design.

REMEMBER

Templates are for reference only and won't be saved with your project.

Design Space offers two types of card templates under the Templates button on the left side of the Canvas: Cutaway Cards and Cards. Follow the steps illustrated in Figure 12-7 to add a Cutaway Card Template to your Canvas:

1. **Click on Templates.**
2. **Choose Cutaway Card.**
3. **Choose your card size from the available options: S40CA, R10CA, R20CA, or R40CA.**
4. **Follow the instructions on the Cutaway Card Guide to begin creating your design, making sure to stay within the dashed line design area.**

Follow the steps illustrated in Figure 12-8 to add a Legacy (basic) Card Template to your Canvas:

1. **Click on Templates.**
2. **Select Legacy Templates at the bottom.**

162 PART 3 Projects Using Paper and Cardstock

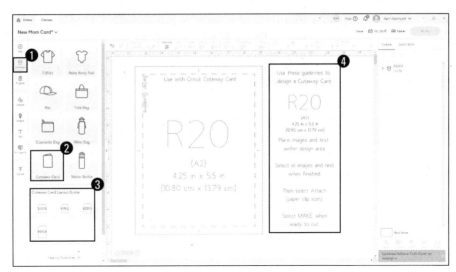

FIGURE 12-7: Finding and using a Cutaway Card Template.

Source: design.cricut.com

3. **Click on Cards to add a blank folded card design to your Canvas.**

   Note: The action of clicking on Cards occurs in a new window, so Step 3 is not shown in Figure 12-8.

4. **Click on the Type drop-down menu at the top of the Canvas.**

   Here you can choose from

   - **Bi-fold – Vertical:** Creates a template with a vertical score line for a card that folds open like a book.
   - **Bi-fold – Horizontal:** Creates a template with a horizontal score line for a card where the top folds upwards.

5. **Click on the Size drop-down menu to choose the dimensions of your card.**

   If you don't see the size that you want listed, click on Custom and enter the width and height of your card.

6. **Change the color of your card template using the Color square at the top.**

   Color changes on the template are for visualization purposes only.

7. **Edit your template.**

   Follow these guidelines:

   - **Accessing template edit tools:** After adding elements like text or shapes to the Canvas, the Template edit tools (Type, Size, Color) may disappear, as Design Space shifts focus to the new elements. To regain access to these template editing options, click on Cards at the bottom of the Layers panel. This action brings the Template edit tools back into view.

CHAPTER 12 Making Cards 163

- **Managing template visibility:** If you need to work without the template in the way, use the Eye tool next to Cards at the bottom of the Layers panel to temporarily hide your template. Click on the Eye tool again to make it reappear.

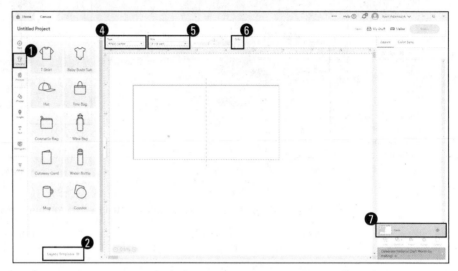

FIGURE 12-8: Working with Legacy Card Templates.

Source: design.cricut.com

REMEMBER

The card templates are for visualization only; they won't be cut by your Cricut. They're designed to assist you in positioning your designs accurately. When you procced to Make, the mat preview will display only the designs you placed on the template, not the template itself. If you need the Cricut to cut out the entire card shape, you must create the design using Shapes tools.

Here's how to create your own template using Shapes (see Figure 12-9):

1. **Decide on the finished size of your card.**

   For example, a standard 5 x 7-inch (12.7 x 17.8-cm) card works well for most occasions.

TIP

   For folded cards, double the width of your design (for example, 10 x 7 inches [25.4 x 17.8 cm]) to account for the fold.

2. **Select a square from the Shapes toolbar.**
3. **Resize the square to match your desired card dimensions.**

TIP

   To resize your square easily, enter the dimensions in the Size boxes found in the top toolbar. When the Lock icon is closed, your design stays proportional. If you unlock the design by clicking the Lock icon, you can change the dimensions independently, allowing you to transform the square into a rectangle.

164 PART 3 **Projects Using Paper and Cardstock**

4. **Click the Shapes tool and select Score Line, which is used for creating a fold line in the middle of your card.**

5. **Position the score line in the center of your rectangle to mark where the fold will be.**

   TIP

   Use the Align tool at the top of the screen to center the score line horizontally or vertically.

6. **Attach the score line to the rectangle so that they stay together during cutting and scoring.**

   Highlight the rectangle and score line by holding shift and clicking each element, and then click Attach at the bottom of the Layers panel.

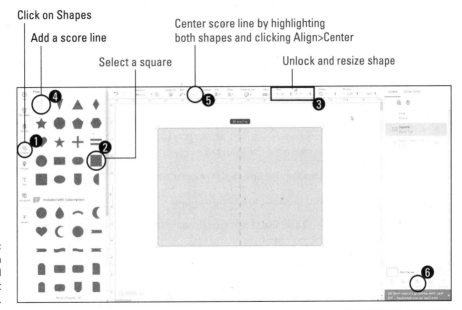

FIGURE 12-9: Creating a custom card template in Cricut Design Space.

Source: design.cricut.com

Step 3: Adding your designs

Now the fun begins — designing your card! Here are some ways you can further customize your card:

1. **Use the Shapes, Images, and Text tools in Design Space to create cutouts, decorative elements, or written messages for your card.**

   TIP

   To find fonts designed for writing with Cricut Pens, use the Filters option in the Font drop-down menu and select Writing.

CHAPTER 12 **Making Cards** 165

TIP

If you're making a custom Insert Card, search for "Insert Card Corners" in the Images section of Cricut Design Space. These designs create the corner slots needed to hold the decorative insert in place, making it easier to create a professional-looking Insert card from scratch.

2. **Arrange your design elements on the card base as desired.**

Step 4: Adjusting operations

Your Cricut needs clear instructions to create your card perfectly. This involves choosing an operation for each design element, such as cutting with a blade or drawing with a pen. Follow these steps to control what your Cricut does with each part of your design:

1. **Select your design element.**

   Click on each element within your design on the Canvas. This can be text, images, or custom shapes you've added.

2. **Open the Operation drop-down menu.**

   At the top of the Canvas, you'll find the Operation drop-down menu (refer to Figure 12-9). This allows you to assign a specific action that the Cricut will perform for the selected element.

3. **Choose the appropriate operation.**

   You have the following options:

   - **Basic Cut:** Use this operation to cut out shapes, text, or designs from your card.

   - **Pen:** Select this to write text, draw designs, or add decorative elements with Cricut Pens or Markers. Use a writing font for the best results.

   - **Foil:** Choose this option to apply shiny accents or details using Cricut Foil Transfer Sheets.

   - **Score:** For folded cards made from cardstock, use the scoring operation to create precise fold lines.

   - **Deboss:** Choose this option to press intricate designs into your material, creating a depressed effect. This adds texture and a touch of sophistication to any card.

   Repeat this process for each design element.

Step 5: Preparing to make your card

You're almost ready to make your card!

1. **Attach all elements.**

   When you're satisfied with your edits, highlight all the design elements and click Attach in the Layers panel to lock everything in place for proper cutting or drawing.

2. **Click Make to move to the Prepare screen.**

3. **Set the Material Load Type.**

   For Insert and Cutaway Cards, use the drop-down menu to change the Material Load Type to On Card Mat.

   For custom cards made with cardstock, set the Material Load Type to On Mat.

4. **Position your design on the mat preview.**

   Design Space automatically places your card design in the upper-left corner of the mat. You have the flexibility to move your design to any panel on the card mat by dragging and dropping it. This is helpful for avoiding excessive wear on any single area of the mat, helping the mat wear more evenly over time.

   If you are creating multiple cards at once, Design Space will initially sort your designs onto separate mats by color. If you prefer to cut all your designs on the same mat, click on your design in the mat preview. Then, click on the three dots in the upper-left corner and select Move Object. Choose the mat you want to move your design to and click Confirm.

   REMEMBER

   If you're cutting multiple cards on the same Card Mat at once, all cards must be the same size.

5. **Choose the Material Size.**

   From the Material Size drop-down menu, select the size that matches the card or material you're using.

   TIP

   If the size you need isn't listed, the project may only support specific dimensions. Consider choosing a different project if you don't see the correct size.

6. **Click Continue to advance to the Make screen.**

7. **Select the right material type from the Browse All Materials menu, such as Cardstock, Insert Card – Cardstock, or Cutaway Card + Backer.**

   Cardstock (for intricate cuts) also works well for most card-making projects.

CHAPTER 12 **Making Cards** 167

Step 6: Loading your material onto the mat

Remove the protective cover(s) from your mat.

Make sure the mat is facing the right way up — you should be able to see the Cricut logo in the top left. Unlike other machine mats that can be loaded from either end, the 2x2 Card Mat must always be loaded top-first.

Follow the steps in the following sections to load your card on the mat, depending on the type of card you're making.

Cutaway Cards

For Cutaway Cards:

1. **Prepare the card base.**

    Open the card and peel off the paper liner from the inside to expose the sticky adhesive underneath.

2. **Attach the decorative insert.**

    Stick the decorative insert onto the adhesive with the decorative side facing down toward the adhesive. The white side, or non-decorative side, should face up. This side with the decorative backer attached becomes the front of your card where the design elements will be cut.

    Use a brayer or scraper to ensure that the backer adheres smoothly without air bubbles.

3. **Position the card on the Card Mat.**

    Slide the card into the left side of the pocket on the Card Mat. Ensure that the white backer is facing up on the left, and the colored bottom side of the card is tucked underneath the pocket's panel. Slide the card all the way into the top-right corner of the pocket on the mat.

4. **Secure the card.**

    Close the card and press the front firmly onto the mat's adhesive. Use your hands or a brayer to ensure that it sticks well.

Insert Cards

For Insert Cards:

1. **Position the card on the mat.**

    Open the card and slide the bottom of the folded card under the plastic divider from the left side of the Card Mat panel. Slide the card all the way into the top-right corner of the pocket on the mat.

TIP

If lifting the plastic divider with your fingers is challenging, use a weeding tool or spatula to slightly lift the edge, allowing you to smoothly slide the card underneath.

2. **Secure the card.**

   Press the front of the card into the adhesive on the mat using your hands or a brayer to ensure that it sticks well.

Custom cards

For custom cards made from cardstock:

1. **Place your cardstock on a StandardGrip mat, aligning it to match the mat layout on the Prepare screen in Design Space.**

2. **If you want to write or draw on the inside of your card, fold it inside out before loading it onto the mat.**

   In Design Space, check the project Preview screen to make sure your Draw design is positioned and oriented correctly.

Step 7: Loading your tools and mat

Design Space will guide you through which tool to use, which clamp to put it in, and when to change it. (For more detailed information on these tools, see Chapter 4.) Depending on your design, you may want to do the following:

- Insert the Scoring Stylus or Wheel if your card includes a score line for folding.
- Load a pen or marker for written or drawn elements, if applicable.
- Ensure that the Fine-Point Blade is installed for cutting.
- Insert the Debossing Tip if your design includes debossed details.
- Use the Foil Transfer Tool if your design includes foiled designs. Make sure to select Fine, Medium, or Bold in Operations to control the thickness of the foil lines.
- Adjust the machine's *star wheels* (small white rings on the roller bar) to prevent track marks on your cards.
  - **For Cricut Maker and Explore machines:** Move the star wheels to the center of the bar so they align with the middle column of the Card Mat (see Figure 12-10).

- **For Cricut Joy Xtra:** Move the star wheels to the sides of the rail, ensuring that none of them will roll over the top of the card to prevent unwanted track marks.
- **For Cricut Joy:** This model does not have star wheels, so no additional adjustments are needed.

Doing so ensures that the wheels align with the middle column of the card mat for clean, accurate cuts.

FIGURE 12-10: Moving the star wheels to the center of the Cricut Maker to prevent track marks on the cards.

Source: Kerri Adamczyk

Before loading your mat, make sure your Cricut machine is positioned far enough away from any walls or obstacles behind it. This ensures that the mat doesn't hit the wall as it moves in and out during the cutting process.

Insert the mat into your Cricut machine and press the Load button to feed it in. If you're using a Cricut Joy or Cricut Joy Xtra, these models don't have a Load button — simply insert the mat, and the machine will pull it in automatically.

Step 8: Making your project

Get ready!

1. **Start the process.**

   Press the Go button to begin the process. The Cricut will draw, score, cut, foil, and/or deboss in the correct sequence, depending on your design. Design

Space will guide you through any necessary tool changes, providing clear instructions on when and how to switch them.

2. **Once the machine finishes its tasks, unload the mat.**

Step 9: Assembling your card

After your card has been cut, scored, debossed, and/or drawn to perfection, it's time to put it all together. This final step is where your project truly comes to life. Follow these instructions to complete your card:

1. **Carefully remove the card from the mat.**

   Use a scraper tool to gently lift the card from the top of the mat. Once the edges are slightly lifted, gently pull the rest of the card up from the panel. Slowly slide the card out, taking care to avoid tearing or bending. If the card feels stuck, gently wiggle it from side to side to ease it out.

   - **For Insert Cards:** If the material settings for the cut were correct, the card should peel away cleanly, leaving the cut pieces behind on the sticky mat. The sticky mat should take care of the weeding process for you! To remove any bits and pieces left on the mat, use the scraper tool again, scraping from top to bottom rather than side to side. This keeps small pieces of paper from getting stuck in the crevices of your mat.

   - **For Cutaway Cards:** Remove the card from the mat the same way as with an Insert Card. The design cutouts will still be attached at this state — you'll remove them in Step 4.

   - **For Standard Mat Users:** Start by peeling the mat away from the card rather than pulling the card away from the mat. This technique helps minimize bending or damage to the edges of your cardstock. Use a flat spatula tool to carefully lift the edges of the card, starting from one corner and slowly working your way around.

2. **Fold the card along the score line.**

3. **For Insert Cards, add the decorative insert.**

   Slide the decorative insert into the precut corner slots from behind the front of the card. Start by tucking one top corner into a slot, then do the same with the opposite top corner. Repeat for the bottom corners, adjusting as needed so the insert sits evenly behind the design.

CHAPTER 12 **Making Cards** **171**

4. **For Cutaway Cards, remove design cutouts.**

   Carefully remove the cutouts to reveal your design. Use your fingers to pick out large pieces. Carefully remove small or more intricate pieces with a weeding tool or tweezers to avoid scratching or damaging the backer. This process is similar to weeding vinyl, except instead of removing excess vinyl, you're peeling away the top layer of the card to expose the decorative backer underneath.

5. **Attach layers and embellishments.**

   Use adhesives to attach any additional layers, embellishments, or decorative elements.

6. **Add final touches like handwritten messages or decorative details using pens or markers.**

7. **Once your card is complete, slide it into the included envelope.**

4

Vinyl and Heat Transfer Projects

IN THIS PART . . .

Understand the basics of working with vinyl and how to apply it to various surfaces.

Layer vinyl to make colorful and complex designs.

Customize fabric projects like T-shirts and tote bags with heat transfer vinyl.

Try out Infusible Ink for vibrant-looking crafts that last longer.

Use vinyl stencils to make etched designs on glass.

IN THIS CHAPTER

» Discovering creative project ideas for vinyl crafting

» Steering clear of surfaces vinyl won't stick to

» Exploring the many types of vinyl

» Mastering the art of weeding vinyl

» Moving vinyl designs with transfer tape

» Gathering everything you need for vinyl crafts

» Following a step-by-step guide to working with (and caring for) vinyl

Chapter **13**
Working with Vinyl

Vinyl is one of the most versatile materials for Cricut projects. Think of it as a giant roll of durable sticker paper you can cut into endless shapes and sizes to stick on all kinds of surfaces. It comes in a wide range of finishes, colors, textures, and sizes — from huge rolls to individual sheets.

Once your Cricut cuts your design into the vinyl, the real fun begins. You'll *weed out* (remove) the parts you don't need to reveal your final masterpiece. But vinyl doesn't work alone — its trusty sidekick, transfer tape, helps you move your design to its final destination, whether that's a mug, a sign, or even a wall.

In this chapter, you explore the many types of vinyl, from glittery and holographic, to permanent and removable. Plus, I walk you through step-by-step instructions on cutting, weeding, and applying vinyl. (Check out the color section to see some vinyl projects.)

Exploring Vinyl Project Ideas

Vinyl sticks to almost any smooth surface you can think of. Apply it to glass windows, wooden signs, plastic containers, or metal tumblers. Vinyl is also durable, making it perfect for car decals that need to withstand the elements. It's great for creating everything from personalized home décor to outdoor signage.

Need some ideas for your next project? Here are some creative ways to use vinyl:

- **Customizing glass items:** Personalize mugs, mirrors, or windows.

  Metallic gold vinyl is perfect for adding an elegant touch to bridal party wine glasses. Use a script font to personalize each glass with a name or role like *Bride* or *Maid of Honor*.

- **Designing wood signs:** Apply vinyl to smooth, painted, and sealed wood surfaces to create signs for home décor. You can also use heat transfer vinyl (HTV) on wood signs for a durable and unique finish. Check out Chapter 15 to get more information about HTV.

- **Creating stencils:** Use vinyl as a one-time stencil for painting crisp designs on walls, wood, or fabric. This technique is also popular for wood-burning projects using Torch Paste. Chapter 17 covers steps for making stencils.

- **Crafting shadow boxes:** Create meaningful keepsakes by decorating shadow boxes with vinyl designs on the glass and adding personal mementos inside. Shadow boxes are also fun to fill with rolled paper flowers, which I cover in Chapter 11.

- **Making Christmas ornaments:** Add names, dates, or fun designs to ornaments to give your tree a personal touch.

- **Personalizing car decals:** Create vinyl decals to highlight your interests or advertise your business on your vehicle's windows. For a detailed tutorial on how to make and sell car decals using your Cricut, watch this video on my YouTube channel: `https://youtu.be/D7S1OV6frxw`.

  When creating vinyl decals, choose thicker fonts. They're easier to cut and weed, and they stick to surfaces better.

- **Adding magic to kids' cups:** Apply color-changing vinyl to cups that also change color when filled with hot or cold liquid for a fun surprise. I have a tutorial for this project on my YouTube channel: `https://youtu.be/tIUijXtSrME`.

- **Customizing back-to-school supplies:** Add names, subjects, or fun designs to pencil cases, notebooks, or binders.

TIP Want to see how to make more of my favorite vinyl Cricut projects? Check out this playlist on my YouTube channel, Kerri Crafts It, with over 40 tutorials: www.youtube.com/playlist?list=PL-sW1stz54sleAN4mFREJWp7GJd0fwLZM.

Avoiding Surfaces Vinyl Doesn't Stick To

Although vinyl sticks well to many things, some surfaces just don't work with it. Avoiding the following surfaces will ensure that your vinyl projects last longer and look their best:

- » **Porous surfaces:** Unsealed wood, rough concrete, or untreated stone won't provide a smooth, solid bond for vinyl.

- » **High-heat surfaces:** Stay away from items like pots, pans, oven mitts, or surfaces exposed to direct heat, as the vinyl can melt, peel, or catch fire.

- » **Food-contact areas:** Vinyl isn't food-safe, so don't apply it directly on plates, cutting boards, utensils, or anything that will come into contact with food.

WARNING Vinyl isn't microwave-safe, so think twice before using it on coffee mugs. If you're someone who frequently reheats your coffee, consider using Infusible Ink instead. See Chapter 16 for details.

- » **Fabric:** Standard adhesive vinyl doesn't stick well to most fabrics. For clothing or fabric items, use HTV instead (see Chapter 15).

- » **Dirty, greasy, or dusty surfaces:** Always clean surfaces with rubbing alcohol before applying vinyl.

- » **Flexible or rubbery materials:** It may be difficult to get vinyl to stay in place on items made of silicone or things that have a squishy surface.

Checking Out Types of Vinyl

Vinyl comes in many colors, finishes, and textures, making it perfect for all kinds of projects. This section shows you the different types of vinyl and helps you pick the best one for your project.

TIP Just starting out? Grab a vinyl starter kit or bundle with an assortment of vinyl colors, transfer tape, and weeding tools to explore the basics. The GO2CRAFT All-in-One Accessories Bundle on Amazon comes with 90 pieces to get you started with most projects. This bundle includes permanent adhesive vinyl, transfer tape,

CHAPTER 13 **Working with Vinyl** 177

cutting mats, glitter heat transfer vinyl (see Chapter 15), vinyl sticker paper (see Chapter 19), stencil sheets, weeding tools, a scraper, and a pen adapter allowing you to use non-Cricut brand pens — all for under $40. Check it out via my affiliate link: https://amzn.to/3DeSxd6.

Deciding between permanent and removable vinyl

Permanent vinyl is perfect for projects that need to last, like car decals, outdoor signs, or water bottles. It's durable but may peel if exposed to hot water or the dishwasher. Oracal 651 permanent vinyl is water-resistant and can last up to six years, making it great for outdoor use.

Removable vinyl is best for temporary projects like wall decals, window clings, and seasonal decorations. It won't leave any sticky residue when removed. Oracal 631 is ideal for temporary use; Oracal 651 is better for permanent designs.

Glossy vinyl provides a vibrant, polished finish, perfect for projects like water bottles and Christmas ornaments, and matte vinyl offers a subtle, nonreflective look, making it ideal for wall decals that blend seamlessly with painted surfaces.

Exploring specialty vinyl for unique designs

Specialty vinyl offers unique effects that can make your projects stand out. Whether you're looking for interactive designs or eye-catching finishes, there's a specialty vinyl for every style. Here are some popular types to try:

- **Color-changing vinyl:** Adds a fun twist by changing color in different lighting or temperature, perfect for interactive designs
- **Etched vinyl:** Ideal for glass and metal projects, giving a frosted, etched look that mimics sandblasting
- **Fluorescent vinyl:** Provides bold, bright colors that pop, great for signage or attention-grabbing designs
- **Glitter vinyl:** Adds sparkle and shine to your projects, perfect for anything that needs a little extra glam
- **Glow-in-the-dark vinyl:** Absorbs light and glows in the dark, making it ideal for nighttime projects like costumes and décor
- **Holographic vinyl:** Creates a shimmering, rainbow effect that changes color in different lighting, perfect for a futuristic look

- **Printable vinyl:** Allows you to print full-color designs, ideal for detailed, multicolored projects
- **Printed pattern vinyl:** Features pre-designed patterns like florals or animal prints, adding personality to your projects
- **Reflective vinyl:** Shines brightly and reflects light, perfect for projects that need high visibility, like safety gear
- **Stencil vinyl:** Designed specifically for creating custom stencils, making it easy to transfer detailed designs onto surfaces

TIP

Keeping your vinyl collection neat doesn't have to be overwhelming. Use over-the-door shoe organizers to store rolls, cube shelves to combine sheets and scraps, or rolling craft carts for a portable solution. File folders or magazine holders are great for smaller pieces, and hanging wire baskets offer easy access to both rolls and sheets. Choose a system that fits your space and style, and keeps everything tidy.

Using Smart Vinyl for mat-free cutting

Cricut's Smart Vinyl lets you skip the cutting mat, making it perfect for large or continuous projects like banners. Available in permanent and removable versions, it works with Cricut machines that support Smart Materials, such as the Cricut Maker 4, Maker 3, Explore 4, Explore 3, Joy, Joy Xtra, and Venture (see Chapter 2 for details).

To use Smart Vinyl, load it directly into your Cricut machine without a mat. Align the edge of the vinyl with the guides on your machine and make sure it's straight. Select Smart Vinyl from the Browse All Materials menu in Design Space (see Part 2), and let your machine do the cutting. Then weed and apply your Smart Vinyl just like regular vinyl — but without the extra step of dealing with a mat!

Weeding Vinyl to Reveal Your Design

TIP

Weeding is the process of removing the extra vinyl (called the *negative space*) from your design, leaving only the parts you want to transfer. Here are some helpful tips to make weeding easier and less stressful:

- **Do a test cut first.** Before cutting your entire design, try a small test cut to confirm your settings. Select a small shape like a star in Design Space and cut it with your current settings. If it weeds easily, your settings are correct. Use

CHAPTER 13 **Working with Vinyl** 179

the Eye tool in the Layers panel to temporarily hide your main design while you test, or assign a different color to the test shape so Design Space places it on a separate mat for cutting. This ensures that the vinyl will weed cleanly and saves material if adjustments are needed.

» **Weed on the mat.** Keep your vinyl design on the cutting mat while you're weeding. The mat holds everything flat, preventing the vinyl from curling and making it easier to work on.

» **Start in the center.** When weeding small vinyl cuts, begin in the center and work outward. This keeps the outer edges in place and helps you avoid shifting or damaging the design. For example, remove the inside of a letter O before the outer piece.

» **Use the right tools.** A weeding hook, tweezers, *pin pen* (a pen with a sharp metal tip, also called a *weeding pen*), or other precision tools can help you grab and pull away small pieces without damaging the design.

» **Double-check your design.** Keep Cricut Design Space open while you work to confirm what stays and what goes. It's easy to accidentally pull off small details, so having a reference helps you stay on track. (Flip to Part 2 for more on Cricut Design Space.)

» **Watch for sticky mishaps.** Be careful not to let the sticky side of the excess vinyl touch your design. Vinyl tends to stick to itself, and pulling it apart can stretch or distort the design image.

» **Take your time.** Weeding requires patience, especially when you're working with intricate designs. Taking it slow and steady helps you avoid mistakes.

» **Troubleshoot tough vinyl.** If your vinyl doesn't peel away easily, it may need to be recut with a higher pressure setting. This adjustment can make a big difference for clean weeding. You can increase your Cricut's cutting pressure by changing the pressure setting from Default to More after choosing your material in Design Space.

» **Try reverse weeding for intricate designs.** For more complex designs, apply transfer tape over your unweeded cut vinyl while it's still on the backing paper. Flip the design over and peel away the backing paper, leaving the vinyl on the transfer tape. Weed the excess vinyl directly off the transfer tape and then apply the design to your project as usual.

If you're struggling with weeding your project, it may be time to replace your Cricut blades. For detailed instructions, see Chapter 5.

180 PART 4 **Vinyl and Heat Transfer Projects**

Using Transfer Tape

Transfer tape is used to move your vinyl design from the backing paper to your project surface without losing pieces or messing up the alignment. Without it, you'd be stuck transferring each tiny piece by hand — not fun! Transfer tape comes in low-, medium-, and high-tack options. Low tack is best for delicate surfaces, medium tack works for most projects, and high tack is great for thicker vinyl like glitter or reflective types. You can also choose clear transfer tape for easier alignment or grid-lined transfer tape for precise placement. Masking paper transfer tape is another option for delicate surfaces.

TIP

My favorite transfer tape is the YRYM HT Vinyl Transfer Tape on Amazon (https://amzn.to/4h3CTPM). This paper transfer tape provides a perfect blend of features — it's clear for easy alignment, features red grid lines for precise placement, and has a medium tack that's perfect for most projects.

After your design has been cut and weeded, you're ready to transfer it to your blank with transfer tape. Properly applying transfer tape is crucial for keeping your vinyl design intact. Here's how to do it:

1. **Prepare the tape.**

   Cut the tape so it's slightly larger than your design.

2. **Attach the tape to your design.**

   Peel off the transfer tape's backing to expose the sticky side. Use the taco method to stick the transfer tape to the vinyl: Bend the tape into a U-shape (like a taco), touch the center to the design first, and then smooth the tape outward with a scraper or brayer.

3. **Transfer the vinyl to your blank surface.**

   Once the vinyl is attached to the transfer tape, it's time to apply it to your project surface. You can use one of these methods to get it just right:

   - **Standard method:** This straightforward approach is perfect for simple designs. Press the transfer tape down firmly over the vinyl with a scraper and peel it from the backing carefully, lifting your vinyl design with it. You can then position the vinyl on your blank surface and press down to secure it. Carefully peel off the transfer tape to reveal your finished project.

TIP

If the vinyl doesn't lift with the tape, firmly rub it down again with a scraper. Or you can flip the vinyl and transfer tape upside down so the tape is touching your work table. Press down firmly across the liner with your scraper and then slowly peel the liner away from the tape — this reverse approach often helps the vinyl stick to the tape better. If it's still stubborn, use a weeding tool to gently lift a corner of the vinyl — once the edge lifts, the rest should follow.

TIP

- **Taco method:** Tacos are awesome, and so is the taco method for applying vinyl! This technique is perfect for handling larger designs with ease. After you've lifted your design off the liner with transfer tape, gently fold it into a U-shape, like a taco. Apply the vinyl to your surface, starting from the center and smoothing outward to the edges.

  The taco method allows for more precise placement and reduces the likelihood of wrinkles or bubbles in your project.

- **Wet method:** This method may sound strange, but spraying your surface with soapy water before applying your vinyl can actually make the process easier. Unlike the other methods, the wet method allows you to reposition your vinyl design after placing it on your surface.

  Fill a spray bottle with water and add a couple of drops of dish soap. Lightly spray this mixture onto the project surface and the sticky side of your vinyl. This helps you move the vinyl around more easily and gets rid of air bubbles. Once you've placed the vinyl on your blank, use a scraper to press out the liquid underneath. Make sure it's completely dry before you take off the transfer tape.

TIP

If your transfer tape is too sticky, press it onto your clothes a few times before using it. This reduces the tackiness, making it easier to lift the vinyl without tearing or stretching it.

Gathering Your Materials for Vinyl Projects

Before you start your vinyl project, make sure you have the following materials (see Chapters 2 and 4 for more details):

- **Blanks or a blank surface:** You can apply your designs to customizable objects (also called *blanks*) made of glass, metal, plastic, wood, and other vinyl-friendly material.
- **Brayer or scraper:** This tool helps you smooth transfer tape over your vinyl designs.
- **Cricut machine:** Any model will cut vinyl.
- **Fine-Point Blade:** This is the blade you need for clean cuts on vinyl.
- **Rubbing alcohol and lint-free wipes:** You'll need these to clean your project surface before applying vinyl to make it stick better.

- **StandardGrip Mat (optional for Smart Vinyl):** This mat holds vinyl securely in place during cutting.
- **Transfer tape:** This helps you move your vinyl design to your project smoothly. You can see which type works for your project in the earlier section "Using Transfer Tape."
- **Vinyl or Smart Vinyl:** Choose from different finishes like matte, glossy, or textured. Smart Vinyl is great for quick, no-mat projects. Get the details on different types of vinyl in the next section.
- **Weeding tools:** Use tools like hooks and tweezers to remove extra vinyl after cutting your designs.

Working with Vinyl: A Step-by-Step Guide

Mastering vinyl projects is easier than you think. The simple guide in this section walks you through each step.

TIP

The following sections focus on single-layer vinyl projects. If you're working with multicolored designs, you'll need to layer your vinyl or use printable vinyl. For help layering vinyl, check out Chapter 14. To find out more about printable vinyl, see Chapter 19.

Step 1: Designing your project

Follow these steps to bring your ideas to life in Cricut Design Space (see in Part 2):

1. **Create or upload your design.**

   Open Design Space and start by creating or uploading your design.

   TIP

   SVG files are the best choice for vinyl projects because they're easy to resize without losing quality. When downloading designs from external websites, the files typically come in various formats like PNG, JPG, and SVG. These sites usually specify the file types included with each download, allowing you to choose the most suitable one for your project.

2. **Measure and resize.**

   Measure the surface where you'll apply the vinyl and then resize your design to match your measurements. Simply select the design and use the resize handles in the corners to adjust its dimensions. You can also use the Size tool in the edit bar at the top of the Canvas. The Lock tool next to the Size tool plays an important role in maintaining the aspect ratio of your design. When the lock is closed, resizing the width will automatically adjust the height to keep your design proportional. If you unlock it, you can change the width and height separately, giving you flexibility but possibly altering the design's original shape.

3. **Unite your design elements.**

   If your design has multiple pieces you want to keep together, use the Unite feature, found under the Combine tool at the bottom of the Layers panel. This is especially helpful for script fonts, because it keeps the letters connected and prevents your Cricut from making slice marks between them.

REMEMBER

   You don't need to *mirror,* or flip, your design when working with regular vinyl. The only exception for regular vinyl is if you're applying it inside glass and want the design to face outward. I do this when making memorial lanterns. Placing the vinyl inside the glass preserves the design and makes it easier to clean the glass. This tutorial on my YouTube channel (https://youtu.be/9_X_-0VFo5A) walks you through how to make custom lanterns with vinyl.

4. **Set your operation.**

   Before moving on, make sure Operation (in the toolbar at the top of the Canvas) is set to Basic Cut. This ensures that your Cricut will cut the vinyl instead of trying to draw or score it.

5. **Click Make.**

   Once you're finished editing your design, click Make to proceed to the Prepare screen, where you can set the number of project copies, choose your mat size, and mirror your design (or not). For tips on navigating these screens, see Chapter 9.

REMEMBER

   Where you place your design on the mat preview in Design Space is exactly where you need to stick your vinyl on the cutting mat. Design Space automatically places your design in the upper-left corner, so unless you move it, that's where your vinyl should go.

Step 2: Preparing the materials

Get everything ready for a smooth cutting and application process:

1. **Clean your surface with rubbing alcohol and a lint-free wipe and let it dry completely.**

2. **Cut your vinyl.**

   Use a Cricut trimmer or scissors to cut a piece of vinyl slightly larger than your design — or place a longer piece or roll of vinyl directly on the mat and trim it after cutting. Experiment to see which method works best for you.

   Don't toss your vinyl scraps! Save them for smaller projects like labels, decals, or test cuts. Keep your scraps organized by size or color in a folder or clear plastic bag for easy access.

3. **Place the vinyl, paper liner side down, in the upper-left corner of a StandardGrip Mat to match the placement in Design Space.**

   If your mat is new or extra sticky, a LightGrip Mat may be easier to work with.

4. **Press the vinyl firmly onto the mat.**

   Smooth out any wrinkles or air bubbles with your hands, a scraper, or a brayer to make sure it stays in place during cutting.

Smart Vinyl needs to be at least 6 inches (15.2 centimeters) long for mat-free cutting. For shorter pieces, place the Smart Vinyl on a StandardGrip Mat.

Step 3: Loading and cutting the vinyl

For regular vinyl, follow these steps:

1. **In Browse All Materials, select your material, such as Vinyl for permanent vinyl.**
2. **Load the cutting mat into the machine by aligning it under the guide tabs and pressing the Load button.**
3. **Press the Go button to begin the cutting process.**

For Smart Vinyl, follow these steps:

1. **Select Without Mat in Design Space.**
2. **In Browse All Materials, choose Smart Vinyl.**
3. **Align the Smart Vinyl with the machine guides, ensuring that the edge is straight for accurate cutting, and press the Load button.**
4. **Press the Go button to begin the cutting process.**

Step 4: Weeding the excess vinyl

Remove the excess vinyl to reveal your clean design:

1. **Once the cutting is complete, remove the mat (or Smart Vinyl) from the machine.**

2. **Weed your vinyl design while it's still on the mat to keep it flat and easier to work with.**

   Use a weeding tool to carefully remove all the unwanted vinyl. See the earlier section "Weeding Vinyl to Reveal Your Design" for more tips.

Step 5: Applying transfer tape

Use transfer tape to move your design from the paper backing to your material:

1. **Cut a piece of transfer tape slightly larger than your design.**

2. **Peel the backing paper off and use the taco method to apply the tape, sticky side down, starting at the center.**

   See the earlier section "Using Transfer Tape" for details.

3. **Smooth the tape over the vinyl with a scraper or brayer to attach it firmly to your design.**

4. **Carefully peel the tape from the vinyl backing, lifting your design with it.**

   If you have difficulty lifting your design from the backing, smooth your scraper over the tape again or use a weeding tool to lift the edge.

Step 6: Transferring your design

Apply your design to the desired surface for a beautiful finish:

1. **Choose a transfer method, such as the taco method for larger designs or the wet method for easier repositioning.**

   See the earlier section "Using Transfer Tape."

2. **Use a scraper to press the vinyl down firmly onto your blank surface.**

3. **Slowly peel back the transfer tape at a sharp angle, leaving the vinyl design in place.**

   If you're using the wet method, be sure to let your project dry fully before peeling off the transfer tape.

TIP If air bubbles appear under your vinyl, pop them with a sewing needle and smooth over the area with your finger to flatten the vinyl.

Caring for Your Vinyl Projects

TIP Vinyl projects are durable and beautiful, but a little extra care can go a long way in keeping them looking their best. Avoid sealing vinyl, as it can cause peeling or warping. Hand-wash with mild soap and warm water, and avoid abrasive sponges. Never put vinyl items in the dishwasher or microwave, as heat can damage them and release fumes. Handwashing is the safest option.

For tips on maintaining cutting mats and other tools for vinyl projects, check out Chapter 5.

IN THIS CHAPTER

» Picking the best vinyl for layering

» Managing multilayered designs in Cricut Design Space

» Mastering different techniques for precise alignment

Chapter **14**

Layering Vinyl for Colorful Designs

Layering vinyl, whether it's adhesive vinyl or heat transfer vinyl (HTV), is a popular Cricut technique that lets you create colorful multidimensional designs on everything from T-shirts and tumblers to home décor and signs. By stacking different layers of vinyl, you can bring your designs to life with bold colors, intricate details, and added depth that a single layer of vinyl just can't achieve.

In this chapter, you discover how to work with layered designs in Cricut Design Space, from organizing your layers to deciding the best order for stacking them. You also find out how to use registration marks and the Slice tool to keep your designs perfectly aligned. Plus, I walk you through step-by-step instructions for layering both adhesive vinyl and HTV so that you can choose the technique that works best for your project.

REMEMBER

There's no single "right" way to layer — it all comes down to what works best for your designs and crafting style. With a little patience and a bit of practice, you'll soon be layering like a pro!

Choosing the Right Vinyl for Layering

Selecting the right type of vinyl is the key to making the layering process easier and ensuring that your design lasts over time. Not all vinyl is created equal — some types layer smoothly, but others can cause frustration and may eventually peel or lift.

For everything you need to know about vinyl, including detailed descriptions of each type, see Chapter 13. Chapter 15 gives you the lowdown on heat transfer vinyl (HTV). In this section, you find out which types of vinyl work best for layering and which types to avoid.

Sticking with the easiest vinyl to layer

If you're new to layering, start with vinyl that's easy to work with. Adhesive vinyl and HTV, in both matte and glossy finishes, are the easiest to layer. They stick well and create clean, professional-looking designs. Matte finishes give your projects a soft, muted look; glossy finishes add a bit of shine. Because both types are great for layering, your choice comes down to the look you want to achieve.

Avoiding vinyl that's hard to layer

Some types of vinyl may look great but shouldn't be used as the base of a layered design.

Never layer on top of holographic, glitter, flock, or metallic vinyl. It's difficult to get other vinyl to stick to the textured or shiny surface of these specialty vinyls, and your design may peel or lift over time because of the poor adhesion.

If you still want to incorporate specialty vinyl in your project, you can try a workaround. For example, you can use the Slice tool in Cricut Design Space to cut out overlapping sections and fit the vinyl pieces together like a puzzle rather than stacking them. Alternatively, you can use specialty vinyl as the top layer in your design, so nothing needs to stick to it.

Layering dark colors last

When you're layering vinyl, especially HTV, it's important to consider the color of your layers to determine the order in which you'll apply them.

REMEMBER Whenever possible, place light colors on your surface first and stack darker colors on top. This prevents the darker colors from bleeding through the lighter layers, especially when you apply heat.

For example, if you're layering white and black HTV, place the white layer down first and add the black layer on top. This keeps the lighter color vibrant and clean, and ensures that the dark vinyl maintains its boldness without affecting the layer beneath it. This technique is especially important when you're working with fabrics, where color bleeding is more likely to occur.

Working with Multilayered Designs in Design Space

After you know which vinyl to use — and which to avoid — you're ready to move on to the design process. Before you start cutting your vinyl, it's important to organize and prepare your layers in Cricut Design Space. Multilayered designs require careful alignment, and Design Space offers several tools to help, as you find out in the following sections.

TIP Create simple two-layered designs quickly and easily using the Offset tool at the top of the Canvas. Just type some text, add an offset in a contrasting color, and layer the vinyl for a bold, eye-catching look. Part 2 has full details on working in Design Space.

Ungrouping layered designs

Before you can start layering, you need to split your design into individual parts to see the different layers. This helps you visualize how the pieces stack together, making it easier to assemble your project correctly later on.

Many designs in Cricut Design Space come grouped together by default. To separate them into individual layers, you'll use the Ungroup tool, located in the upper left of the Layers panel. You may need to click Ungroup multiple times to fully separate all the layers.

For example, take a look at the cow design in Figure 14-1. The cow on the left is the completed design as it appears when you first open it in Design Space. After ungrouping, the design is broken down into five separate layers, each representing a different color or detail.

CHAPTER 14 **Layering Vinyl for Colorful Designs** 191

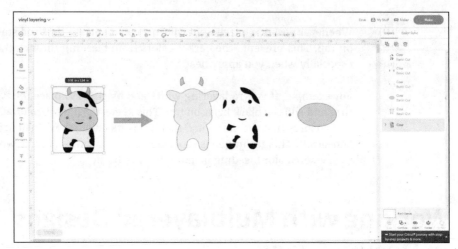

FIGURE 14-1: Ungrouping a cow design in Design Space to reveal individual layers.

Source: `design.cricut.com`

Deciding the stack order

Figuring out the order to stack your vinyl layers can be tricky, but the Layers panel in Design Space (on the right side of the screen) is a great guide.

REMEMBER

The Layers panel shows the stack order in reverse — what's on top in the panel should usually be the top layer of your finished project. For example, in the cow design in Figure 14-1, the top layer is the black spots and features, followed by the orange horns, dark pink nostrils, light pink nose, and finally, the white body as the base layer.

TIP

However, keep in mind that the Layers panel may not reflect the exact stack order for complex or imported designs. It's a good idea to double-check your design on the Canvas to make sure everything lines up as it should. You can click and drag to rearrange the pieces on the Canvas, which helps confirm the correct stacking order.

Considering the maximum number of layers

Once you ungroup your design and can see all the different layers, you should think about how many layers you actually need. Some designs have lots of layers, but stacking too many can cause issues later on.

WARNING

TIP

Too many layers can make your project stiff, bulky, and more likely to peel or lift — especially on items that need to stay flexible like clothing. For the best results, stick to three or four layers. Going beyond that can affect how your project feels and holds up over time.

If your design seems overly complicated, you can simplify it in the following ways:

- » You can use the Color Sync tool at the top of the Layers panel to reduce the number of colors in your design, which can help cut down on unnecessary layers. To find out more about Color Sync, check out Chapter 8.
- » Another helpful technique is using the Slice tool at the bottom of the Layers panel to cut out overlapping sections, so you can assemble your vinyl pieces like a puzzle instead of stacking them on top of each other. See the next section for details.

Simplifying designs with the Slice tool

If your multilayered design seems too complicated, you can use the Slice tool in Design Space to simplify it. Think of it as a cookie cutter — it cuts out overlapping sections so that your vinyl pieces fit together like puzzle pieces instead of stacking on top of each other.

Here's how to use the Slice tool to reduce layers:

1. **Select the overlapping layers.**

   Highlight the two layers you want to slice. You can slice only two at a time. Additionally, you can hold down the Shift key while selecting your design on the Canvas or in the Layers panel to easily select multiple layers.

2. **Click Slice.**

   In the Layers panel on the right side of your screen, click on the Slice button at the bottom. This will cut the top shape out of the bottom layer.

3. **Remove extra pieces.**

   Delete any unnecessary shapes, keeping only the parts you want.

4. **Repeat as needed.**

   Continue slicing until your design is simplified.

TIP

The slicing technique is especially useful for materials like glitter vinyl or holographic HTV, which shouldn't be layered underneath other vinyl because of their textures. Slicing allows these materials to fit together neatly without overlapping. This method is also incredibly useful for layering Infusible Ink Transfer Sheet projects, where the layers of ink cannot overlap or else it will cause color bleeding. See Chapter 16 for more details to help you visualize this slicing method.

Exploring Layering Techniques

When it comes to layering vinyl, there's no one-size-fits-all method. The technique you choose depends on the complexity of your design and what seems easiest for you. Here are a few ways to layer vinyl that will help you get clean, perfectly aligned results.

Layering from bottom to top

The bottom-to-top method is the most common approach for layering vinyl. You build your design one layer at a time, starting with the base and working your way up. Here's how to do it:

1. **Place your base layer (for example, the white cow body in Figure 14-1) directly on your mat.**

   The mat keeps your design steady and secure while you assemble the layers.

2. **Use transfer tape to apply each additional layer, starting with the next color (in Figure 14-1, the light pink nose), and continue until the top layer is applied.**

   Each new layer builds upon the last until the design is complete.

3. **Once all the layers are assembled, use a fresh piece of transfer tape to lift the entire layered design off the mat and apply it to your project surface.**

   Smooth it down with a scraper or brayer, and then carefully remove the transfer tape. (Flip to Chapter 13 for some helpful pointers on using transfer tape.)

Layering from top to bottom

In the top-to-bottom method, you build your layered design directly onto one piece of transfer tape before applying it to your project. This method allows you to transfer all layers at once, keeping everything aligned. Follow these steps to layer from top to bottom:

1. **Start with the top layer.**

   Stick your transfer tape to the topmost layer of your design.

2. **Stack each layer underneath.**

   Without removing the first layer from the transfer tape, place it onto the next layer down and smooth it out. Repeat this process, stacking each lower layer until you reach the base layer. When looking at your transfer tape from above, you should see your entire design on a single sheet of transfer tape before applying it to your project.

3. **Apply your design in one step.**

   Once all the layers are stacked on the tape, transfer the entire design to your project in one go.

TIP

This method works well for simple designs with a few layers but can be tricky for complex or detailed projects. If you're using the top-to-bottom technique, stick to simple designs with fewer layers to keep things manageable.

Imagine you're adding vinyl to an acrylic key chain. You want to add a brushstroke with pink vinyl and a name with gold vinyl. Rather than putting transfer tape onto the brushstroke, applying it to the key chain, removing the tape, reapplying the transfer tape to the name, and sticking the name to the brushstroke vinyl, you could simply stick the transfer tape to the name, lift up, and immediately press it down on the brushstroke. Then you could lift up both pieces onto the same piece of tape and transferring it in one go. Since this design is simple and doesn't require super-precise alignment, the top-to-bottom method is straightforward and works well for this project.

Using registration marks for precise layering

Although layering from the bottom up is usually the best approach, you may need a little extra help to get everything perfectly aligned when you're working with complicated designs. Even the slightest misalignment can throw off your whole design and make it look uneven or crooked. That's where registration marks come in — they help you line up your layers with pinpoint accuracy, making sure every piece ends up exactly where it should.

Registration marks are small shapes, like stars or triangles, that you add to each layer of your design in the exact same spot. These marks act as alignment guides, so you can line up each layer perfectly when it's time to assemble your project.

TIP You can use any shape for registration marks, but stars work especially well because their points make it easy to spot even the slightest misalignment, giving you more precise control when layering.

Setting up registration marks

Follow these steps and see Figure 14-2 for guidance:

1. **Choose a shape.**

    Open the Shapes menu in Design Space (on the left side of your screen) and select a simple shape (for example, a star) as your registration mark.

2. **Position the registration mark.**

    Place the star near your design without overlapping it. For instance, in Figure 14-2, the star is positioned between the cow's legs in the design.

3. **Duplicate the registration mark.**

    Duplicate the star by selecting it and clicking the Duplicate button at the top of the Layers panel, or by right-clicking and choosing Duplicate. Repeat this step until there's one for each layer of your design (for example, you need five stars for a design with five layers).

4. **Color match the registration mark with your layers.**

    Assign a color to each layer and change each star's color to match its corresponding layer. Start by clicking on one of the stars and then clicking on the colored box next to the Operation menu at the top of the screen. Cricut conveniently displays all the material colors in a row at the top of the color selection tool as you choose them. Repeat this process for each star.

5. **Align the registration marks.**

    Now it's time to stack all the stars on top of each other so they line up correctly during cutting. To do this, hold down the shift key and click each star in the Layers panel to select them all. Then, click the Align tool in the top toolbar and choose Center. This will stack all the stars into one perfect pile, which is why it will look like there's only one star on the Canvas.

6. **Position the grouped registration marks.**

    Drag the aligned group of stars back to the desired spot on your Canvas, such as between the cow's legs (see Figure 14-2). Make sure they stay grouped.

7. **Attach the registration marks to the layers.**

    See the next section for guidance on this process.

FIGURE 14-2:
Aligning and positioning registration marks in Design Space.

Source: `design.cricut.com`

Attaching registration marks to layers

To keep your registration marks and design layers in place while your Cricut is cutting, you'll need to attach them together. Here's how:

1. **Select the layers.**

   Hold the shift key and click both the registration mark and its matching design layer in the Layers panel (for example, in Figure 14-2, the pink star and the pink layer of the cow).

2. **Lock the layers together.**

   Click Attach (at the bottom of the Layers panel) to lock them together for cutting.

3. **Repeat for all the layers.**

   Follow Steps 1 and 2 for the rest of your layers.

After you're finished attaching your layers and registration marks, each set will update in the Layers panel to show the word *Attach*. If you click the drop-down arrow next to each attachment, you'll see the two elements listed underneath: the registration mark and its matching design layer. Figure 14-3 shows how this looks in the Layers panel. If you try dragging your design apart on the Canvas, you'll notice that all five layers of the design stay aligned with the registration mark attached in the same spot on each layer.

CHAPTER 14 **Layering Vinyl for Colorful Designs** 197

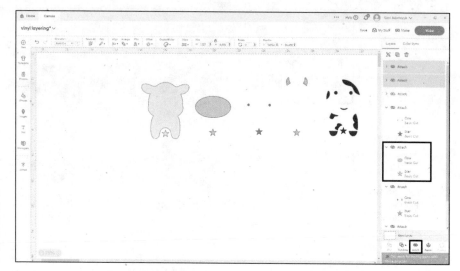

FIGURE 14-3: Attaching registration marks to design layers for precise cutting.

Source: design.cricut.com

TIP

Attaching registration marks often shifts the stacking order in the Layers panel. If this happens, use the Arrange tool in the top toolbar, or right-click on the registration mark and choose Send to Back, Move Backward, Move Forward, or Bring to Front to adjust its position. If you lose track of the original stack order, reimport the design as a reference.

Aligning and applying layers

With your registration marks in place, you're ready to cut, weed, and assemble your layers. Here's how to align and apply them step by step:

1. **Cut and weed your layers.**

   Click Make, select your material, and then decide if you need to mirror your image. For adhesive vinyl, no mirroring is required. For heat transfer vinyl (HTV), toggle on mirroring so that your design transfers correctly onto the fabric. Design Space's Auto Mirror function will automatically adjust the mirror setting after you select your material. Once set, cut each layer with its attached registration mark and carefully weed the layers, keeping the registration marks intact.

2. **Prepare the surface of your blank.**

   Clean your *blank* (the object you're applying your design to) with rubbing alcohol and a lint-free wipe. Allow the surface to fully dry before applying the vinyl.

198 PART 4 **Vinyl and Heat Transfer Projects**

3. **Align and layer your design.**

   Stick the base layer to a StandardGrip Mat. Use transfer tape to lift and align the next layer, relying on the registration marks to guide you. Once a layer is aligned, press the vinyl down with a scraper or brayer and remove the transfer tape. Repeat for each layer.

4. **Transfer your layered design to your project.**

   Use fresh transfer tape to lift the entire design off the mat and apply it to your project, using a scraper or brayer to smooth it down. Once the design is applied, remove the registration marks.

Layering HTV with registration marks

Layering HTV is similar to stacking adhesive vinyl but involves heat pressing between steps. Here's how to do it:

1. **Mirror your design.**

   Make sure that your design is *mirrored* (flipped so you don't transfer it to your blank backward) before cutting the layers. Design Space's Auto Mirror feature automatically adjusts this setting after you select HTV as your material, so your design faces the right direction when applied.

2. **Cut and weed each layer, keeping the carrier sheets intact.**

3. **Prepare your fabric.**

   Press the fabric with your heat press for 10 seconds to remove moisture and wrinkles. Use a lint roller to clean the surface.

4. **Align the layers.**

   Stack all the layers on their carrier sheets, aligning the registration marks so everything stays in place during pressing. Don't worry about the layers sticking to each other — HTV doesn't have a sticky side like adhesive vinyl. You'll be able to peel these layers apart before heat pressing without affecting your design.

5. **Position the base layer.**

   Place the stacked layers on your fabric in the correct position. Hold down the base layer with one hand to keep it in place while carefully peeling off the stack of upper layers. Remember, you can't heat press all layers at once because the carrier sheets would block the transfer.

REMEMBER

Don't forget to trim off the registration mark with scissors right before heat pressing each layer. Since they're only used for alignment, you don't want to mistakenly heat press them onto your fabric.

CHAPTER 14 **Layering Vinyl for Colorful Designs** 199

6. **Tack down the base layer.**

   The upper layers should still be stuck together — set them aside for now. Cover the base layer with a protective sheet (like Teflon or parchment paper). Use your heat press to lightly press it for 2–5 seconds to tack it down.

   Because layering HTV requires multiple heat presses, tacking down for just a few seconds prevents the glue from melting off, bubbling, overheating, and causing the vinyl to shrink. Shrinking can throw off alignment, making it difficult to layer correctly. Only the top layer of your design should be pressed for the full duration.

   Once the base layer is secure, peel off its carrier sheet.

7. **Position the next layer and repeat the process.**

   Take your stack of upper layers and carefully align it over the base layer you just heat pressed. Hold down the next bottom layer with one hand to keep it in place while peeling away the remaining stack of upper layers. Set aside the upper layers and trim off the registration mark from the layer you're about to press.

   Cover the layer with a Teflon sheet, lightly press it for 2–5 seconds to tack it down, then remove its carrier sheet. Repeat this process for each remaining layer, always using the registration marks to keep your design properly aligned and removing them before pressing

8. **Make the final press.**

   Once all the layers are applied, cover the design with a protective sheet again and press for the full recommended time to secure everything to the fabric.

   Check the Cricut Heat Guide (https://cricut.com/heatguide) or your heat press manufacturer's instructions for recommended heating times and temperatures.

Layering with parchment paper

Registration marks are an excellent way to keep your layers aligned, but many crafters find another technique even easier — layering with parchment paper.

Using parchment paper is a simple trick that makes layering adhesive vinyl super simple. Because parchment paper is nonstick and slightly see-through, you can position each vinyl layer with transfer tape without sticking it down right away. This gives you time to adjust the placement until it lines up perfectly. Here's how to layer using parchment paper:

1. **Place the base layer on a mat.**

   Stick your vinyl base layer directly onto a StandardGrip Mat, with the backing still attached. This keeps it in place while you align the remaining layers.

2. **Cover the base layer with parchment paper.**

   Cut a piece of parchment paper larger than your design and place it over the base layer. Parchment paper prevents the transfer tape from sticking while allowing you to see through it.

3. **Apply transfer tape to the next layer up.**

   Place transfer tape over the second layer (the next one that needs to be stacked) and burnish it well. Peel the second layer off its backing so that it's now on the transfer tape.

4. **Align the second layer over the base layer.**

   Holding the transfer tape, position the second layer over the parchment-covered base layer. Since the vinyl won't stick to parchment paper, you can adjust it until it's perfectly aligned.

5. **Tack down one side and remove the parchment paper.**

   Once aligned, peel back a small section of the transfer tape so it sticks to the base layer, securing that side in place. Then, carefully slide out the parchment paper while smoothing the second layer down onto the base layer with a scraper or your fingers.

6. **Repeat for additional layers.**

   Continue layering from the base up, repeating Steps 3–5 until all vinyl layers are stacked and aligned.

7. **Transfer the completed design to your project.**

   Once all layers are combined, apply transfer tape over the entire design, lift it from the backing, and apply it to your final project surface as usual.

IN THIS CHAPTER

» **Exploring HTV project ideas and types**

» **Choosing the perfect size and placement for T-shirt decals**

» **Identifying essential materials for HTV projects**

» **Mastering how to cut and apply HTV**

» **Caring for your HTV projects**

Chapter **15**

Using Heat Transfer Vinyl

eat transfer vinyl, also known as *HTV* or *iron-on vinyl,* is a special type of vinyl with a heat-activated adhesive. Much like cooking, you have to heat it for the right amount of time and at the correct temperature to get it just right. If you overcook it, you'll end up with a burnt, melted mess. But if you undercook it, your design will be as flaky as a croissant. The exact time and temperature you need varies depending on the brand, so always check the application guidelines on your HTV to avoid a crafting catastrophe.

HTV is most commonly used to print designs on clothing or fabrics. However, some materials you can put HTV on — such as wood — may surprise you. In this chapter you find out about the different types of HTV, discover which materials you can apply it to, and master the art of using it with an easy, step-by-step guide plus project ideas and care instructions. (See the color section for photos of HTV projects.)

Exploring HTV Project Ideas

HTV can be applied to a variety of materials, making it perfect for countless projects. Some of the best surfaces include cotton fabrics (T-shirts, hoodies), canvas (tote bags, home décor), denim (jackets, jeans), polyester (athletic wear, pillow covers), and even leather and faux leather (wallets, patches). You can also use HTV on burlap, felt, microfiber, neoprene, and smooth, sealed wood surfaces for custom creations. Whether for clothing, accessories, or home décor, HTV offers endless possibilities.

TIP

You can apply HTV to a wide variety of blanks. *Blanks* are premade items without any designs, typically used as a base for customization. For instance, a blank T-shirt is a common item used for HTV application. Here are some fun project ideas and the best surfaces to customize with HTV:

- » **T-shirts:** Personalize with quotes, messages, or layered vinyl designs. Everyday Iron-On is my go-to for easy, durable results. See Chapter 14 for layering techniques.

- » **Tote bags:** Add motivational quotes, fun sayings, or labels like *Dairy* and *Meat* for grocery organization. Personalize them for teachers or special gifts. Use glitter HTV for extra sparkle.

- » **Stuffed animals:** Personalize with names or designs using HTV for birthdays or special occasions. Glitter or flock HTV works great on plush. Check out my tutorial on YouTube (`https://youtu.be/3k1BdEGIOJ8`).

- » **Hats and caps:** Create custom beanies or matching Mama and Mini hats with glitter HTV. Apply Everyday Iron-On to a leather patch for unique hats, perfect for gifts.

- » **Pillow covers:** Add a personal touch with seasonal or holiday designs. Search for ideas like "Farmhouse Bundle" or "Family Quotes" on Creative Fabrica for custom designs, perfect for wedding or anniversary gifts.

TIP

If you're looking for more inspiration or want to follow along with step-by-step video tutorials, check out my YouTube channel (`www.youtube.com/@KerriCraftsIt`). I share tons of HTV projects, tips, and tutorials to help you bring your ideas to life!

Checking Out Types of HTV

HTV comes in many different types, giving each of your projects unique finishes and effects. From bold and glittery to smooth and sleek, there's a type of HTV for every style.

REMEMBER

Different brands and types of HTV require specific temperature and pressure settings, so always check the manufacturer's instructions to get it right.

Here are some popular types of HTV you may want to try:

- **Everyday Iron-On:** The go-to choice for most projects, including custom T-shirts, bags, and home décor on cotton, polyester, and blends.
- **Flock HTV:** Adds a soft, fuzzy texture to designs on fabrics like flannel or fleece, perfect for blankets, pillows, and stuffed animals.
- **Foil HTV:** Provides a shiny, metallic finish that's great for satin fabrics, like bridal party robes.
- **Glitter HTV:** Brings sparkle to your projects, though its thicker texture may require a StrongGrip Mat for cutting. Chapter 4 has details on different kinds of mats.
- **Glow-in-the-dark HTV:** Absorbs light and glows brightly in the dark, perfect for costumes or kids' pajamas. Keep in mind that the glow may fade over time and may need to be recharged by exposure to light.
- **Holographic HTV:** Adds a dazzling, rainbow-like finish that shines and changes color when light hits it.
- **Patterned HTV:** Offers fun designs like animal prints, florals, or tie-dye to make your projects stand out.
- **Printable HTV:** Lets you print full-color designs using an inkjet printer, available for both light and dark fabrics (see Chapter 20).
- **Reflective HTV:** Shines brightly and reflects light, making it ideal for visibility in low-light conditions.
- **Smart HTV:** Designed for matless cutting on compatible machines (see Chapter 2).
- **Stretch HTV:** Perfect for stretchy fabrics like spandex or Lycra, making it ideal for activewear or swimsuits. Cricut's SportFlex Iron-On is popular.
- **UV-activated, color-changing HTV:** Changes color when exposed to sunlight, adding a fun twist to outdoor projects.

TIP

HTV and adhesive vinyl may look similar, but you can easily tell them apart by feel. Adhesive vinyl has a paper backing, and HTV has a plastic carrier sheet, which makes them easy to distinguish.

CHAPTER 15 **Using Heat Transfer Vinyl** 205

Finding the Right Size and Placement for T-shirt Decals

Making sure your decal is the right size is important for creating professional looking T-shirts. A decal that's too small on a large shirt can look awkward, and one that's too big can be overwhelming. To help you get the perfect size, here are some recommendations:

>> **Baby shirts (0–12 months):** Vinyl decal size between 3 inches and 5 inches, placed 1 inch below the neckline.

>> **Toddler shirts (18 months to 5T):** Vinyl decal size between 4 inches and 6.5 inches, placed 1 inch below the neckline.

>> **Youth shirts (XS to XL):** Vinyl decal size between 6.5 inches and 8.6 inches, placed 2 inches below the neckline.

>> **Adult shirts (XS to 4XL):** Vinyl decal size between 8.5 inches and 11 inches, placed 3 inches below the neckline.

For more details, check out the Cheat Sheet by heading to www.dummies.com and searching for "*Cricut For Dummies* Cheat Sheet."

Getting your decal perfectly aligned on your shirt can make a huge difference in the final look of your project. After all that work designing and cutting, the last thing you want is a crooked design. Follow these tips to ensure that your design is centered and straight:

>> **Finding the center of your shirt:** To find the center of a shirt, fold it in half lengthwise, aligning the sleeves and edges. Lightly press the fold with your heat press or iron to create a crease. Unfold the shirt and lay it flat. Use the crease line as a reference to center your design.

>> **Finding the center of your decal:** Fold your decal in half, pinching only the top and bottom of the carrier sheet. Line up the creases on your carrier sheet with the creases on your shirt to align the decal perfectly in the center.

>> **Using T-shirt ruler guides:** T-shirt ruler guides are handy tools that make aligning your designs a breeze. These guides have markings that help you center and position your decals accurately. Simply place the ruler guide on your shirt and use the markings to align your design perfectly. T-shirt ruler guides can be purchased on Amazon or at your local craft store.

Gathering Everything You Need for HTV Projects

REMEMBER

Before you start your HTV project, make sure you have all the materials you need (see Chapter 4 for an intro to tools and materials). Having everything ready helps you work faster and get the best results. Here's what you'll need:

» **Base material:** The item you're decorating, like a shirt, hoodie, or pillow cover.

» **Heat source:** Such as a heat press, EasyPress, or household iron to apply your HTV.

» **HTV:** The main material for your design; I describe various types of HTV in the previous section.

» **Lint roller:** To remove any lint or debris from your base material before you apply the HTV.

» **Mat:** A StandardGrip or StrongGrip Mat to hold your HTV in place while your Cricut cuts it.

» **Protective material:** A Teflon sheet or parchment paper to place over your design to protect your project during heat application.

» **Ruler or measuring tape:** For measuring how big to make your design.

» **Scraper or brayer:** For securing your HTV to the mat.

» **Thermal tape:** To hold your design in place on your base material.

» **Vinyl trimmer or scissors:** To cut your HTV to the desired size.

» **Weeding tools:** Tools to remove excess vinyl from your design.

Cutting and Applying HTV: A Step-by-Step Guide

Almost all HTV projects follow a similar process. Use the easy guidelines in the following sections to master cutting and applying HTV.

Step 1: Designing your project

First up is creating your HTV design.

1. **Choose a design.**

   Search for a design in Cricut Design Space's Images library. Use the filter options to narrow your search to Cut or Single Layer images for easy cutting and weeding. For designs with multiple colors, you'll need to layer the vinyl by cutting each color separately and assembling them on your project. (For detailed instructions on layering HTV, see Chapter 14.) You can also browse the Projects library by clicking the All Projects drop-down menu and selecting Iron-On for ready-to-go designs.

2. **Resize your image.**

   Use a ruler to measure the area where you want to apply your design. Adjust the size of your image by typing in the dimensions in the Edit bar at the top or dragging the corners until it fits perfectly. Not sure how big to go? No worries! I've included T-shirt decal size tips earlier in this chapter.

3. **Adjust settings on the Prepare screen.**

   Click "Make" to go to the Prepare screen. Adjust the number of copies, material load type (On Mat or Without Mat), material size, and whether to mirror your image.

   REMEMBER

   Heat transfer vinyl must always be mirrored before applying. The Auto Mirror feature in Design Space automatically mirrors your design on the next screen when you select heat transfer materials like HTV or Infusible Ink, so you can skip the mirroring step here. Place your HTV where your design appears on the mat preview and click Continue.

4. **Adjust settings on the Make screen.**

   Under Set Base Material, choose the correct HTV type in Design Space. The software has preset cut settings for nearly every kind of HTV. Click Browse All Materials if you can't find what you're looking for.

   After selecting your material, the Auto Mirror feature automatically mirrors your design when you select materials like HTV that require it. However, it's always a good idea to double-check that this setting is correct after selecting your material.

Step 2: Preparing the materials

After you've created your design, get your materials ready.

1. **Prepare the material you're applying your HTV to.**

   Use a lint roller to remove fur, hair, and lint. Press your base material for 10 seconds to eliminate moisture and wrinkles.

2. **Cut your vinyl.**

   Use a Cricut trimmer or scissors to cut a piece of vinyl slightly larger than your design — or place a longer piece or roll of vinyl directly on the mat and trim it after cutting. Experiment to see which method works best for you.

3. **Place your HTV on the mat.**

   Place your HTV with the shiny carrier sheet side down in the upper-left corner of a StandardGrip or StrongGrip Mat. Use a scraper or brayer to secure it. If you're using Smart Iron-On, no mat is needed.

Step 3: Loading and cutting the HTV

It's time to load and cut your HTV. Follow these steps:

1. **Load your mat or Smart Iron-On.**

   For regular HTV, slide the mat into the Cricut, aligning it with the tabs, and press the Load button. For Smart Iron-On, load the material directly, shiny side down, making sure that there is at least 6 inches for the rollers to grip.

2. **Begin the cut.**

   Once the mat is pulled in, press the Go button to begin the cut.

Step 4: Weeding and transferring your design

After your HTV is cut, you're almost done!

1. **Weed your design.**

   After your machine finishes the cut, unload your mat and weed your vinyl. *Weeding* means removing the extra vinyl, leaving only your design on the carrier sheet. Carefully peel away the small bits from the inside of letters like O and B.

2. **Heat press your project.**

   Place your design on the material and cover it with a protective sheet. Make sure it's exactly where you want it, as it becomes permanent once heated. For curved items, like hats, use heat-resistant tape to keep the design in place. Apply heat with an EasyPress, heat press, or iron, following the recommended time and temperature for best results.

3. **Peel the carrier sheet.**

   Once you've heat pressed your design, remove the carrier sheet. If you're using hot peel HTV, peel it off immediately while the vinyl is still hot. If you're using cold peel HTV, wait until the vinyl is cool to the touch before removing the carrier sheet.

Choosing between hot peel and cold peel depends on the HTV brand you're using. Always check the manufacturer's instructions for the best results.

Following Washing and Care Instructions for HTV Projects

Proper care is key to keeping your HTV projects looking great. Wait at least 24 hours before washing to allow the HTV to cure. Always turn your project inside out before washing to protect the design. Wash in cold or warm water on a gentle cycle, and avoid hot water, as it can weaken the adhesive. Use a mild detergent and avoid stain removers or eco-friendly detergents, which can be too harsh. Never use bleach or fabric softeners, as they can damage the adhesive and appearance.

For drying, air-dry your project flat or hang it up. If you're using a dryer, tumble dry on low heat to prevent damage. Avoid direct heat sources, and never place HTV directly under a heat vent. Don't iron directly on the vinyl; instead, iron the garment inside out or place a cloth between the iron and HTV. Lastly, avoid dry-cleaning, as it can damage the HTV.

If you decide to sell your HTV projects, be sure to include these care instructions for your customers. You can find printable care instructions on Creative Fabrica (www.creativefabrica.com) or Etsy (www.etsy.com).

IN THIS CHAPTER

» Checking out Infusible Ink project ideas

» Organizing everything you need for Infusible Ink projects

» Crafting projects with Infusible Ink Transfer Sheets

» Creating artwork using Infusible Ink Pens and Markers

» Keeping your Infusible Ink projects looking great

Chapter 16

Trying Infusible Ink

Cricut Infusible Ink is a line of unique materials that lets you add vibrant permanent designs to your projects. Unlike heat transfer vinyl (see Chapter 15), which just sticks to the surface of your base material, Infusible Ink becomes part of the material itself, resulting in a professional finish that looks like it came from a store. Infusible Ink is available in transfer sheets, pens, and markers.

Infusible Ink Pens and Markers allow you to draw custom designs either freehand or with your Cricut. Unlike regular Cricut Pens and Markers, which use standard ink for paper crafts like greeting cards and scrapbook pages, these pens and markers contain heat-activated ink that fuses permanently into compatible blanks. You can even heat press hand-drawn pictures onto coffee mugs, T-shirts, tote bags, and other surfaces — something regular Cricut Pens can't do.

In this chapter, you explore inspiring project ideas and find step-by-step guides for working with transfer sheets, pens, and markers.

Exploring Infusible Project Ideas

Looking for some inspiration? Here are some fun project ideas to get you started:

» **Baby bodysuits:** Add a baby's name or fun sayings to create adorable outfits.

» **Coasters:** Craft seasonal designs or create monogrammed coasters for weddings or anniversaries.

» **Cosmetic bags:** Make personalized cosmetic bags with names or initials surrounded by pretty floral borders.

» **Hats:** Customize hats for sports, hobbies, or other interests.

» **Mugs:** Have your kids draw pictures with Infusible Ink Pens and Markers to create special gifts for grandparents.

REMEMBER

For any text, instead of handwriting with Infusible Ink Pens, type out messages directly in Cricut Design Space so you can mirror them. This ensures that the text appears correctly oriented when transferred.

» **Pillow covers and home décor:** Add unique designs to pillows, framed art, and other home accents.

» **Tote bags:** Create custom tote bags that make awesome gifts for teachers.

» **T-shirts:** Personalize T-shirts with bright designs, quotes, or cute patterns.

» **Wine bags:** Design monogrammed wine bags for special occasions like weddings, anniversaries, or holidays.

These projects use blanks sold exclusively by Cricut, designed for their line of Infusible Ink projects. Once you get comfortable with Infusible Ink, the possibilities are endless.

Gathering Your Materials

Before diving into an Infusible Ink project, it's important to have all your materials and tools ready. The following sections include everything you need for all types of Infusible Ink projects, but for a deeper dive into Cricut machines, tools, and materials, check out Chapters 2 and 4.

Common materials for all Infusible Ink projects

Here's what you'll need for any project using Infusible Ink, whether you're working with pens, markers, or transfer sheets:

- **Butcher paper:** Absorbs excess ink and moisture during heat pressing, preventing unwanted ink transfer.
- **Cricut machine:** Any Cricut can cut Infusible Ink Transfer Sheets.
- **Heat press, EasyPress, or mug press:** Applies the necessary heat and pressure to transfer the ink onto your blank.

WARNING

Don't use a regular iron. Infusible Ink requires consistent pressure at 400 degrees Fahrenheit (205 degrees Celsius), which household irons can't provide.

- **Heat-resistant tape:** Secures the design in place, preventing shifting and ghosting during pressing.
- **Infusible Ink–compatible blanks:** For example, polyester T-shirts and tote bags, or specially coated coasters and mugs.
- **Lint roller:** Removes dust and fibers from fabric blanks to prevent imperfections in the final transfer.
- **Ruler or measuring tape:** To check that your design is the right size.
- **Vinyl trimmer or scissors:** For cutting Infusible Ink Transfer Sheets to the correct size.
- **White cardstock:** Placed inside fabric blanks or under projects (not on top) to prevent ink bleed-through onto your heat press or work surface.

Specific materials for projects using Infusible Ink Transfer Sheets

Here's what else you need when working specifically with Infusible Ink Transfer Sheets:

- **Brayer:** Helps press Infusible Ink Transfer Sheets firmly onto the mat for a secure cut
- **Infusible Ink Transfer Sheets:** Pre-inked sheets that transfer vibrant designs when heated onto compatible blanks

CHAPTER 16 **Trying Infusible Ink** 213

- » **Fine-Point Blade:** The blade required for cutting Infusible Ink Transfer Sheets
- » **StandardGrip Mat:** Holds Infusible Ink Transfer Sheets in place for cutting with a Cricut machine
- » **Tape (with low tack like washi tape or painter's tape):** Helps secure Infusible Ink Transfer Sheets to the mat, preventing movement or curling during cutting
- » **Weeding tools (optional):** Helps remove excess material from detailed designs, though finger-weeding is often recommended to avoid pressing ink into the liner

Specific materials for projects using Infusible Ink Pens and Markers

Here's what else you need when working with Infusible Ink Pens and Markers for drawing and transferring designs:

- » **Infusible Ink Pens and Markers:** Choose pens (0.4 mm) for fine details or markers (1.0 mm or thicker) for bolder strokes.

TIP

Infusible Ink Freehand Markers (available in Marker, Brush, and Dual Tips) let you draw designs by hand on laser copy paper. Once you're finished, transfer your artwork onto compatible blanks with heat, perfect for designs that can't be made using a Cricut. Be sure to protect your work surface when you're coloring by hand. Place a second sheet of copy paper beneath your primary sheet so the ink doesn't bleed onto your work surface.

TIP

Store Infusible Ink Pens and Markers with the tip down to keep the ink flowing and prevent drying.

- » **Laser copy paper:** This paper is designed to handle high-heat temperatures and has a special coating that helps Infusible Ink Pens and Markers transfer better. It holds the ink on the surface rather than absorbing it like regular paper, allowing for a more vibrant and even transfer when heat is applied.

REMEMBER

Don't draw directly on blank surfaces using Infusible Ink Pens and Markers. Always draw on laser copy paper first, then transfer the design onto your blank, ensuring that it's mirrored before pressing.

- » **LightGrip Mat:** Holds laser copy paper in place during drawing.

Choosing the right blanks for Infusible Ink

To get great results with Infusible Ink, choosing the right blanks is key.

Infusible Ink works best on light-colored polyester fabrics or polymer-coated *blanks* (specially treated surfaces designed to accept Infusible Ink), which limits your options but ensures a strong bond when you use it correctly. Cricut offers blanks like T-shirts, tote bags, mugs, and coasters specially designed to work seamlessly with Infusible Ink. You can also try third-party blanks labeled as sublimation-compatible or as having a high polyester content, but test them first to ensure durability.

Steer clear of cotton and dark-colored items, because Infusible Ink won't bond well or appear as vibrant on those surfaces. Untreated surfaces like regular ceramic mugs won't work either — mugs must have a polymer coating for the ink to infuse properly.

Working with Infusible Ink Transfer Sheets: A Step-by-Step Guide

Infusible Ink Transfer Sheets are preprinted sheets infused with solid colors or patterns that transfer onto compatible blanks when heated. Unlike Infusible Ink Pens and Markers, which require drawing a design, Infusible Ink Transfer Sheets let you easily cut shapes, text, or intricate designs with your Cricut machine. Follow the steps in this section to create stunning projects with Infusible Ink Transfer Sheets.

Step 1: Create your design

First, design your project in Cricut Design Space. If you're new to Design Space, check out Part 2 for a detailed introduction.

1. **Create your design.**

   Open Cricut Design Space and create your design using the Text tool or the Images library. Combine parts of your design into a single layer using the Unite or Weld options from the Combine drop-down menu in the Layers panel.

2. **Resize your design.**

   Use a ruler to measure the area on your blank where the design will be applied. In Design Space, click on your design, then adjust the Width (W) and Height (H) boxes in the top toolbar to match your blank.

Step 2: Slice multilayer designs (if necessary)

If your design includes overlapping colors, modify it using the Slice and Set technique. Each color of Infusible Ink must sit side by side, without overlapping, to prevent colors from bleeding and to allow a single-press application. Follow these steps to apply the Slice and Set technique:

1. **Select your design and click on the Ungroup tool at the top of the Layers panel to separate your multilayered design into individual layers, making each layer adjustable.**

2. **Use the Slice tool at the bottom of the Layers panel to cut through overlapping areas, but note that you can slice only two elements at a time.**

   Before slicing, use the Arrange tool to perfectly align the elements of your design.

3. **After slicing, delete any unwanted pieces.**

4. **Continue adjusting and slicing pairs of layers until all components fit together seamlessly without overlapping.**

Step 3: Adjust settings in Design Space

With your design finalized, you're ready to prepare it for cutting.

1. **Adjust settings on the Prepare screen.**

   Once your design is ready, click Make to move to the Prepare screen. Here, you can adjust the number of copies, select your material load type (On Mat), and choose your material size. Skip the mirror option — Design Space's Auto Mirror handles this automatically.

   Design Space automatically places your design in the upper-left corner of the mat preview. Position your Infusible Ink Transfer Sheet in the same location on your cutting mat. Once everything looks good, click Continue to proceed to the Make screen.

2. **Adjust settings on the Make screen.**

   Under Set Base Material, select Infusible Ink Transfer Sheet. If you don't see it listed, click Browse All Materials and type it in the search bar. If you're using a Cricut Explore Air 2 or an older model, set the machine's dial to Custom before selecting your material in Design Space.

REMEMBER

   Once you've selected Infusible Ink Transfer Sheet as your material, Design Space's Auto Mirror feature will automatically mirror your design. Infusible Ink designs must always be mirrored to ensure that they transfer correctly — if it's not mirrored, your design will appear backwards on the blank.

Step 4: Clean and prepare your materials

Wash and dry your hands before handling Infusible Ink Transfer Sheets. Your materials should be clean and free of any oils, lint, hair, and wrinkles before applying your design. Follow these steps to ensure a smooth transfer process:

1. **Turn on your heat press and set the recommended time and temperature using the Cricut Heat Guide.**

   You can find Cricut's Heat Guide at https://cricut.com/heatguide. This guide lets you select your heat transfer material (Infusible Ink Transfer Sheet), your base material (like a T-shirt or coaster), and a Cricut heat press model, including the EasyPress, Mug Press, or Autopress. If you're using a different brand of heat press, you can still follow the same temperature and time settings for the machine that most closely matches yours. (If the guide isn't loading, try disabling your ad blocker.)

2. **Clean your blanks.**

   How you clean your blanks depends on what they are.

   - **For fabrics:** Use a fresh lint roller to clean your blanks and remove any dust or fibers.

   - **For hard blanks:** Wipe the surface with a lint-free wipe and rubbing alcohol to remove oils and debris. Let the blanks dry completely before applying your design.

3. **Preheat fabric blanks for 15 seconds to prevent any unexpected transfer issues due to moisture and wrinkles.**

   Hard blanks, like mugs, coasters, and tumblers, don't require preheating.

WARNING

   Preheated blanks will be hot to the touch. Use caution and handle them carefully to avoid burns.

4. **Place the Infusible Ink Transfer Sheet on the StandardGrip mat, ink side up and shiny side down.**

TIP

If the sheet isn't sticking well to the mat, try pressing it down with a *brayer* (a small roller) or securing the edges with low-tack tape like washi tape or painter's tape.

Step 5: Cut and weed your design

After prepping your materials, you're ready to cut your Infusible Ink Transfer Sheet.

1. **Load your mat into the Cricut machine and press Go.**

   TIP

   To load your mat, insert it into your Cricut under the guides until it touches the rollers. Press the Load button on the front of your Cricut to feed the mat into the machine before you press Go.

2. **When the cut is complete, remove the mat from your Cricut and carefully peel the mat away from your cut design instead of lifting the design off the mat.**

   This method helps prevent the design from bending, curling, or stretching.

3. **Gently *crack* (bend and roll the paper) to loosen the design from the transfer sheet and separate the cuts.**

   This technique makes the cut lines more visible, making the weeding process easier. Don't worry if the design lifts off the liner slightly; this is normal.

4. **Weed (pick off) any excess material, leaving only your design on the backing.**

   TIP

   Try weeding with your fingers instead of hook tools. This method helps prevent the ink from being pressed into the transfer sheet, reducing the risk of leaving unwanted marks on your design.

5. **Trim the clear liner with scissors or a vinyl trimmer so it doesn't extend past the edges of your heat press plate.**

Step 6: Position and apply the design

After your blank is clean, smooth, and cooled down, you can carefully position and apply your design. Follow these steps to prevent shifting, ink blowouts, and other transfer issues:

1. **Arrange and set your design (for multicolor designs using the Slice and Set technique).**

   Begin with the largest carrier sheet as your base, building your design directly onto it. Using your fingers or tweezers, pick up each piece of your Infusible Ink design and carefully place it onto the carrier sheet. Start from the outer edges and work your way inward, fitting each piece tightly together for a clean, single-press transfer.

2. **Place the assembled design, ink side down and shiny side up, on the blank.**

   WARNING

   Never place your Infusible Ink design on a warm or hot blank. The heat can cause premature transfer, leading to ghosting or misalignment. Always let your blank cool completely before positioning your design.

3. **Use heat-resistant tape to secure the design in place and prevent shifting during the heat press.**

4. **Prevent ink blowouts.**

   Depending on the type of blank you're using, follow these guidelines.

   - **For fabrics:** Insert a sheet of white cardstock inside fabric blanks to prevent ink from bleeding onto the back of your project. For extra ink blowout protection, place a second sheet of cardstock on the bottom of your heat press, underneath your blank.
   - **For hard blanks:** Place a sheet of cardstock or butcher paper on the bottom of your heat press to protect it from ink blowouts.
   - **For mugs:** Wrap mugs and tumblers in a sheet of butcher paper before placing them in the mug press, securing it with heat-resistant tape.

5. **Cover the design with a sheet of butcher paper that extends beyond the edges of your project to protect your heat press from ink blowout.**

   WARNING

   Don't reuse butcher paper for other projects, because it may transfer stray ink or residue to your heat plate or blank.

   WARNING

   Wear heat-resistant gloves when handling materials during the heat pressing process. Infusible Ink projects are extremely hot when they come out of the heat press, and gloves will help protect your hands from burns. Even the handles may be hot, so be cautious when touching any part of the project.

CHAPTER 16 **Trying Infusible Ink** 219

6. **Use the heat press for the recommended time and temperature to transfer your design.**

WARNING

Don't heat your design longer than recommended. Excessive heat can cause colors to fade instead of making them darker.

Step 7: Cool and reveal your design

Allow your project to cool completely to prevent ghosting or smudging. Carefully peel away butcher paper and transfer sheets. Use tweezers if any liner sticks. For long-lasting results, follow the care instructions in the later section "Caring for Your Infusible Ink Projects."

Drawing with Cricut Infusible Ink Pens and Markers

Infusible Ink Pens and Markers let you create hand-drawn or machine-drawn designs that transfer permanently onto polyester or specially coated blanks. For the best results, use Infusible Ink Pens or Markers with your Cricut to draw a mirrored design on laser copy paper, which will then be heat-transferred onto your blank.

TIP

Unless you've mastered the art of writing backwards, skip the handwritten words and let your Cricut do the work. Because Infusible Ink transfers in reverse, using your Cricut to mirror and write the text will help it transfer in the correct orientation.

WARNING

Don't draw directly on your blank, even if you plan to heat press it — Infusible Ink must be applied to laser copy paper first for proper transfer. Drawing directly on a blank won't allow the ink to bond correctly, resulting in dull, faded, or inconsistent results.

The following sections explain how to use Infusible Ink Pens and Markers for your next Cricut project.

Step 1: Create and mirror your design

Follow these steps to create your design, customize settings, and mirror your image before drawing:

1. **Open Cricut Design Space and select or create your design.**

   Use the Text tool to write out messages, names, or quotes. Click on the Font drop-down menu, then select the Filter menu (a small icon with two lines and circles) located just below and to the right of the Font search bar. In the filter options, check Writing to display fonts specifically designed for use with Cricut Pens and Markers. These fonts have a single-line appearance, making them ideal for drawn designs.

   To add drawable images, click on Images in the left-side toolbar. Then, click the Image filter and check Draw to filter for images that work with Cricut Pens and Markers. If you're looking for free designs, you can also check Free to display images available at no cost.

2. **Measure your blank and resize your design as needed.**

   Adjust the size of your design by typing the dimensions in the Edit bar at the top of the canvas or dragging the corners until it fits perfectly on your blank.

3. **Change the Operation setting to Draw and select pen colors.**

   To ensure that your Cricut draws your design instead of cutting it, you need to change the Operation setting to Draw. If you previously filtered for Writing fonts or Draw images, this setting may already be applied, but it's always good to double-check. Select all parts of your design that you want to be drawn by clicking and dragging over them or holding Shift while selecting each element. Then, click on the Operation drop-down menu in the top toolbar and choose Pen.

4. **Assign pen or marker colors.**

   Assign pen or marker colors to different parts of your design. Click on each design element, then select the Color box next to the Operation menu to choose either Fine Point (0.4 mm) or Marker (1 mm). Then, scroll through the options until you find the color that matches your Infusible Ink Pen or Marker. This step ensures that Design Space prompts you to load the correct pen colors when drawing.

TIP

Use the Attach feature to keep your design elements in place so they draw exactly as arranged on the Canvas. For example, if you're combining a quote and an illustration, Attach will ensure that they stay aligned when sent to your Cricut. To do this, select all the elements, then click Attach at the bottom of the Layers panel on the right side of the screen.

5. **Adjust settings on the Prepare screen.**

   Once your design is ready, click Make It to move to the Prepare screen. Here, you can adjust the number of copies, select your material load type (On Mat), and choose the correct material size — such as 8.5 x 11 inches for standard laser copy paper.

   Because Infusible Ink Pens and Markers create a mirrored transfer, you'll need to manually mirror your design on this screen. Click the Mirror toggle to ensure that your design transfers correctly — if it's not mirrored, it will appear backward when pressed onto your blank.

   By default, Design Space positions your design in the upper-left corner of the mat preview. When placing your laser copy paper on the LightGrip Mat, position it in the same location to match the screen preview. Once everything looks correct, click Continue to move to the next step.

6. **Select your material on the Make screen.**

   Under Set Base Material, select Laser Copy Paper. If you don't see it listed, click Browse All Materials and type it in the search bar. If you're using a Cricut Explore Air 2 or older, make sure to turn the dial on the outside of the machine to Custom first.

   At this stage, many users expect Design Space to Auto Mirror their design, as it does when selecting HTV or Infusible Ink Transfer Sheets. However, Auto Mirror doesn't activate when Laser Copy Paper is selected, even if you chose an Infusible Ink Pen type in Step 3. Since Design Space doesn't recognize laser copy paper as a heat transfer material, you must manually toggle the Mirror setting on to prevent your design from transferring backward. Double-check your mirror settings here before moving forward, as this is the last chance to correct it before cutting begins.

7. **Follow the prompts in Design Space to load an Infusible Ink Pen or Marker into Clamp A of your machine.**

   If your design includes multiple colors, Design Space will notify you when it's time to switch to the pen color.

8. **Place laser copy paper on the LightGrip Mat.**

   When you're drawing on laser copy paper with Infusible Ink Pens and Markers, use the blue LightGrip Mat. For Infusible Ink Transfer Sheets, use the green StandardGrip Mat.

Step 2: Draw your design

After your design is set up, it's time to draw it onto laser copy paper using your Cricut machine. Follow these steps to load your mat, start the drawing process, and remove your design when finished:

1. **Load your mat into the Cricut machine and begin drawing.**

   Slide your mat into your Cricut, aligning it under the two tabs on the left and right sides. Press the blinking Load button on your machine to load the mat and press Go to begin drawing.

2. **After your Cricut has finished drawing the design, unload the mat and remove the design.**

   Press the Load button to release the mat. Carefully peel the laser copy paper off the mat. If needed, use a spatula tool to help lift the edges without tearing the paper. Then, use scissors or a paper trimmer to cut around your design, removing any excess paper before transferring it to your blank.

Step 3: Prepare your blank

Before transferring your design, it's important to properly prepare your blank. Infusible Ink bonds permanently to the material, so any dust, wrinkles, or moisture can interfere with the transfer. Follow these steps to get your blank ready for pressing:

1. **Turn on your heat press and set the recommended time and temperature using the Cricut Heat Guide.**

   You can find Cricut's Heat Guide at https://cricut.com/heatguide. This guide lets you select your heat transfer material (Infusible Ink Pen/Marker on Copy Paper), your base material (like a T-shirt or coaster), and a Cricut heat press model, including the EasyPress, Mug Press, or Autopress. If you're using a different brand of heat press, you can still follow the same temperature and time settings for the machine that most closely matches yours. If the guide isn't loading, try disabling your ad blocker.

2. **Insert a sheet of white cardstock inside fabric blanks to prevent ink from bleeding through.**

3. **Clean your blank.**

   Depending on your blank material, follow these guidelines.

   - **For fabrics:** Use a fresh lint roller to clean your blank and remove any dust or fibers.
   - **For hard blanks:** Wipe the surface with a lint-free wipe and rubbing alcohol to remove oils and debris. Let it dry completely before applying your design.

4. **Preheat fabric blanks for 15 seconds to prevent any unexpected transfer issues due to moisture and wrinkles.**

   Hard blanks, like mugs, coasters, and tumblers, do not require preheating.

WARNING

Preheated blanks will be hot to the touch. Use caution and handle them carefully to avoid burns. Allow the blank to fully cool before placing your design to prevent premature ink transfer, which can lead to ghosting or uneven results.

Step 4: Position and apply your design

After your blank is prepared, it's time to position your design and transfer it using heat. Follow these steps to apply your design:

1. **Place your design, ink side down, on the blank.**

TIP

   Avoid seams, zippers, or buttons, which create uneven pressure during pressing and can lead to patchy results.

2. **Use heat-resistant tape to secure the design in place and prevent shifting during the heat press.**

3. **Cover the design with butcher paper and secure it with heat-resistant tape.**

TIP

   Always cover your design with a fresh sheet of butcher paper that's larger than the heat plate. Don't reuse butcher paper for other projects, because it may transfer stray ink or residue to your heat plate or blank.

WARNING

   Wear heat-resistant gloves when handling materials during the heat pressing process. Infusible Ink projects are extremely hot when they come out of the heat press, and gloves will help protect your hands from burns. Even the handles may be hot, so be cautious when touching any part of the project.

4. **Use the heat press for the recommended time and temperature to transfer your design to the blank.**

Step 5: Cool and reveal

Let the project cool completely before removing the copy paper to reveal your design.

Caring for Your Infusible Ink Projects

Your Infusible Ink project is complete! With proper washing and care, your design will remain bright and beautiful, just like the day you made it. Follow these care guidelines to keep your project looking its best:

>> **For fabric items**: Machine wash inside out in cold water with mild detergent. Avoid bleach, dryer sheets, or fabric softeners. Tumble dry low or line dry.

>> **For mugs and coasters**: Hand-wash or place in the top rack of the dishwasher. Avoid steel wool, scrubbing pads, or harsh cleaning agents.

IN THIS CHAPTER

» **Coming up with etched glass project ideas**

» **Getting the right supplies for glass etching**

» **Creating your vinyl stencil design**

» **Etching glass with Armour Etch cream**

Chapter 17
Etching with Vinyl Stencils

Want to create long-lasting designs on glass that won't peel or fade? Etching cream, like Armour Etch, is a great way to create permanent frosted designs on clear glass. It works by gently roughening the glass surface, giving it a frosted look that won't peel or fade. The process is quick and easy, usually taking just a few minutes to complete.

In this chapter, you explore how to add durable custom designs to glassware using vinyl stencils, etching cream, and your Cricut machine. Vinyl stencils are incredibly versatile and can be used for a variety of Cricut crafts, from etching glass to painting wood signs. (For more on using vinyl stencils for painting wood signs, check out Chapter 22.) With permanent vinyl, you can create stencils with clean, sharp designs that stick well to smooth surfaces, so your project turns out perfect every time.

WARNING

This method is best for decorating glassware, mugs, and other items that won't touch food, as etching cream is not food-safe.

Exploring Glass Etching Projects

Etching glass with etching cream like Armour Etch opens up endless possibilities for creating personalized gifts and décor. Here are some popular ideas to get you started:

- **Bathroom accessories:** Customize items like glass soap dispensers or storage jars with etched designs or labels to add decorative touches. Use etching to distinguish toiletries like hand soap, lotion, and bath salts for an organized, stylish bathroom setup.

- **Beer mugs:** Etched beer mugs make excellent gifts, especially for Father's Day or as wedding party favors. Customize mugs with messages like *Best Dad Ever, IPA lot when I drink, Groomsman,* or even hobby-themed designs such as fishing lures or team logos. Dollar Tree often has beer mug blanks perfect for etching. Flip to the color section to see an etched beer mug I made for my husband.

- **Casserole dishes:** An etched casserole dish is a thoughtful gift for a wedding, housewarming, or holiday. Personalize it with a name, design, or fun phrase like *Baked with Love* or *Mom's Famous Lasagna*. These dishes are especially useful at potlucks and family gatherings, making it easy to identify who brought what.

WARNING

Never put etching cream on the inside of a casserole dish! Etching cream is a strong chemical that isn't food-safe. Instead, you can mirror your design and apply etching cream to the bottom of the dish so it's visible through the glass without touching food.

- **Decorative vases:** Glass vases with etched floral patterns, monograms, or inspirational quotes can be used as beautiful home décor. They also make great gifts for weddings, Mother's Day, or a housewarming.

- **Glass coasters:** Customize glass coasters with monograms, patterns, or fun designs for home décor or personalized gifts. They make lovely wedding or housewarming gifts, and you can create sets featuring names, dates, or meaningful symbols etched into the glass.

- **Glass jars and canisters:** Etch labels or designs onto kitchen storage jars for a practical and stylish way to organize ingredients. You can etch words like *Sugar, Flour,* or *Coffee* onto canisters for quick identification.

- **Holiday ornaments:** Glass ornaments etched with seasonal designs, names, or dates can become memorable keepsakes for family and friends during the holiday season. For added color, many crafters like to pour paint or glitter inside ornaments before etching, giving them a festive touch.

- » **Shot glasses:** Etched shot glasses are popular wedding favors and can be customized with the couple's names, wedding date, or fun phrases like *Cheers!* or *Bottoms up!*

- » **Wine glasses:** Etched wine glasses make perfect custom gifts. Personalize them with names, dates, or fun sayings like *Wine a little, laugh a lot; I tend to wine a lot;* or *Cheers to pour decisions.* You can find affordable stemmed or stemless blanks at Dollar Tree.

WARNING

Etching cream contains corrosive chemicals like ammonium bifluoride that should never touch surfaces where food is prepared or consumed. Even after thorough washing, residues may remain, posing a risk of accidental ingestion. Etched glass can become porous, which makes it harder to clean and can trap food particles and bacteria. Over time, these surfaces may release chemicals, especially when exposed to acidic foods or high temperatures, so be sure to use it on non-food surfaces only.

Gathering Your Materials for Glass Etching Projects

These are the materials you'll need for your glass etching projects (see Chapters 2 and 4 for details on these items):

- » **Cricut machine:** For cutting vinyl stencils. (Any model will do the job.)
- » **Etching cream:** Armour Etch is a popular and reliable brand used to create a frosted effect on glass surfaces.
- » **Fine-Point Blade:** The blade required for cutting vinyl.
- » **Glass blanks:** Smooth, clear glass items such as wine glasses, mirrors, or mugs.

TIP

Before you rush out to buy an expensive new blank for your project, try etching something you already have at home, like an old drinking glass or coffee tumbler. If you don't have anything to spare, check thrift stores or dollar stores for affordable blanks to practice on.

- » **Lint-free wipe:** To wipe the glass before and after etching.

TIP

Coffee filters are an inexpensive lint-free wipe many people have at home.

- » **Paintbrush:** Use bristle brushes instead of foam brushes. The bristles help spread the etching cream evenly, but foam brushes can trap air bubbles and cause uneven results.

CHAPTER 17 **Etching with Vinyl Stencils** 229

- » **Painter's tape:** To mask off areas that shouldn't be etched.
- » **Protective gloves and glasses:** Essential for handling etching cream safely.
- » **Respirator or face mask:** To protect against fumes.
- » **Rubbing alcohol:** For cleaning the glass to ensure proper adhesion of the stencil.
- » **Ruler:** To check that your design is the right size.
- » **Scraper:** To press the transfer tape evenly over your stencil and your blank.
- » **Soft brush:** For removing excess cream after etching.
- » **Transfer tape:** For lifting your design off the vinyl and transferring your stencil onto the glass.
- » **Vinyl:** Use stencil or permanent vinyl for best results.

WARNING

Avoid using removable vinyl for stenciling because it doesn't stick well enough to the surface, which can cause the etching cream to leak under the stencil and create blurry edges. For the best results, use stencil vinyl or permanent vinyl, as they stick better and keep the cream in place.

- » **Weeding tools:** To remove unwanted vinyl from the stencil.

TIP

Etched glass vinyl, often called *frosted vinyl*, is a type of vinyl that mimics the look of etched glass. Unlike vinyl used for stencil-making, this vinyl is designed to be applied directly to the surface to create actual designs. It's a quick, mess-free alternative to etching cream, but it's not permanent and can peel over time, especially with frequent washing or heat exposure. It's best for decorative items and should never be used on food-contact surfaces.

REMEMBER

Not all glass is created equal when it comes to etching. Choosing the right glass can make or break your etching project. By selecting the correct type, you'll ensure that your designs turn out beautifully every time. For the best results, use clear uncoated glass. Here are some additional tips for choosing the right glass:

- » **Avoid Pyrex and borosilicate glass.** Pyrex and similar heat-resistant glass is designed to withstand thermal shock, making it resistant to the chemical reaction that etching cream uses to create a frosted effect. Attempting to etch these types of glass often leads to faint or uneven results. For customizing heat-resistant glass like Pyrex, laser engraving may be a better option.
- » **Steer clear of colored glass.** Colored or tinted glass often contains additives that can interfere with the etching process, leading to unclear or patchy designs. Stick to clear glass for the most consistent outcome.

> » **Check for coatings.** Some glassware, including certain drinkware, may have coatings that resist etching. Test a small, inconspicuous area first to ensure that the cream reacts as expected.

Creating Your Stencil in Cricut Design Space

Vinyl-made stencils are great for so many Cricut crafts. You can use them to customize T-shirts, applying ink or fabric paint only to the areas you want. They're also great for coated metal surfaces like tumblers — apply a vinyl stencil and use a paint stripper like Citristrip to remove the coating, revealing the shiny metal beneath (discover how in Chapter 22 and see an example in the color section). Want to make custom wall art? Simply paint on wood or canvas signs using vinyl stencils. And of course, you can use them for etching (see "Etching Glass with Your Cricut: A Step-by-Step Guide" later in this chapter).

Use the following steps to create your own vinyl stencil in Cricut Design Space (see Part 2):

1. **Open Cricut Design Space and create or upload your design.**

   Choose a single-layer cut file, which is a design that cuts as one single piece, without separate parts or different colors that Cricut would treat as multiple layers. If your design has multiple parts or colors, use the Weld or Unite tool at the bottom of the Layers panel on the right to combine them into one layer before cutting. Both tools achieve the same result, but although Unite can be undone, Weld is permanent.

   TIP

   If you're unsure whether your design is a single-layer cut file, check the Layers panel on the right. There should only be one layer listed. If there are multiple layers, you may need to Weld or adjust the design.

   TIP

   When using Cricut's Images library, you can filter results by checking Single Layer Only to find designs that are already a single layer. If you're uploading your own design, use the Preview Single Layer option to check how it will cut. See Chapter 8 for more details on this feature.

2. **Resize the design to fit your glass *blank* (the item you're customizing).**

   Use a ruler to measure your blank and determine the exact size for your design. Then, adjust the size of your design by typing the dimensions in the Width (W) and Height (H) fields in the Edit bar at the top of the Canvas. You can also adjust the size by dragging the corners of your design until it's the perfect size for your blank.

If you need to adjust the width and height separately, click the Lock icon above the Width and Height fields to unlock the aspect ratio. This allows you to change the dimensions independently instead of scaling the design proportionally.

3. **Add a background shape.**

   Since your design will become a stencil, it needs to be sliced (cut out) from a background shape. Click the Shapes tool in the left toolbar and select a square (or another shape if needed). Resize the shape to be slightly larger than your design. Click and drag your design over the shape until it's centered (see Figure 17-1). If your design disappears behind the shape, right-click on it and select Bring to Front to make it visible again. To center your design exactly within the shape, select both objects, then use the Align option at the top and choose Center.

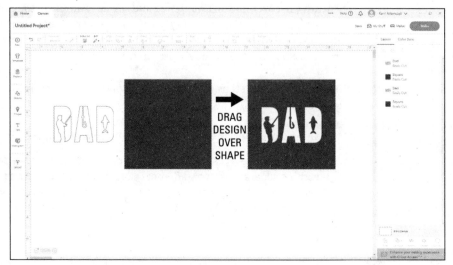

FIGURE 17-1: Drag your design over the shape to create a stencil.

Source: design.cricut.com

4. **Use the Slice tool to separate the layers of your design.**

   Highlight both the shape and the design, and then click on Slice at the bottom of the Layers panel. Think of Slice like using a cookie cutter — your design acts as the cutter, punching through the background shape. And just like with a cookie cutter, you end up with extra pieces in the middle. If you were making cookies, you'd keep the cutout and toss the scraps. But for your stencil, you do the opposite — you discard the cutout (the "cookie") and keep the outer part (the "scrap") to use as your stencil.

TIP   If the Slice tool isn't available, it's likely because your design has multiple layers. The Slice tool works only when two layers are selected at the same time. This is why it's important to make your design a single-layer cut file in Step 1 before slicing it into the background shape. If you place a multilayer design over a shape and try to use Slice, the tool will be unavailable. To fix this, select your multilayer design and use Weld (or Unite) (under Combine at the bottom of the Layers panel) to merge it into a single layer before slicing into the background shape.

5. **Remove the extra layers.**

   After slicing, drag the pieces apart and you'll see three layers. Delete the two "trash" layers, leaving only the design with a border (see Figure 17-2). Now you have your finished design, ready to send to your Cricut!

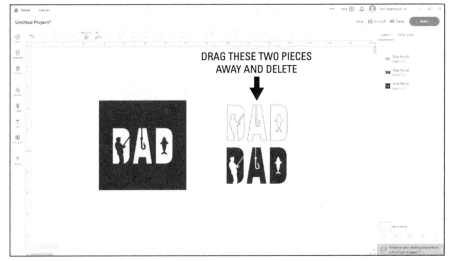

FIGURE 17-2: Delete the sliced parts of your design.

Source: design.cricut.com

6. **Adjust settings on the Prepare screen.**

   Once your design is ready, click the Make button to proceed to the Prepare screen. Here, you can adjust the number of project copies, choose your material load type, and set your material size (for example, 12 x 12 inches for a standard mat or 12 x 24 inches for a long mat). You'll also have the option to mirror your image, but I suggest skipping this step on the Prepare screen since Design Space's Auto Mirror feature will automatically handle it on the next screen.

CHAPTER 17 **Etching with Vinyl Stencils**   233

Your design will be placed in the upper-left corner of the mat preview by default. Make sure to position your vinyl in the same location on your actual mat as it appears in Design Space. When everything looks good, click Continue to proceed to the Make screen.

7. **Adjust settings on the Make screen.**

Under Set Base Material, choose Vinyl. Once you've selected your material, Design Space's Auto Mirror feature will automatically mirror your design for materials that require it. Since vinyl typically doesn't need to be mirrored, the Mirror option should be toggled off. However, it's always a good idea to double-check this setting after selecting your material to ensure that it's correct.

8. **Prepare your mat.**

Place your adhesive vinyl paper side down on a StandardGrip Mat, with the colored vinyl side facing up. Align the vinyl with the upper-left corner of the mat, matching its placement in Design Space. If needed, use a brayer or scraper tool to smooth it down so that it sticks well to the mat.

Once your vinyl is secured, you're ready to load the mat into your machine.

9. **Load your mat or Smart Vinyl and begin the cut.**

Gently slide your mat into the Cricut machine, making sure it's aligned under the two tabs on the left and right sides. Press the Load button on your machine to load the mat.

For Smart Vinyl, load the material directly into the Cricut without a mat, ensuring that the paper backing is facing down and the colored vinyl side is facing up. Make sure there's at least 6 inches of material for the rollers to grip properly. If there's not, stick the Smart Vinyl to a StandardGrip Mat.

Once the mat or Smart Vinyl is pulled in, press Go to begin the cut.

10. **Weed your vinyl stencil.**

When your machine finishes cutting, it's time to *weed* (remove) the excess vinyl to create your stencil. Normally, when working with vinyl designs, you remove the outside vinyl so that you're left with the design itself. However, when making stencils, you need to weed away the inside of the design, leaving behind the outer vinyl and the open spaces where the etching cream will go.

Take a look at the sliced design on the left in Figure 17-2. You'll want to remove the white areas of your design, being careful not to remove the centers of letters, as these small pieces are part of your stencil and need to stay in place. Using weeding tools can help you remove only the areas you need while keeping the letter centers intact. Chapter 13 provides more guidance on crafting with vinyl.

234 PART 4 Vinyl and Heat Transfer Projects

Etching Glass with Your Cricut: A Step-by-Step Guide

Forget an expensive laser engraver — you can etch glass beautifully with your Cricut machine and some basic supplies. Just follow the steps in the following sections to create permanent dishwasher-safe designs with Armour Etch cream.

Step 1: Preparing your design

See the earlier section "Creating Your Stencil in Cricut Design Space" for a detailed guide on creating your stencil design. This includes steps for resizing, slicing, and weeding your stencil to ensure a clean and accurate application.

Step 2: Cleaning the glass

Before applying your stencil, it's important to start with a clean surface. Any dust, oil, or residue on the glass can prevent the stencil from sticking properly, leading to uneven etching. Follow these steps to prepare your glass blank:

1. **Clean your glass blank with rubbing alcohol and a lint-free wipe to remove oils or dust.**

   TIP

   Coffee filters are my go-to lint-free wipe!

2. **Allow the glass to dry completely before applying the stencil.**

   TIP

   Keep your glass from rolling around while you work! A cup cradle (available on Amazon) holds round glasses, tumblers, and mugs steady. If you don't have one, place two lint rollers on either side of the glass to create a simple DIY cradle.

Step 3: Applying your transfer tape

Using transfer tape helps lift the stencil off its backing and place it smoothly onto the glass without distorting the design. Here's how to use it:

1. **Apply transfer tape over your stencil.**

   Cut a piece of transfer tape to fit your design and peel off the paper backing. To apply it smoothly, use the taco method: Hold the transfer tape with both hands and fold it into a U-shape like a taco. Touch the center of the tape to your stencil first (the bottom of your taco), then lay it flat from the center outward. Smooth the tape over the stencil using a scraping tool. This is called *burnishing* and helps the tape stick better.

2. **Use transfer tape to lift your vinyl stencil off the liner.**

   Burnish the tape over the stencil using a scraper tool, working away from your starting point and applying steady pressure. Flip the stencil over and burnish the scraping tool over the back side. Many people find it easier to peel the paper backing away from the transfer tape while it's flipped upside down, rather than pulling the tape upward. You can also lift the transfer tape from the top if you prefer. Go slowly when you begin to peel the stencil off the liner — if parts of it are still stuck to the liner, use your scraper to burnish it again.

3. **Transfer your stencil to the glass blank.**

   When your stencil is attached to the transfer tape, use the taco method again to carefully position it on your glass. Hold the stencil in a U-shape, let the center touch the glass first, and then gently press down the sides. If you're working with a curved surface, cut small slits in the transfer tape to make it easier to apply. Once the stencil is in place, use your scraper or brayer to smooth out any air bubbles for a tight seal.

4. **Peel the transfer tape off the glass.**

   Slowly peel the transfer tape at a sharp angle, keeping it close to the surface rather than pulling straight up. This helps prevent the stencil from lifting. Take your time and don't rush this step — resist the urge to rip it off like a bandage! If you peel too quickly, you risk stretching the vinyl, tearing it, or accidentally losing small design elements. If any part of the stencil starts to lift with the tape, press it back down and burnish it again with your scraper before continuing.

5. **Apply a border of painter's tape around the outside of the stencil to protect the glass from drips of etching cream.**

   If there's not enough vinyl around your stencil, use painter's tape to create a protective border. Carefully place painter's tape along all four sides of the stencil, making sure it slightly overlaps the edges of the vinyl without covering any of the weeded design where you'll apply the etching cream. Press the tape down firmly to prevent any etching cream from seeping underneath.

Step 4: Applying the etching cream

After your stencil is in place and the surrounding glass is protected, it's time to apply the etching cream. Because etching cream is a strong chemical, it's important to take safety precautions and prepare your workspace before you begin.

1. **Put on protective gloves, eyewear, and a face mask, and work in a well-ventilated area.**
2. **Make sure your work area, glass blank, and etching cream are at room temperature (about 70 degrees Fahrenheit or 21 degrees Celsius).**

   REMEMBER

   If the etching cream gets too cold, it can start to crystallize, which may interfere with the etching process and result in an uneven finish. Letting everything reach room temperature helps the cream spread evenly. If you notice crystallization, place the sealed bottle in a container of warm (not hot) water for 15–20 minutes, then stir or shake it well before use.

3. **Cover your work area with newspaper, a drop cloth, or some other protective barrier to catch stray drips of etching cream.**
4. **Shake the bottle first and use a paintbrush to apply a thick layer of Armour Etch over the stencil.**

   Brush the etching cream with a bristle brush using side-to-side, up-and-down, and diagonal motions to ensure that it covers all areas. Avoid scrubbing with the brush, as this can cause the vinyl to lift. Apply a thick coating, but be careful not to let the cream run all over the glass. The etching cream should stay on for at least 3–5 minutes.

Step 5: Rinsing off the etching cream

After the etching cream has done its job, the next step is to thoroughly rinse it off:

1. **After 3–5 minutes, rinse the glass under cool running water, using a soft brush to help remove excess etching cream.**
2. **Before peeling off the vinyl, inspect your etching.**

   If the results look patchy or uneven, you can add more etching cream and try again, as long as your stencil still has a tight seal.

3. **Remove the vinyl stencil and clean the glass with alcohol.**

   Then, thoroughly wash the glass with soap and water before use to make sure that it's completely clean.

5
Projects Using Printable Materials

IN THIS PART . . .

Master Cricut's Print Then Cut feature to create detailed and colorful designs.

Make your own stickers and labels with printable materials.

Try printable heat transfer vinyl for complex, colorful designs on fabric projects.

IN THIS CHAPTER

» **Understanding the basics of Cricut Print Then Cut**

» **Discovering project ideas using Print Then Cut**

» **Following a step-by-step guide to completing Print Then Cut projects**

Chapter **18**

Mastering Cricut Print Then Cut

Print Then Cut is an amazing feature that lets you print designs in full color on your home printer and then cut them precisely with a compatible Cricut machine. All Cricut models I discuss in this book (Explore Air 2 and newer), except the Cricut Joy, support Print Then Cut. Imagine the possibilities: custom stickers, labels, gift tags, and even wedding invitations! In this chapter, you discover how Print Then Cut works, explore project ideas, get tips on setting up your machine and choosing materials, and follow a step-by-step guide to create your own designs.

Knowing How Print Then Cut Works

Remember: Your Cricut isn't a printer. With Print Then Cut, you print your design using a printer. Once it's printed, you place it on a mat and load it into your Cricut. You'll see four black L-shaped marks around the corners. These are the registration marks that help your Cricut cut exactly around your design (see Figure 18-1).

FIGURE 18-1: The black L-shaped marks in the corners are the registration marks your Cricut reads to figure out where to cut your designs.

Source: Kerri Adamczyk

REMEMBER

Print Then Cut follows these three basic steps:

- **Design:** Choose or upload an image in Cricut Design Space (see Part 2).
- **Print:** Send your design to a printer, which adds the black registration marks around the image.
- **Cut:** Place the printed paper on a Cricut mat. The machine reads the registration marks using its sensors and then cuts precisely around the design.

Exploring Print Then Cut Project Ideas

Print Then Cut is perfect for projects that have lots of color or detail, letting you skip the hassle of layering different materials. Just print your design in full color and let your Cricut handle the cutting. Here are some fun ideas:

- **Custom bookmarks:** Print designs or quotes onto cardstock, and cut them out for cute, functional bookmarks. Chapter 21 has more details.
- **Gift tags:** Personalize your gift tags with a recipient's name and a special message.
- **Invitations:** Create unique invitations for birthdays, showers, or weddings.

>> **Iron-on transfers:** Use printable iron-on material to make custom pillows, tote bags, or T-shirts. Great for kids' birthday shirts with colorful, detailed designs. Flip to Chapter 20 for more on printable HTV.

>> **Labels:** Organize your stuff with color-coded or custom-sized labels.

>> **Magnets:** Use printable magnet sheets to make custom magnets for your fridge or to pass out as party favors.

>> **Photo booth props:** Design and cut props to add a fun, interactive element to your photo booth at parties or weddings.

>> **Stickers:** Make custom full-color stickers for planners, laptops, or gift bags. For detailed instructions on making stickers, see Chapter 19.

Testing Different Print Then Cut Materials

With Print Then Cut, you're not limited to paper projects. Cricut lets you print and cut on all kinds of materials. Here are some popular materials you can try out with Print Then Cut:

>> **Printable cardstock:** Add a sturdy, professional feel to your greeting cards, gift tags, bookmarks, or scrapbook pages.

>> **Printable iron-on transfer paper:** Create colorful designs without needing to layer heat transfer vinyl (see Chapter 14). Perfect for custom tees and tote bags.

>> **Printable magnet sheets:** Make your own fridge magnets or photo magnets. Great for family pictures!

>> **Printable sticker paper:** Design custom stickers for planners or journals. Sticker paper comes in both clear and white options.

>> **Printable tattoo paper:** Make custom temporary tattoos for parties or events — always a hit with kids!

>> **Printable vinyl:** Create waterproof stickers, labels, and decals for decorating water bottles, laptops, and phone cases.

>> **Printable window cling:** Craft seasonal and holiday décor you can stick on and peel off windows easily.

CHAPTER 18 **Mastering Cricut Print Then Cut** 243

TIP

For the best results, use matte or nonreflective materials. Shiny surfaces can throw off Cricut's sensors and lead to inaccurate cuts, particularly in older models like the Explore Air 2. Newer models handle a wider range of materials but still perform best with light-colored and simple patterns.

Preparing Your Cricut for Print Then Cut

Print Then Cut seems straightforward — just print your design and have your Cricut cut it out. But there's a lot more involved behind the scenes. Your Cricut must be properly calibrated for accuracy, and the printer settings must be correct to avoid grainy, low-quality images. You'll also need to understand the size limits for Print Then Cut projects and when to use the Bleed feature to avoid unwanted white edges on your designs. This section helps you set everything up for great results.

Calibrating your Cricut

Calibrating your Cricut machine (adjusting its alignment) is key for precise cuts, especially with Print Then Cut. It's recommended to do a calibration before your first Print Then Cut project or when you notice alignment issues, like uneven white edges around your printed designs or cuts that appear slightly off-center. Here's how to calibrate your Cricut for Print Then Cut on a computer or phone.

For Windows PC or Mac:

1. **In Design Space, click the drop-down menu next to your name in the upper-right corner.**
2. **Go to Settings > Machines > Machine Calibration.**
3. **Select your Cricut device and click Start.**
4. **Choose Print Then Cut Calibration and follow the on-screen instructions.**

For iOS or Android:

1. **Tap the menu icon (three horizontal lines) in the top-left corner.**
2. **Go to Settings > Calibration.**
3. **Select Print Then Cut and follow the prompts to calibrate.**

For detailed calibration instructions, go to Cricut's online Help Center (https://help.cricut.com/hc/en-us).

Understanding Print Then Cut size limits

The maximum print area for Print Then Cut projects depends on the following factors:

>> **Your Cricut model:** Each model has different Print Then Cut size limits.

>> **Your printer's maximum material size:** Standard options are usually Letter (8.5 x 11 inches) or A4 (8.3 x 11.7 inches), but some printers can handle larger sizes like Tabloid (11 x 17 inches) or A3 (11.7 x 16.5 inches).

>> **Your project size:** Keep your design within the recommended boundaries.

The following sections provide additional guidance to help you fit your design within Cricut's Print Then Cut limits.

Auto-resizing your image

The easiest way to determine the largest possible size for your design is to resize it directly in Design Space and check the Layers panel. If you see a warning icon (a red exclamation point), this indicates that your image is too big. You'll also get an Image(s) Too Large error when selecting Make It. You can resize it to fit within your Cricut's Print Then Cut limits with these steps:

1. **Click the red exclamation point in the Layers panel.**

2. **Select Auto-Resize Image.**

    Design Space will automatically adjust your design to the largest size that works with your Cricut model (see Figure 18-2).

Changing your paper size

If you have a wide-format printer or your printer handles large paper sizes, you may be able to print even bigger designs. To adjust the paper size

1. **Locate the Change Page Size button (see Figure 18-2).**

2. **Select your Cricut model, mat size, and paper size from the drop-down menus, and then click Done (see Figure 18-3).**

3. **Resize your design as needed.**

    If your design is still a bit large, use the Auto-Resize Image option again (see the previous section).

CHAPTER 18 **Mastering Cricut Print Then Cut** **245**

FIGURE 18-2: Auto-resizing your image to the maximum cut size.

Source: design.cricut.com

FIGURE 18-3: Changing your paper size.

Source: design.cricut.com

Getting the best print quality

For the best results, start with high-quality images, aiming for a resolution of around 300 dpi (dots per inch) to prevent grainy prints. If Cricut Design Space alerts you with a Low Resolution warning in the Layers panel (refer to Figure 18-2), reduce the image size or replace it with a higher-resolution one. For the clearest details, consider shooting photos in RAW format.

When preparing to upload, choose PNG for transparent backgrounds or JPEG for other images. Before uploading, tweak your images in editing software like Canva or Adobe Express to adjust lighting and colors, enhancing overall print quality.

Distinguishing Bleed on from Bleed off

When you use the Print Then Cut feature on your Cricut, you can choose whether to turn the Bleed setting on or off. Here's how each setting affects your design:

- » **Bleed on:** This setting adds a small colored border around your design, which helps prevent white edges if the cut is slightly off. This is especially useful for colored or complex images, such as the gift tags shown on the right in Figure 18-4. You'll notice that the presents in these tags have a red bleed around them. The white parts of the design shrink slightly to allow for this bleed, ensuring that no white edges are visible if the cuts are slightly off. This extra border is trimmed away in the final cut, leaving a perfectly finished tag.

- » **Bleed off:** With Bleed off, what you see is what you get — your design prints exactly as it looks on the screen, with no added border. It's good for designs that don't need cutting or are simple enough that precision isn't a concern. The gift tags on the left in Figure 18-4 are printed this way. They look exactly like the digital design, but any small misalignment during cutting may show white edges.

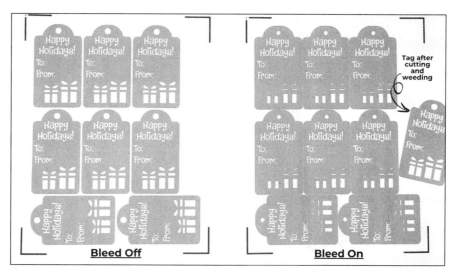

FIGURE 18-4: Comparing Bleed on to Bleed off prints.

Source: design.cricut.com

Using Print Then Cut: A Step-by-Step Guide

Follow the steps in the following sections to get clean, professional-looking results when you design, print, and cut your project with Cricut's Print Then Cut feature. With a bit of practice, you'll quickly master this feature and find it an essential tool for personalizing everything from cards to home décor.

Gathering your materials

To get the best results with Print Then Cut, here are some basic materials you'll need (see Chapters 2 and 4 for details):

- » **Cricut machine:** Make sure that you have a compatible machine. Print Then Cut works with the Cricut Joy Xtra, Explore series, Maker series, and Venture machines.

REMEMBER

  The Cricut Joy doesn't have the sensors for Print Then Cut. Also, older machines like the Explore Air 2 can use this feature only with nonreflective white materials.

- » **Fine-Point Blade:** The standard blade works well for most Print Then Cut projects.
- » **LightGrip Mat:** This mat is perfect for holding your printable materials in place while cutting.
- » **Home printer:** Inkjet printers work best with most Print Then Cut materials. Laser printers can be used with some materials, but avoid them for heat-sensitive blanks like printable vinyl or iron-on and HTV, because the printer's heat may damage the adhesive.
- » **Printable materials:** Examples include printable vinyl, sticker paper, and iron-on transfers.
- » **Scraper tool:** Helpful for quickly removing leftover bits from your mat after cutting.
- » **Spatula tool:** Handy for lifting designs cleanly off your cutting mat.

Step 1: Setting up your design

With Print Then Cut, you have unlimited creative possibilities — bright colors, detailed graphics, even your favorite photos. Nothing is off-limits! The Cricut Images library offers tons of ready-made options — simply filter by Print Then Cut to find compatible designs. You can also easily turn any image into a Print

Then Cut design by choosing Print Then Cut in the Operation menu at the top of your Canvas. Follow these steps to start:

1. **Start a new project.**

   Open Design Space and start a new project.

2. **Choose a design.**

   Browse Cricut's premade designs or upload your own file.

   TIP

   Print Then Cut-compatible designs are easy to find in Design Space. Just select Images, click the Filter icon, and check Print Then Cut. Once you've chosen a design, add it to your Canvas for quick customization.

   TIP

   Send and receive images the right way. Avoid using screenshots, social media messaging apps, and texting for sharing images, as they often compress files, reducing the quality. Use email or file-sharing services like Google Drive or Dropbox to keep the image quality intact before uploading to Cricut Design Space.

3. **Resize your design for Print Then Cut.**

   Keep your design within the maximum size limit. If you see a warning that your design is too large, click Auto-Resize Image to adjust the size automatically. I provide details on how to do this in the earlier section "Auto-resizing your image." If you need to make your image bigger or smaller, keep the aspect ratio the same by keeping the Lock icon closed to avoid stretching or distortion.

4. **Flatten multilayered designs.**

   If your design has multiple layers, use the Flatten tool at the bottom of the Layers panel to merge everything into one printable image.

   TIP

   If you're working on a small project like gift tags, consider duplicating your design to fill the printable area. This way, you'll make the most of your material and print multiple copies in one go.

5. **Change the Operation Type.**

   Check your Layers panel to make sure the Operation type is set to Print Then Cut. You can easily convert any image or design file to a Print Then Cut project by selecting it on your Canvas, then changing the operation type to Print Then Cut from the Operation drop-down menu at the top.

6. **Save your project.**

   Click Save in the upper-right corner and name your project clearly so that you can find it easily later.

Step 2: Printing your design

After your design is set up and ready to go, the next step is printing it out. Cricut will guide you through this process, starting right from your Canvas:

1. **Click Make.**

   Once your design is ready, click Make to proceed with printing.

2. **Mirror the image (if necessary).**

   REMEMBER

   Most printable materials, like paper and sticker paper, don't require mirroring (flipping) your design. However, certain brands of printable HTV may require it. For example, StarCraft InkJet Printable Heat Transfers for Light Materials require mirroring, but Cricut Printable Iron-On for Light Fabrics don't. Always check the manufacturer's instructions.

3. **Select the paper size.**

   Click on the Material Size drop-down menu and choose the paper size that matches your material. Then click Continue.

4. **Click Send to Printer.**

5. **Acknowledge Sensor Marks.**

   A pop-up that says "Sensor Marks Added" may appear. Click Next. To skip this pop-up in the future, check the Don't show this again box.

6. **Choose your printer.**

   Select your printer from the drop-down menu.

7. **Turn Bleed on or off.**

   Turning Bleed on adds a color-matching border around the design for clean cuts, which is especially helpful for detailed edges. Turning Bleed off removes the border, which is ideal for simpler shapes. Find out more in the earlier section "Distinguishing Bleed on from Bleed off."

8. **Toggle System Dialog on.**

   This will bring up printer settings on the next page, where you can adjust your preferences, such as paper type and print quality. Click Print.

9. **Select your printer, and then click on Preferences.**

10. **Select paper type.**

    Under your printer preferences, choose your paper type from the drop-down menu. This page may look slightly different depending on the type of printer you're using.

    TIP

    For best results, choose a printer setting that closely matches the printable material you're using, such as matte photo paper for sticker paper, and glossy photo paper for glossy or shiny materials.

11. **Select Print Quality.**

    Under your printer preferences, locate the Print Quality drop-down menu. If it's not automatically selected, change Print Quality to Best. Press OK, and then Print.

Head over to your printer and grab your freshly printed sheet. You now have a printed copy of your design ready to cut with your Cricut.

Step 3: Cutting your project

With your printed design in hand, you're now ready to cut it out precisely using your Cricut machine:

1. **Set your Base Material in Design Space.**

   After your design prints, Design Space automatically loads a new screen where you'll select your base material (your paper or other printable material type). Make sure your Cricut machine is powered on and connected, or these material options won't appear. Choose your material from the list shown. If your material isn't listed, click Browse All Materials to find additional options.

2. **Prepare your mat.**

   Place your printed design in the upper-left corner of your mat (refer to Figure 18-1).

   TIP

   Use a LightGrip Mat for thin paper and a StandardGrip Mat for thick materials like printable vinyl.

3. **Load the mat.**

   Insert your mat into your Cricut under the guides until it touches the rollers. Press the Load/Unload button on the front of your Cricut to feed the mat into the machine.

4. **Begin the cut.**

   Press the Go button on your Cricut to begin the cut. Your Cricut machine will move the mat around, reading the registration marks, and then begin cutting.

5. **Unload the mat.**

   Press the Load/Unload button to remove your mat.

6. **Remove your design from the mat.**

   Gently bend the mat to lift the design without curling or tearing. Use a spatula to carefully remove the design, leaving excess paper behind. Clean any leftover pieces from the mat with a scraper tool.

CHAPTER 18 **Mastering Cricut Print Then Cut** 251

IN THIS CHAPTER

» Discovering unique uses for your stickers

» Preparing everything you need for sticker-making

» Enhancing your designs with creative borders

» Waterproofing your stickers

» Checking out the differences between kiss-cut and die-cut stickers

Chapter **19**

Creating Custom Stickers

Ready to make some awesome stickers with your Cricut? The Print Then Cut feature (which I introduce in Chapter 18) will spark your creativity, and you'll soon find yourself eager to decorate and label everything in sight — your planner, your water bottle, and even your craft room!

In this chapter, you find out everything you need to know about using printable sticker paper and printable vinyl. You explore the different types of materials available, get design tips and step-by-step guidance on making stickers, and check out some waterproofing options to keep your stickers looking fresh and vibrant. So dive in and get sticking!

REMEMBER

Your Cricut isn't a printer. Instead, it reads special marks to cut around your printed designs. You'll need a compatible model and a separate printer to get started with Print Then Cut projects like sticker-making.

Exploring Project Ideas Using Stickers

Stickers can do so much more than just decorate! They're perfect for organizing your kitchen, creating classroom incentives, or adding a personal touch to your belongings. Here are some creative uses for stickers:

» **Customizing your planner:** Create stickers that make organizing your life fun. Customize them with special icons, important dates, or inspirational quotes.

TIP

For cute ready-made designs, search "planner stickers" in the Project library on Cricut Design Space (see Part 2) or explore Creative Fabrica (www.creativefabrica.com).

» **Organizing your kitchen:** Get your spices, pantry items, or storage containers in order with stylish printed labels. If you prefer a label without a white or clear background, you can cut letters or designs from adhesive vinyl instead. For more on creating vinyl decals, check out Chapter 13.

» **Styling your phone case:** Give your phone a makeover with small custom stickers that match your style.

» **Elevating your scrapbooking:** Add a personal touch to your scrapbook pages with themed stickers that match your memories, whether it's a birthday party or beach vacation.

» **Creating Halloween treats:** One year, I added some cute Halloween stickers to the candy bowl, and the kids went for the stickers more than the candy! Make your own fun and spooky designs for trunk-or-treats, Halloween parties, or trick-or-treating.

» **Decorating your laptop:** Add custom stickers with your favorite quotes, cool designs, or motivational sayings to give your laptop a personal touch and make it stand out.

» **Crafting classroom stickers for teachers:** Print sheets of kiss-cut stickers with rewarding and motivational sayings like *Great Job, Keep It Up,* and *Fantastic Work* for your kids' teachers. Teachers often purchase these supplies out of their own pockets, so they'll truly appreciate this thoughtful and practical gift. Find info on how to make kiss-cut stickers later in this chapter.

» **Promoting your brand:** Create custom stickers to market your small business. Design thoughtful *Thank You for Your Order* stickers or add your logo to items like water bottles to increase visibility.

» **Crafting convenient address labels:** Make customized address labels so you never have to handwrite your return address again. They're perfect for sending a ton of mail at once, like holiday cards or wedding invitations.

- **Adorning holiday gifts:** Festive *To* and *From* stickers add a personal touch to your gifts and replace messy permanent markers and sloppy handwriting. (For another option, use Cricut's Print Then Cut feature to create cardstock gift tags — see Chapter 10 for instructions.)

Gathering Your Materials

Before you get started on your stickers, make sure that you have the following supplies on hand (see Chapters 2 and 4 for more details):

- **Cricut machine:** Compatible machines include the Maker and Explore series, Venture, and Joy Xtra. The Cricut Joy doesn't support the Print Then Cut feature.
- **Fine-Point Blade:** This is the standard blade used for cutting printable sticker paper and printable vinyl.
- **Laminating sheets or sealants (optional):** You can add a protective waterproof barrier for extra durability *before* cutting your stickers. For detailed instructions on waterproofing techniques, including laminating sheets and sealants, see the later section "Waterproofing Your Stickers."
- **LightGrip Mat:** You'll use this mat to hold your sticker paper or vinyl securely in place while cutting.
- **Printable sticker paper or printable vinyl:** You can choose from matte, glossy, white, or transparent finishes. For help deciding which type of printable material to use, keep reading!

TIP

My favorite printable paper for making stickers is Joyeza Premium Printable Vinyl Sticker Paper in Matte White.

- **Printer:** Inkjet printers are the best choice, but laser printers also work if your sticker paper is compatible. Just keep in mind that some materials, like vinyl, may not handle the heat of a laser printer and can cause jams.
- **Scraper:** This versatile tool is used for securing printable paper to the mat, smoothing down laminate films for waterproofing, and removing stickers from the mat.
- **Spatula:** This tool allows you to carefully lift and remove stickers from the mat without damaging them.

CHAPTER 19 Creating Custom Stickers **255**

Choosing your printable sticker paper

When deciding on sticker paper, consider both durability and appearance. Printable sticker paper is great for indoor projects like planners and labels but is not water-resistant, so it's best for dry use. If you need something more durable, printable vinyl is tougher and water-resistant, making it perfect for items like water bottles and phone cases.

For colors, white sticker paper makes your colors stand out and works well for designs with white details; transparent sticker paper is better for clear surfaces. Just remember that inkjet printers can't print white ink, so any white parts of your design will appear clear on transparent sticker paper.

In terms of finish, matte offers a non-shiny, writable surface perfect for simple designs, and glossy provides a shiny, vibrant finish — just be sure to adjust your printer settings and let the ink dry to avoid smudging.

TIP

If you're printing on glossy paper and need it to dry fast, place it in front of a fan or use a hair dryer on the lowest heat setting.

Making sure your sticker paper works with your Cricut model

When selecting the right paper for your machine, it's important to consider both the type of material and your machine's capabilities. Different Cricut models have varying sensitivities to certain finishes, which can affect cutting accuracy, especially when using the Print Then Cut feature.

- » **For Cricut Explore Air 2 and older machines:** Only print on nonreflective matte white or transparent materials. Reflective materials, glossy finishes, or darker colors may interfere with the Print Then Cut sensor, preventing the machine from reading the cut sensor markings correctly. To avoid alignment issues, stick to lighter-colored materials that are simple and nonreflective.

- » **For Cricut Joy Xtra or machines from the Maker, Explore, or Venture series:** These machines are more versatile with a wider range of materials. It's best to print on white, lightly colored, or simple-patterned materials for the best results. Cricut's Printable Vinyl and Waterproof Sticker Sets in gold, silver, and holographic finishes are compatible with these models. However, avoid using non-Cricut materials with darker colors, high-gloss finishes, or holographic patterns, because these can disrupt the sensor scan and affect cutting accuracy.

- » **For the Cricut Joy:** The Cricut Joy doesn't support the Print Then Cut feature.

Designing Your Stickers in Cricut Design Space

There are many different tools in Cricut Design Space to help you create perfect, professional looking stickers. In this section, you explore several different methods, such as using the Create Sticker tool, the Offset tool, and shapes to add attractive borders around your designs. However, not all stickers need borders to look great.

REMEMBER

You can quickly turn any design into a sticker by selecting it and choosing Print Then Cut from the Operation drop-down menu in the top toolbar. If your design includes multiple layers, like text on top of a shape, you need to merge these layers into one. Do this by selecting your design and clicking Flatten at the bottom of the Layers panel. This step prepares your design for the Print Then Cut process.

Using the Create Sticker tool with Cricut Access

For some designs, especially those with text, adding a border makes the design look better and ensures that it cuts out as one piece. This way, text is cut as a single sticker rather than each letter being cut individually. One easy way to add a border is by using the Create Sticker tool in Cricut Design Space.

The Create Sticker tool is a fast and easy way to add borders to your stickers, but it's available only to Cricut Access subscribers (find out more about this program in Chapter 6).

To make stickers with the Create Sticker tool, select your design in Cricut Design Space, and then click on the Create Sticker button in the top toolbar, next to the Offset tool (see Figure 19-1). Unlike the Offset tool, the Create Sticker tool combines border creation with a streamlined sticker-making process.

Here's how to use the Create Sticker tool:

1. **Upload or create your design in Cricut Design Space.**
2. **Highlight the entire design and click the Create Sticker tool.**
3. **Choose Kiss Cut or Die Cut.**

    See the later section "Cutting Both Ways: Kiss-Cut Stickers versus Die-Cut Stickers" to discover the differences.

CHAPTER 19 Creating Custom Stickers   257

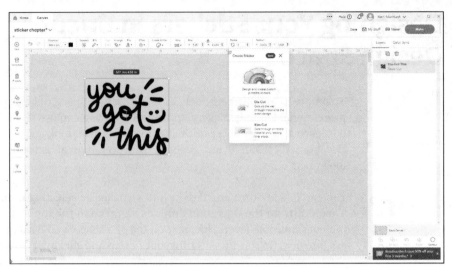

FIGURE 19-1:
Using the Create Sticker tool.

Source: design.cricut.com

4. **Choose your border settings.**

   - **Select a border size:** From the drop-down menu, choose Thin, Standard, Wide, or Custom.

   - **Choose a border color:** Click on white, black, or the plus icon for a custom option.

5. **Click Apply.**

   The Create Sticker tool flattens everything for you, preparing the design for Print Then Cut.

Adding borders to your stickers without Cricut Access

Adding borders to your stickers makes them easier to cut and gives you nice, clean edges. Even without Cricut Access, you can still add borders using free tools in Design Space, like the Offset tool or by flattening your design onto a background shape.

Figure 19-2 shows how four different border options look on the same design in Cricut Design Space. I imported a simple text design that says "You got this." Here's how each border option affects the design:

» **No border:** If you make the sticker without adding a border, your Cricut will cut out each letter as a separate piece.

- » **Small offset:** If you add a small offset to the design, your Cricut will make one continuous cut around the design, but there will be cutout sections in the middle.

- » **Large offset:** If you add a large offset, you'll get a thick, lumpy-looking border.

- » **Shape placement:** Instead of using the Offset tool, you can place the text inside a circle (or some other shape), which gives you a smooth, even border around the edge.

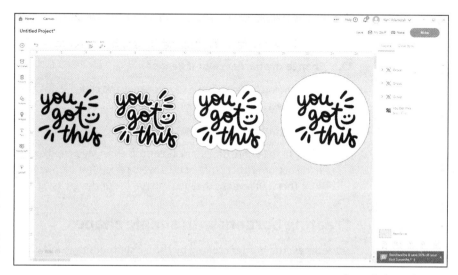

FIGURE 19-2: Different border options for a simple text sticker in Cricut Design Space.

Source: design.cricut.com

TIP

If you're working on a design with a white background and your Canvas is also white, it can be difficult to see the borders of your sticker. To make your designs easier to see, change your Canvas color to a light gray or any other light color that contrasts with the white background (refer to Figure 19-1). This will help you clearly distinguish the borders of your sticker. To change your Canvas color, click Blank Canvas at the bottom of the Layers panel, then select the Color box in the Edit bar at the top and choose a color.

Using the Offset tool

The Offset tool in Cricut Design Space creates a border, or *offset*, around your design. This is a quick and easy way to add a border without changing the design itself.

CHAPTER 19 **Creating Custom Stickers** 259

To make a border with the Offset tool, select your design, and then click on the Offset button located in the top toolbar, right above your design area, next to other editing tools like Flip and Create Sticker. Here's how it works:

1. **Upload or create your design in Design Space.**
2. **Highlight your design and click on the Offset tool in the top toolbar.**
3. **Adjust the slider to set the thickness of the border.**

   Move it left for a thin outline or right for a thicker one.
4. **Choose whether you want rounded or square corners for the border.**
5. **Click Apply to add the border.**
6. **Change the border color if needed.**

   Select the offset layer in the Layers panel and click the Color box in the Edit bar to choose a color for your border.
7. **Flatten your design and border together.**

   Highlight the entire design, including the offset layer, and click the Flatten button in the bottom-right corner of the Layers panel. This merges the layers into a single Print Then Cut layer so that you can print your design using an inkjet printer.

Creating borders with simple shapes

TIP

Sometimes, the border created by the Offset tool may look uneven or lumpy, especially with text-based designs (refer to Figure 19-2). In these cases, it's better to place your design inside a premade shape to achieve a smoother, more consistent border. Here's how to do it:

1. **Click on the Shapes icon in the Design panel on the left and select any shape, such as a circle, square, or rounded rectangle, to add to your Canvas.**
2. **Position your text or image inside the shape.**
3. **Highlight both the design and the shape and click on Flatten at the bottom of the Layers panel to turn them into a single-layer sticker.**

Printing Your Stickers

After you've designed your stickers, printing is the next step. You'll use Cricut's Print Then Cut feature to bring your stickers to life. (For a deeper dive into Print Then Cut, see Chapter 18.)

Follow this step-by-step guide to set up your printer and achieve great results:

1. **Confirm that your stickers are flattened and set to the Print Then Cut operation, and then click Make.**

   Flatten your design by selecting it and clicking the Flatten button in the Layers panel. Then, look at the Layers panel and make sure your design says Print Then Cut. Once confirmed, click Make.

2. **Click Send to Printer and choose your printer from the drop-down menu.**

   A pop-up that says "Sensor Marks Added" may appear. Click Next. To skip this pop-up in the future, check the Don't show this again box.

3. **Turn Bleed on or off, depending on your design.**

   TIP

   Turning Bleed on extends the color beyond the edges of your design for clean cuts, which is helpful for detailed edges. Turning Bleed off removes the border, which is ideal for simple shapes without needing extra color around the edges. See Chapter 18 for more details.

4. **Turn on Use System Dialog to find advanced printer settings.**

5. **Match your paper type to the sticker material and set the print quality to High Quality or Best.**

   The Glossy or Photo Paper setting works best for glossy sticker paper or vinyl.

6. **Print and cut a test page on plain paper to check alignment and color accuracy.**

   If you're unsure about your bleed settings, the test print is a great way to check and compare the differences.

   If your stickers aren't cutting out right, you may need to calibrate your machine. See Chapter 18 for steps on calibrating your Cricut for Print Then Cut projects.

7. **Load your sticker paper into the printer with the smooth printable side facing the print direction.**

   This varies by printer type — check your user's manual to figure out whether the printable side should face up or down.

8. **Click OK and Print.**

   TIP

   Let the printed stickers dry completely before handling them to prevent smudging.

CHAPTER 19 Creating Custom Stickers   261

Waterproofing Your Stickers

If you're making stickers for water bottles or other items that will be exposed to moisture, waterproofing is a must. Here are some options to protect your stickers and keep them looking great and lasting longer:

- **Cricut Printable Waterproof Sticker Set:** This kit includes a printable vinyl layer and built-in laminate sheet. Apply the protective laminate over your printed design before cutting to create a durable, water-resistant finish. After applying the laminate, click Browse All Materials in Cricut Design Space and choose from the four Printable Waterproof Sticker Set options: transparent, transparent holographic, white, or white holographic. Select the one that matches the finish of your sticker set and proceed with cutting.

- **Laminating sheets:** This clear protective film gets applied over your printed design before being cut with your Cricut. Choose from glossy, matte, or holographic finishes, depending on your desired look. When I use TeckWrap holographic laminating sheets, I select the Holographic Vinyl setting for a kiss cut and the Glitter Vinyl setting for a die cut.

TIP

Applying laminating sheets can be tricky — they're super thin, and it's like handling a giant sheet of packing tape. If you're not careful, they can stick to themselves and get ruined. (I ruined quite a few before I got it right!) If you'd like to see the process in action, check out my YouTube video where I show how to apply a laminate film to a sticker sheet (`https://youtu.be/ZFcVT--HhB8`).

- **Spray sealants:** Sealants like acrylic spray (for example, Krylon Triple-Thick Crystal Clear Glaze) or polyurethane spray offer additional waterproofing. Apply in three light layers, allowing each layer to dry completely (about 30 minutes) before applying the next. Always work in a well-ventilated area for safety.

REMEMBER

Always seal your stickers before cutting, and let the sealant dry completely to avoid damage to your machine or design.

Cutting Both Ways: Kiss-Cut Stickers versus Die-Cut Stickers

When you're ready to cut your stickers, you must decide whether you want them to stay on a sheet (kiss cut) or be cut out as individual pieces (die cut). If you're using the Create Sticker tool, you'll be asked to choose one of these cut styles — so it's important to know the difference.

- **Kiss cut:** Cuts only the top sticker layer, leaving the backing intact — perfect for sticker sheets, planner stickers, or organized labels. When selecting your material on the Make screen, use a light-pressure setting like Washi Tape.

- **Die cut:** Cuts through both the sticker and backing, giving you stand-alone stickers — great for selling, gifting, or handing out (like the Halloween stickers in Figure 19-3). When selecting your material on the Make screen, use a stronger setting like Cardstock or Vinyl to cut all the way through.

FIGURE 19-3: Halloween die-cut stickers I made for individual giveaways.

Source: Kerri Adamczyk

After selecting the right base material setting for your cut type, it's time for the fun part — cutting out your stickers!

1. **Place the printable sticker paper or vinyl on the mat.**

   Stick the printed sticker paper onto the upper-left corner of your LightGrip Mat, with the printed side facing up.

2. **Load the mat.**

   Insert your mat into your Cricut machine and press Load.

3. **Start cutting.**

   Press Go to begin the cut.

CHAPTER 19 Creating Custom Stickers 263

4. **Unload the mat.**

   When the cutting is complete, press the Unload button and carefully remove the mat from the machine.

5. **Carefully lift your individual stickers off the mat with a spatula.**

   Make sure to slide your spatula under the backing material so you don't separate the sticker from its backing when you're removing die-cut stickers from the mat. You can also bend the mat slightly to help loosen the stickers before lifting them off.

IN THIS CHAPTER

» **Knowing the pros and cons of printable HTV**

» **Checking out projects you can craft with printable HTV**

» **Choosing the materials you'll need for printable HTV projects**

» **Making crafts with printable HTV and taking care of your finished projects**

Chapter **20**

Crafting with Printable Heat Transfer Vinyl

rintable iron-on vinyl is a special type of vinyl that you can print on using an ordinary inkjet printer. This material, often referred to as *printable heat transfer vinyl* or *printable HTV*, is then transferred to fabrics using a heat press or an iron. In this chapter, you get the full scoop on printable iron-on.

Understanding the Pros and Cons of Printable HTV

Printable HTV is a great choice for many crafting projects, allowing you to print full-color designs like photos or detailed artwork. Unlike traditional HTV (see Chapter 15), there's no need to layer colors, because you print the entire design in one go, keeping your project smooth and less bulky. The designing, printing, and cutting process is the same as for making stickers (see Chapter 19), except the design is applied with heat instead of a sticky adhesive. It's easy to use — simply cut around the design and heat press it onto a wide variety of fabrics, including cotton, polyester, and blends. If you want to create a border around your entire design, use the Offset tool and flatten the design before printing (see Chapter 8 for details). This makes it easier to pull your design up in one piece like a sticker.

WARNING

Because printable HTV ink can fade and bleed over time, especially with frequent and improper washing, it's best for projects that won't need to be washed often, like decorative items. Be sure to follow the care instructions at the end of this chapter to keep your designs looking their best. It works well on most fabrics but isn't ideal for stretchy fabrics like spandex, because it may crack. For more durable designs, consider using Cricut's SportFlex Iron-On for stretchy fabrics or explore Infusible Ink (see Chapter 16) or heat transfer vinyl (see Chapter 15) for longer-lasting results.

Exploring Project Ideas with Printable HTV

Need some inspiration for your next crafting adventure? Here are some creative ways to use printable HTV to make everyday items extraordinary:

- **Birthday bash T-shirts:** Create custom T-shirts for the birthday kid.
- **Kids' place mats:** Make mealtime fun and educational by customizing place mats with names, shapes, numbers, animals, maps, and more.
- **Wall art:** Add designs to canvas or smooth, untreated wood signs.
- **Fabric banners:** Perfect for parties or homecomings with personalized messages or colorful designs.
- **Mouse pads:** Create a custom photo collage or add a 12-month calendar to keep track of important dates.
- **Throw pillows:** Personalize with photos, quotes, names, or special dates.
- **Reusable grocery bags:** Make organizing your groceries stylish with labels like *Produce, Cold,* and *Pantry.*
- **Seasonal apparel:** Design custom costumes or holiday outfits.

Gathering Your Materials for Printable HTV Projects

Before you get started with printable HTV crafts, you'll need the following supplies (see Chapters 2 and 4 for details):

WARNING

- » **Cricut machine:** Choose a model with the Print Then Cut feature (see Chapter 18), such as those in the Maker and Explore series, the Joy Xtra, or the Venture.

  The Cricut Joy isn't compatible with the Print Then Cut feature.

- » **Fabric blank:** This can be a T-shirt, tote bag, pillowcase, or any other fabric item you wish to customize.

- » **Fine-Point Blade:** This is the best blade for cutting printable HTV.

- » **Heat press, EasyPress, or iron:** You'll use this to transfer your design onto the fabric.

- » **Inkjet printer:** This is required for printing your designs onto the printable HTV.

WARNING

  Don't use a laser printer with printable HTV! The heat from the printer can damage the vinyl, ruin your design, and potentially harm your printer. Stick with an inkjet printer for safe and reliable results.

- » **LightGrip Mat:** This mat holds your printable HTV in place during the cutting process.

- » **Lint roller:** Clean your fabric blank with this before applying the vinyl.

- » **Printable HTV:** Select the right type — light or dark — to ensure that your design stands out against the fabric background. Get some pointers on choosing your vinyl in the next bulleted list.

- » **Teflon sheet or parchment paper:** This will protect your design during the heat transfer process.

- » **Weeding tool:** To remove excess vinyl from your design after it's cut.

The type of printable HTV you use depends on the color of the fabric you're customizing. There are specific options for light and dark fabrics, and using the wrong one can make your design look dull or not show up at all.

- » **Printable HTV for light fabrics:** Cricut's Printable Iron-On for Light Fabrics is a thin, translucent material that's best used on white fabrics. Since inkjet printers can't print white ink, any white areas in your design will appear transparent. This works well on white fabrics, because the design blends smoothly with the fabric color. However, on dark fabrics, the translucent material doesn't look clear and can give a frosted, parchment paper–like appearance on top of the fabric. Colors won't look as vibrant without the white base, which is why printable iron-on for dark fabrics is your best choice for colored fabrics.

CHAPTER 20 **Crafting with Printable Heat Transfer Vinyl** 267

>> **Printable HTV for dark fabrics:** For dark fabrics, you'll need printable HTV with a solid white background. This helps your design stand out with bright, bold colors. Cricut's Printable Iron-On for Dark Fabrics works well for black shirts, navy blue bags, or any dark-colored project for which you really want the design to pop.

TIP

You can use Printable Iron-On for Dark Fabrics on light-colored shirts, too! The opaque white background keeps your designs looking vibrant and stops them from blending into the shirt color. It's a great choice when you want your design to stay bold and true to what you printed.

Cricut offers its own line of printable iron-on products, but there are also plenty of other affordable brands that work just as well — and often offer much better value. For instance, HTVRONT Heat Transfer Paper for T-Shirts comes with 20 sheets for just $12.89.

Using Printable HTV: A Step-by-Step Guide

After you know how to pick the right printable HTV for different fabric colors, it's time to put that knowledge to work. In the following sections, I walk you through the whole process.

Step 1: Creating your design

The first step is to bring your design to life in Cricut Design Space.

1. **Upload or create your design.**

   Import your image into Design Space by clicking the Upload button, or use Cricut's tools to add images, text, shapes, or a combination of all. Use high-resolution images for the best print quality.

2. **Add a border (optional).**

   If you want your Cricut to cut around the outside of your design, rather than in between elements (like the letters in text), add a small border around your design. You can do this by using the Offset tool or by adding a shape like a circle behind your design.

TIP

Since a white border can be hard to see against a white background, change the color of your Canvas for a clearer view. Click on "Blank Canvas" at the bottom of the Layers panel, then click the color square at the top of your Canvas to choose a new color.

3. **Set the operation.**

   Highlight your completed design and make sure that Operation in the toolbar at the top of your Canvas is set to Print Then Cut. This tells Cricut to print your design before cutting it.

4. **Flatten the design.**

   If your design has multiple layers (like overlapping text, shapes, or an offset), select all the elements and click Flatten in the bottom right-hand corner of the Layers panel. Flattening merges all layers into one printable image and automatically sets the operation to Print Then Cut.

5. **Resize your design.**

   Adjust the size of your design to fit within the Print Then Cut limits. You can resize by dragging the corner of the *bounding box* (the box around your design) or by entering exact dimensions in the Size fields at the top of your Canvas.

REMEMBER

If you see an Image(s) Too Large error, click the red exclamation mark in the Layers panel and select Auto-Resize Image. Design Space will automatically adjust your design to the maximum Print Then Cut size for your Cricut model and paper type.

Step 2: Printing your design

Once your design is ready, it's time to print it onto your printable HTV.

1. **Click Make.**

   After finishing your design, click Make to begin the printing process.

2. **Load the printable HTV.**

   Place the printable HTV, blank side facing up, in your inkjet printer. For Cricut's Printable Iron-On, the back of the light fabric material has a green grid, and the dark fabric material has a QR code sticker. If you're unsure about your printer's orientation, test print with a plain sheet of paper first. Write "front" and "back" on each side of the paper so you can easily determine which is which.

3. **Mirror your design (if needed).**

REMEMBER

   For printable HTV, the need to *mirror* (or flip) your design depends on the brand. To avoid mistakes, always refer to the manufacturer's instructions for the specific product you're using.

4. **Turn Bleed on or off.**

   Turning Bleed on adds a small margin of extra ink around your design to ensure that there are no white edges when the design is cut. This is especially

CHAPTER 20 **Crafting with Printable Heat Transfer Vinyl** 269 useful for intricate shapes or designs with sharp details. Turn Bleed off if your design has a simple, solid shape or an offset border, or if you're confident your machine will cut precisely.

5. **Use the System Dialog to set printing preferences.**

Toggle on Use System Dialog before clicking Print. This will open your printer's advanced settings window after you click Print in Design Space. In the printer dialog box, change the Print Quality to High, Best, and change the paper type to Photo Paper.

Step 3: Cutting your design

After your design is printed, it's time to cut it with your Cricut machine.

1. **Place the printable HTV on the mat.**

Stick the printed HTV onto the upper-left corner of your LightGrip Mat, with the printed side facing up.

2. **Select your material.**

In Design Space, choose the right material setting for your printable iron-on. For Cricut Printable Iron-On, select Printable Iron-On (Light) or Printable Iron-On (Dark), depending on the type you're using.

3. **Load the mat.**

Insert your mat into your Cricut machine and press Load.

4. **Start cutting.**

Press Go to begin the cut.

5. **Unload the mat.**

When the cutting is complete, press the Unload button and carefully remove the mat from the machine.

6. **Weed the excess vinyl (if necessary).**

Use a weeding tool to remove any excess vinyl from the areas inside and around your design, leaving only the parts you want to transfer.

Step 4: Preparing your fabric

Before applying your design, it's important to get your fabric ready. Follow these steps to prepare it for the heat transfer process:

1. **Prewash the fabric.**

   Wash your fabric blank without fabric softener to get rid of chemicals and preshrink the material. This helps the vinyl stick better and last longer.

2. **Clean the fabric surface.**

   Use a lint roller to remove dust, debris, or fibers from the fabric surface.

3. **Preheat the fabric.**

   Set your heat press to the temperature in the printable HTV manufacturer's instructions and preheat the fabric for 10 seconds. This removes moisture and wrinkles, creating a smooth surface for application.

Step 5: Applying the design

Most printable HTVs don't require mirroring, as the printed side faces up when heat pressed. Always refer to the manufacturer's instructions for the correct application method.

Follow these steps to complete the process:

1. **Position the design on your fabric.**

   Use your hands to carefully peel the design off the liner, exposing the adhesive side. Think of it like peeling a sticker off its backing. Don't use transfer tape! Make sure the printed side is facing up and aligned where you want it. Do not place your design ink-side down on the fabric.

2. **Protect your design.**

   Place a Teflon sheet or parchment paper over the design to prevent direct contact with the heat source. Cricut's Printable Iron-On includes a pressing sheet.

3. **Use a heat press to apply the design.**

   Refer to the printable HTV manufacturer's instructions or the Cricut Heat Guide (https://cricut.com/en/heatguide) for the correct temperature and time settings — generally, between 315 and 350 degrees Fahrenheit (157–177 degrees Celsius) for 25 seconds.

Step 6: Peeling the backing (if needed)

Most printable HTV doesn't require peeling a backing after heat pressing. Once you've finished heat pressing, simply remove the Teflon sheet or parchment paper. However, for certain types of printable HTV, you may need to remove a backing or cover sheet, similar to how you would with regular HTV. Follow the instructions for your specific printable HTV to know whether this step is necessary, and whether it requires a hot or cold peel. After removing the backing, inspect the design to make sure no spots are peeling up. If necessary, cover the design with a Teflon sheet or parchment paper and press for another 5–10 seconds.

Following Proper Care Instructions

To keep your designs looking fresh, follow these care tips:

- Wait 48 hours before washing your project.
- Wash inside out in cold water with mild detergent.
- Avoid bleach and fabric softeners.
- Hang or lay flat to dry.
- If ironing is necessary, make sure to iron only the backside of the garment and avoid ironing directly on the design.

WARNING

Not following the care instructions can cause the ink to fade and bleed over time. Repeatedly tossing your Print Then Cut shirt in the washer and dryer with other clothes — like I did — *will* make it fade.

6

The Part of Tens

IN THIS PART . . .

Explore ten beginner Cricut projects that are perfect when you're just starting out.

Challenge yourself with ten advanced Cricut projects designed to take your skills to the next level.

IN THIS CHAPTER

» Creating personalized items like water bottles and bookmarks

» Decorating everyday objects with vinyl and HTV

» Making home and party décor, including banners and throw pillows

» Designing functional and stylish labels for candles and organizing

Chapter 21
Ten Beginner Cricut Projects

Kick-start your Cricut crafting journey with the ten beginner-friendly projects in this chapter. These easy-to-make projects introduce essential techniques and help you build confidence. Each project develops skills you can carry forward into even more exciting crafts. Ready to take your Cricut crafting to the next level? Head over to Chapter 22 to explore intricate designs and techniques that will challenge and inspire you!

REMEMBER

Heat press tools can reach high temperatures; always handle them with care and use heat-resistant gloves if necessary. Find out more about heat presses and other tools in Chapter 4. Chapter 2 introduces you to different Cricut machines, and Part 2 has the scoop on Cricut Design Space.

CHAPTER 21 **Ten Beginner Cricut Projects** 275

Making Birthday Banners

Create the perfect backdrop for your party with a personalized birthday banner. Gather these materials:

- Adhesive
- Cardstock
- Cricut machine (any model)
- Fine-Point Blade
- LightGrip Mat
- Twine or ribbon

Follow these steps:

1. **Plan your banner.**

   Decide what your banner will say so you know how many flags you need. For example, "Happy Birthday" has 13 letters, so you'll need 13 flags.

2. **Design your flags in Cricut Design Space.**

   Open Cricut Design Space and search for "banner" in Images to find a flag or pennant shape. Select the shape and click Duplicate in the Layers panel to create one for each letter. Resize the flags to fit your cardstock or adjust them to match your design needs.

   TIP

   If you don't want to design a custom flag, you can find ready-to-make banner projects in Design Space. Just search for "banner" in the Projects library, choose a design you like, and follow the steps to cut and assemble — it's that simple!

3. **Add and align the letters.**

   Use the Text tool to type out your full phrase in one text box and select a font you like. While the text is still grouped, drag the first letter over a flag and resize it to fit. You may need to zoom out to work with larger designs. Once it looks right, click Ungroup in the Layers panel to separate all letters.

4. **Slice the letters from the flags.**

   Place each letter over its corresponding flag, then select both and use Align > Center to position them correctly. Click Slice to cut the letter out of the flag, then delete the extra pieces. Move the finished flag to the side of your Canvas or hide it using the Eye tool. Just be sure to unhide all flags before clicking Make. Repeat this process for each flag.

5. **Cut the banner pieces.**

   Click on Browse All Materials and set the material to Cardstock. Load your cardstock onto the LightGrip Mat and cut the flags and letters. Use multiple mats for efficiency.

6. **Assemble the banner.**

   Layer the flags, securing the letters onto each one with adhesive, and string the banner together by threading twine or ribbon through the holes your Cricut cut at the top of each flag.

For additional paper crafting projects, see Part 3.

Crafting Custom Bookmarks

Designing custom bookmarks is a fun project to do with kids or by yourself. Gather the following materials:

>> Cardstock

>> Cricut machine (any model)

>> Cricut Pens

>> Fine-Point Blade

>> LightGrip Mat

>> Ribbon or tassels

Follow these steps:

1. **Create the design.**

   Search for "bookmark" in Images for basic bookmark shapes, or in Projects for more elaborate, ready-to-make designs. You can also create your own using the Shapes tool. Start with a rounded rectangle sized to approximately 2 x 7 inches (5 x 18 cm) for the base. Be sure to click the Lock icon to unlock it before entering the dimensions so that you can adjust the width and height independently. Add a small circle (about 0.25 inches [0.6 cm] in diameter) for a tassel, centering it at the top of the rectangle using the Align tool. Select both the bookmark shape and the circle, then click Slice. Delete the extra sliced pieces, leaving a clean hole for the tassel. For added functionality, include a U-shaped flap by searching for #M505D3E40 in Images. Resize and position the flap on the bookmark and then use the Slice tool to cut it into your rectangle.

CHAPTER 21 Ten Beginner Cricut Projects   277

TIP

When using the Slice tool for decorative cutouts or shapes, note that it works with only two elements at a time: the bookmark base and one design element. Position one design element on the bookmark, slice it, and then remove the excess pieces before repeating the process with additional elements.

TIP

If you want to add drawn details to your bookmark, use Cricut Pens. To find the best options, use the Filter tool in the Fonts menu and check off Writing to display fonts that work well with Cricut Pens. You can also use the Filter tool in Images and check off Draw to find images designed for drawing rather than cutting. Set the design elements you want to be drawn to Pen under the Operation drop-down menu, then highlight both the bookmark shape and the drawn elements in the Layers panel and click Attach. This keeps everything in place so that the machine draws the details and cuts in the correct spot.

2. **Cut and draw.**

   Place cardstock on a LightGrip Mat and set the material type to Cardstock in Design Space. Insert a pen into Clamp A, making sure it clicks into place, and load the mat into the machine. Design Space will guide you through the process and prompt you when it's time to switch from drawing to cutting.

3. **Add a tassel.**

   After cutting and drawing, carefully remove the bookmark from the mat. Thread ribbon or a tassel through the hole to finish the bookmark. For added durability, laminate the bookmark.

See Part 3 for more paper projects.

Personalizing Water Bottles

Turn plain water bottles into personalized masterpieces with your Cricut. Gather the following materials:

- Cricut machine (any model)
- Fine-Point Blade
- Lint-free wipe
- Permanent vinyl
- Rubbing alcohol

- » Scissors or trimmer
- » Scraper tool
- » StandardGrip Mat
- » Transfer tape
- » Weeding tool

Follow these steps:

1. **Design the vinyl decal.**

   Use the Text tool in Design Space to type a name or phrase. Resize the decal to fit your water bottle and click Make.

   For a bold, two-layer design, use the Offset tool to add a border around your name or text. This creates a layered effect that makes your design stand out. Simply select your text, click Offset, adjust the size, and choose whether you want rounded or square edges. Cut the offset layer in a contrasting color and apply it first, then place your main text on top.

2. **Cut the vinyl.**

   Click on Browse All Materials and select your vinyl. Place the vinyl colored side up on a StandardGrip Mat and cut the decal using your Cricut. Weed away excess vinyl with tweezers or a weeding tool.

3. **Prepare the bottle.**

   Clean the surface with rubbing alcohol and a lint-free wipe.

4. **Apply the design.**

   Use transfer tape to lift your vinyl from the liner, align it on the bottle, and smooth out air bubbles with a scraper. Peel back the tape carefully.

   Burnishing, or smoothing, the transfer tape over the vinyl with a scraper makes it easier to lift your decal off the liner. For best results, burnish both the transfer tape and the liner on the back of the vinyl. If you have difficulty peeling the decal off the liner, burnish both sides again.

5. **Cure the vinyl.**

   Let the vinyl cure for 24–72 hours before using the water bottle.

See Chapter 13 for more vinyl techniques and Chapter 14 for layering vinyl designs.

Assembling Acrylic Key Chains

Create adorable acrylic key chains with layered vinyl designs. Gather these materials:

- Acrylic key chain blanks (round-shaped bundles with tassels and hardware work great)
- Cricut machine (any model)
- Fine-Point Blade
- Jewelry-making tools (small needle-nose pliers)
- Lint-free wipe
- Permanent vinyl
- Rubbing alcohol
- Scissors or trimmer
- Scraper or brayer
- StandardGrip Mat
- Transfer tape
- Weeding tool

Follow these steps:

1. **Create or upload your design in Design Space.**

   For a custom design, click on the Shapes tool in the left panel and select a circle. Resize it to match your acrylic key chain blank size (typically 2–3 inches [5–8 cm]). This circle serves as a template to help you design your key chain. Layer your text or images on top of the template, arranging them as desired. Before cutting, delete or hide the template using the Eye tool in the Layers panel.

   TIP

   You can search for "key chains" in Projects for ready-made options or explore elements like "brushstroke" in Images to customize your key chain. A popular design idea is layering a name over a brushstroke background for a trendy, personalized look.

2. **Cut the vinyl.**

   Place the vinyl, colored side up, on a StandardGrip Mat, set the material to Vinyl, and cut. Weed the design layers and keep them organized for easy application.

3. **Layer the vinyl.**

   Remove the protective film from the acrylic blank and clean it with rubbing alcohol and a lint-free wipe. Apply the base layer of vinyl using transfer tape, smoothing it down securely with a scraper or brayer as you lift it off the liner and transfer it to the blank. Repeat this process for additional layers, making sure everything is properly aligned before applying each layer.

4. **Assemble the key chain.**

   Attach the hardware using needle-nose pliers and add tassels or charms for extra flair.

See Chapter 13 for additional vinyl tips and Chapter 14 for more on vinyl-layering techniques.

Decorating Throw Pillows

Jazz up throw pillows with heat transfer vinyl (HTV). Gather the following materials:

- Cricut machine (any model)
- Fine-Point Blade
- Heat press or EasyPress
- HTV
- Pillow inserts
- StandardGrip Mat
- Teflon sheets
- Throw pillow covers

Follow these steps:

1. **Create the design.**

   Upload or create your design in Design Space and resize it to fit your pillow.

   TIP

   Designs with HTV always need to be mirrored so that they appear correctly when applied. However, Design Space's Auto Mirror feature automatically mirrors your design on the Make screen when you select an HTV material, such as Everyday Iron-On. It's always a good idea to double-check that the mirror setting is enabled before cutting.

CHAPTER 21 **Ten Beginner Cricut Projects** 281

2. **Cut the HTV.**

   Place the HTV shiny side down on the mat, positioning it in the upper left-hand corner to match the placement on the Preview screen. Set the material to Everyday Iron-On, then load the mat and cut the design. Once the cut is complete, weed the design to remove any excess vinyl.

3. **Prepare the fabric.**

   Clean the pillow cover with a lint roller, place a Teflon sheet inside the pillow to prevent it from sticking together during heat pressing, and press the fabric for 10 seconds at 300 degrees Fahrenheit (149 degrees Celsius) to remove wrinkles.

4. **Apply the design.**

   Position the design on the pillow cover, cover it with a Teflon sheet, and press firmly for 15 seconds at 300 degrees Fahrenheit (149 degrees Celsius), or follow the time and temperature recommendations provided by the HTV manufacturer. After your project cools, peel the carrier sheet off the design according to the manufacturer's instructions.

5. **Insert the pillow.**

   Once the HTV has set, remove the Teflon sheet from inside the pillow cover, then carefully fit the pillow insert into the cover, making sure that the corners are fully aligned.

TIP

For more HTV projects, see Chapter 15, and check out the color section for a fun pocket pillow project idea. You can also watch my YouTube channel (www.youtube.com/@KerriCraftsIt) to see how I made it step by step. If you're looking for blank pocket pillows, you can find them on Etsy.

Designing Custom Hats

Dive into custom hat making with your Cricut and a hat press. Gather your materials as follows:

- Cricut machine (any model)
- Fine-Point Blade

- >> Glitter Iron-On (recommended)
- >> Hat press form or rolled-up towel
- >> Heat press for hats (recommended) or an EasyPress Mini or iron
- >> Lint roller
- >> StandardGrip Mat
- >> Strong heat-resistant tape
- >> Teflon sheet
- >> Weeding tool

Follow these steps:

1. **Create the design.**

   Upload or create your design in Design Space. Resize it to fit the hat (maximum 2.25 x 4.25 inches [5.7 x 10.8 cm]) and mirror the image.

2. **Cut the vinyl.**

   Place the vinyl, shiny side down, on the mat, and set the material to Glitter Iron-On. HTV projects must always be mirrored, but Design Space's Auto Mirror feature automatically mirrors the design when you select your material, so you don't have to do it manually. Cut the design, then weed and trim the carrier sheet to fit the curve of the hat.

3. **Prepare the hat.**

   Clean the surface with a lint roller and insert a hat press form or rolled-up towel into the crown for support.

4. **Apply the design.**

   Position the design on the hat, secure it with heat-resistant tape, and cover it with a Teflon sheet. Press at 320 degrees Fahrenheit (160 degrees Celsius) for 15 seconds, or follow the time and temperature recommendations provided by the iron-on manufacturer.

5. **Cool and reveal your design.**

   Peel the carrier sheet as directed in the manufacturer's instructions.

For more wearable projects, see Chapter 15.

Monogramming Towels

Add a touch of elegance to your bathroom or kitchen with monogrammed towels. Gather these materials:

- » Cricut machine (any model)
- » Fine-Point Blade
- » Heat press or EasyPress
- » HTV (Glitter, Flock, or Everyday Iron-On)
- » Lint roller
- » Teflon sheet
- » StandardGrip Mat
- » Towels (medium-to-low pile)

Follow these steps:

1. **Design the monogram.**

   Create your monogram using the Text tool or Monogram Maker, or browse the Images library by searching "monogram." Resize it to fit your towel and click Make.

2. **Cut the HTV.**

   Place the HTV, shiny side down, on a StandardGrip Mat. Set the material to match the HTV type, and Design Space's Auto Mirror feature will automatically mirror the design for you. Cut the monogram and weed the excess vinyl to leave only the monogram.

3. **Prepare the towel.**

   Use a lint roller to clean the towel. Press it for 10 seconds at 315 degrees Fahrenheit (157 degrees Celsius) to remove moisture and wrinkles.

4. **Apply the HTV.**

   Position the design on the towel, cover with a Teflon sheet, and press at 315 degrees Fahrenheit (157 degrees Celsius) for 30 seconds, or follow the time and temperature recommendations provided by the HTV manufacturer.

5. **Cool and reveal your design.**

   Peel the carrier sheet as directed in the manufacturer's instructions.

See Chapter 15 for more HTV projects.

Creating Infusible Ink Coasters

Make colorful custom coasters with Cricut Infusible Ink. Gather these materials:

- *Brayer* (small roller)
- Butcher paper
- Cardstock
- Cricut machine (any model)
- Fine-Point Blade
- Heat press or EasyPress
- Heat-resistant tape
- Infusible Ink coaster blanks (round ceramic or square cork-backed)
- Infusible Ink Transfer Sheets
- Lint-free wipe
- Scissors or trimmer
- StandardGrip Mat
- Tweezers

Follow these steps:

1. **Design the coasters.**

   Open Design Space and create or choose a design. If you're looking for quick and easy options, search for "coasters" in the Images or Projects library to find tons of ready-to-go designs perfect for Cricut's Infusible Ink-compatible coasters.

   If you're creating a custom design, resize it to fit your coaster blanks: 3.75 inches (9.5 cm) for square coasters or 3.6 inches (9 cm) for round coasters. If you want your design to cover the entire surface of a round or square coaster, you'll need to crop it using the Slice tool. Add a circle or square shape and resize it slightly larger — about 0.25 inches (0.6 cm) bigger than the coaster — to prevent white edges. Place it over your design, then use the Slice tool to trim it to the correct shape. Slicing patterns and images into shapes is a fun and easy way to create custom coaster designs.

2. **Cut the transfer sheet.**

   Place the Infusible Ink Transfer Sheet, ink-side up, on the StandardGrip Mat, positioning it in the upper left-hand corner to match the placement on the

Preview screen. Use a brayer to firmly press and smooth the sheet onto the mat. Set the material to Infusible Ink Transfer Sheet, and Design Space will automatically mirror your design with its Auto Mirror feature, so you don't need to do it manually. Load the mat and cut the design. Once the design is cut, gently bend or roll the sheet to "crack" the cuts and then weed the excess material carefully using your fingers or tweezers to avoid damaging the design.

3. **Prepare the coasters.**

Wipe each coaster with a lint-free wipe (avoid alcohol-based cleaners). Place the design on the coaster blank face down with the ink side touching the surface. Secure it in place with heat-resistant tape.

4. **Position the coasters on your heat press.**

Place a sheet of cardstock on the heat press to protect the bottom platen from ink blowout. Cricut makes two types of Infusible Ink–compatible coasters: round ceramic coasters with a poly-coated surface and square coasters with a cork backing. Because these coasters are made of different materials, they require different positioning methods:

- For **square coasters:** Place the coaster blank side up on the heat press, with the cork backing touching the bottom platen and the transfer sheet on top.

- For **round ceramic coasters:** Flip the coaster upside down before pressing. This means the top of the coaster (with the taped transfer sheet) will be in direct contact with the bottom of the heat press, while the bottom of the coaster faces up. This pressing method is different from square coasters because ceramic coasters require heat from the bottom to ensure even ink transfer.

5. **Use your heat press.**

Cover your coaster with a sheet of butcher paper and set your heat press to 400 degrees Fahrenheit (204 degrees Celsius). Press for the appropriate time based on the coaster type.

- **Square coasters:** 60 seconds

- **Round ceramic coasters:** 240 seconds (4 minutes)

6. **Cool and reveal your design.**

Allow the coasters to cool completely before handling them because they will be extremely hot. Once your project is cool, carefully remove the liner to reveal your vibrant design.

See Chapter 16 for more exciting Infusible Ink projects.

Organizing with Custom Labels

Tidy up your space with custom labels using printable vinyl and Cricut's Print Then Cut feature. Gather the following materials:

- Cricut machine (any model except the Cricut Joy)
- Fine-Point Blade
- Inkjet printer
- LightGrip Mat
- Printable vinyl (recommended: Joyeza Vinyl Sticker Paper, premium matte)

Follow these steps:

1. **Create the design.**

    Open Design Space and create label shapes (for example, rectangles or circles). If you're looking for decorative options, search for "label" in Images to find fancy label shapes. Add text, customize fonts and sizes, and click Flatten to prepare for printing.

2. **Prepare to print the design.**

    Click Make in Design Space and then click on the Material Size drop-down menu and choose the size that matches your printable vinyl — typically 8.5 x 11 inches. Leave the Mirror setting turned off and click Continue.

3. **Print the labels.**

    Load printable vinyl into the printer and click Send to Printer in Design Space. A new window will open where you will select your printer from the drop-down menu. Decide whether to turn the Bleed feature on or off. Toggle the System Dialog on to adjust the printer settings in the next window and click Print. On the System Dialog screen, select your printer again and click on Preferences. In the printer preferences, select a paper type similar to your material, such as Premium Presentation Matte (options may vary depending on your printer), and set the print quality to Best. Click OK and Print.

TIP

Turning Bleed on adds a color-matching border around the design for clean cuts, which is helpful for detailed edges. Turning Bleed off removes the border, which is ideal for simple shapes.

4. **Cut the labels.**

    Set the material type in Design Space to Washi Tape for a *kiss cut,* which leaves the sticker backing intact, or select Cardstock or Printable Vinyl for a *die cut,* which cuts through the backing. Place the printed vinyl in the upper-left corner on a LightGrip Mat and load it into your Cricut. Press the Go button to begin the cut.

5. **Apply the labels.**

   Before applying your labels, clean the surface with a lint-free wipe to remove dust and oils. For nonporous surfaces like glass or plastic, use rubbing alcohol for better adhesion. Peel the labels from the backing and stick them onto your surfaces.

See Chapter 18 for more details on using the Print Then Cut feature and Chapter 19 for guidance on working with printable sticker paper and vinyl.

Creating Custom Candle Labels

Make thoughtful personalized candle labels with Cricut's Print Then Cut feature. Gather these materials:

>> Candle in a jar

>> Cricut machine (any model except the Cricut Joy)

>> Fine-Point Blade

>> Goo Gone (optional)

>> Inkjet printer

>> LightGrip Mat

>> Lint-free wipe

>> Printable vinyl

>> Rubbing alcohol

>> Ruler

>> Scraper or brayer

Follow these steps:

1. **Create the design.**

   Measure the candle jar with a ruler and create a rectangle in Design Space to match. Click the Lock icon to unlock it before entering the width and height separately so that you can adjust them independently. Add text, photos, or patterns, and then use the Flatten tool to finalize the design. In the Layers panel, click on Operation Type and choose Print Then Cut.

2. **Prepare to print the design.**

   Click Make in Design Space and then click on the Material Size drop-down menu and choose the size that matches your printable vinyl. Leave the Mirror setting turned off and click Continue.

3. **Print the label.**

   Load printable vinyl into the printer. Select your printer from the drop-down menu and click Send to Printer. Decide whether to turn the Bleed feature on or off, depending on your design (turn it on for detailed designs; leave it off for simple shapes). Toggle the System Dialog on to adjust the printer settings in the next window and click Print. In the printer preferences, choose Premium Presentation Matte as your paper type and set the print quality to Best. Click OK and Print.

4. **Cut the label.**

   Place the printed vinyl in the upper-left corner on a LightGrip Mat and load it into your Cricut. In Design Space, set the material type to Printable Vinyl. Press Go to begin the cut.

5. **Apply the label.**

   If you're replacing a store-bought candle label, peel off the original label first. For stubborn labels, apply Goo Gone or soak the jar in alcohol to help loosen the adhesive. Once removed, wipe the jar down with rubbing alcohol and a lint-free wipe to ensure a clean surface. Peel your new label from its backing, position it on the jar, and smooth it down with a scraper or brayer.

TIP

For more Print Then Cut projects, see Chapter 18. Check out my YouTube channel, Kerri Crafts It (www.youtube.com/@KerriCraftsIt), to see how I created a personalized candle label as a thoughtful teacher gift using Print Then Cut, featuring my son's school picture and a special note.

CHAPTER 21 **Ten Beginner Cricut Projects** 289

IN THIS CHAPTER

» Working with advanced Cricut techniques

» Enhancing your skills with challenging projects

» Revealing the versatility of your Cricut with intricate and detailed crafts

Chapter 22
Ten Advanced Cricut Projects

Ready to take your Cricut crafting to the next level? In this chapter, you find ten advanced projects that will challenge your creativity and sharpen your skills. From custom leather earrings to detailed puzzles, these projects highlight just how versatile your Cricut can be. *Note:* Some of the projects in this chapter, such as the pet ID tags, quilt blocks, and custom puzzles, can only be made with a machine from the Cricut Maker series, as they require Maker-only tools.

TIP

Check out Chapters 2 and 4 for details on Cricut machines, tools, and materials. Part 2 gives you the lowdown on using Cricut Design Space.

Engraving Pet ID Tags

Engraving ID tags is a fun and practical way to personalize your pet's accessories and ensure that they can always find their way back home. This project uses the Engraving Tip, a tool exclusive to the Cricut Maker series, which allows you to create custom tags complete with your pet's name, your address, and your phone number.

Gather your materials:

- Cricut Maker, Cricut Maker 3, or Cricut Maker 4 only
- Engraving Tip (#41)
- Fine-grit sandpaper
- Lint roller
- Painter's tape
- Soft metal pet tags (aluminum, brass, or copper, no thicker than ⅛ inch [3.2 millimeters])

WARNING: Avoid using any tags that are too thick or hard, as they may damage the tip or the machine.

- StrongGrip Mat

Follow these steps:

1. **Find a template.**

   Start by searching "pet tag" in the Cricut Design Space Images library. Select an image that best matches the shape of your blank tag (like a bone) to use as a template for designing.

2. **Resize the template and create a boundary for your design.**

   Resize the image to fit your tag. Unlock the Lock tool to adjust length and width separately. Set the tag operation to Guide so that it shows as a reference without cutting or engraving. For more on guides, see Chapter 8.

3. **Add text.**

   Use the Text tool to type the pet's name and phone number.

   TIP: To find a font that is best for engraving, click on the filter in the Fonts drop-down menu and check off Multi-layer Cutting. Multilayer fonts show better after engraving because they have two layers for each letter. Choose an easy-to-read font and resize to fit within the tag.

4. **Finalize the design and prepare it for cutting.**

   Finish up your design with these steps:

   - If your design has multiple text boxes or elements, hold Shift and select them (excluding the guide), then click Attach to keep everything together during engraving.
   - Change the operation for these attached elements from Basic Cut to Engrave.

- To engrave the back, create a second pet tag guide and repeat the steps.

- After clicking Make, you'll see a preview of your design on the mat in the Prepare screen. Drag your design to the center of the mat at the 6-inch (15.24-cm) intersection. Where your design appears on this mat preview is where it will be cut on your Cricut. Make sure to place your tag on the StrongGrip Mat in the exact same spot as you see on the screen.

- Click Continue to proceed to the Make screen, choose Browse All Materials, select your material type (for example, Anodized Aluminum), and then click Done.

5. **Prepare the tag.**

   Remove any protective films from the tag and place the tag in the exact center — at the 6-inch (15.24-centimeter) intersection — of the StrongGrip Mat, making sure it matches exactly where you placed your design earlier on the Prepare screen. Use painter's tape to keep the tag from shifting during cutting and make sure that no tape covers the engraving area.

6. **Set up your Cricut Maker.**

   Insert the Engraving Tip (#41) into Clamp B of the Maker. Move the *star wheels* (the white rings on the roller bar) to the side to keep them from getting in the way during engraving.

7. **Engrave the design.**

   Load your mat into the machine and press Go to begin engraving.

8. **Once engraving is complete, remove the tag from the mat and use a lint roller to wipe off any leftover metal flakes.**

WARNING

Don't use your fingers to clean engraved surfaces, because *burrs* (rough areas) and small metal fragments can cause cuts. Instead, use a lint roller for debris removal and fine-grit sandpaper for smoothing burrs.

TIP

Consider using a permanent marker to darken the text, wiping away the excess for added contrast.

"Etching" Coated Metal with Citristrip

After exploring glass etching in Chapter 17, try using Citristrip to stencil designs onto coated metal. While often called "etching," Citristrip removes paint or coating to reveal the shiny metal beneath. It doesn't work on uncoated metals like stainless steel or bare aluminum. See the full transformation of this project in the color section.

Gather your materials:

- Citristrip paint remover
- Coated metal blanks
- Cricut machine
- Fine-Point Blade
- Lint-free wipe
- Paintbrush
- Painter's tape
- Protective gloves and glasses
- Respirator or face mask
- Rubbing alcohol
- Ruler
- Scraper
- Soft brush
- Transfer tape
- Vinyl (stencil or permanent)
- Weeding tools

Follow these steps:

1. **Prepare your stencil.**

   Create or upload your stencil design in Cricut Design Space. If your design includes multiple pieces, select all the elements and use the Weld or Unite tool to combine them into one cuttable layer. Use a ruler to size it appropriately, and cut it out using the Vinyl setting on your Cricut machine. Weed away the parts of the design that will be etched, leaving the rest of the vinyl intact. Need extra help designing your stencil? Check out Chapter 17 for step-by-step instructions on creating stencil designs in Design Space.

2. **Clean the coated metal.**

   Clean the coated metal thoroughly with rubbing alcohol and a lint-free wipe. Allow it to dry completely.

3. **Apply your stencil.**

Transfer your stencil onto the metal blank, smoothing firmly to avoid air bubbles. Secure the stencil edges with painter's tape to protect surrounding areas.

4. **Apply Citristrip.**

Wear protective gear and work in a ventilated area. Brush a thick, even layer of Citristrip onto the exposed stencil areas and let it sit for 10–30 minutes.

5. **Remove the coating to reveal your design.**

Remove the loosened coating by scrubbing with a scraper, brush, or paper towel. Rinse the blank under cool water, remove the vinyl stencil, and wipe clean with a lint-free cloth. Avoid using a heat gun, as excessive heat can damage your project.

Fashioning Leather Earrings

You can create trendy leather earrings using your Cricut and various blades. For example, you can cut thin faux leather with a Fine-Point Blade. For medium-weight leather, you can use the Deep-Point Blade. And for thick tooling leather you use the Knife Blade, which is exclusive to the Cricut Maker series.

Gather your materials:

- Brayer
- Cricut machine (any model)
- Earring findings (supplies like hooks and jump rings)
- Faux leather sheets (or genuine/metallic leather)
- Fine-Point Blade, Deep-Point Blade, or Knife Blade (Maker series only)
- Jewelry pliers
- Leather punch or weeding tool
- Optional embellishments (iron-on vinyl, glitter, foil)
- Painter's tape
- StrongGrip Mat

CHAPTER 22 **Ten Advanced Cricut Projects** 295

Follow these steps:

1. **Create the design.**

   Search for "leather earrings" in Images or Projects in Cricut Design Space, or upload your own design.

2. **Resize the design.**

   Adjust the size of your design, remembering hooks add about ¾ inch (2 cm) to the length. Drop earrings usually range from 1½ to 3 inches (4 to 8 cm) long.

3. **Prepare the leather and load it on the mat.**

   Cut your leather into smaller pieces for each earring to minimize movement on the mat. For most types of leather, place it with the finished, smooth side down on the StrongGrip Mat. Leathers with a coating or specialty finish, such as pull-up leather, should have Cricut Transfer Tape applied to the rough side, then placed with the Transfer Tape side down on the mat. Secure the edges with painter's tape and use a brayer to firmly attach the leather to the mat.

4. **Prepare the design for cutting.**

   On the Preview screen in Design Space, click and drag your design to the spot on the mat where you intend to cut your leather. Because most leather is placed with the finished side down on the mat, be sure to mirror the image so it appears correctly, especially if your design includes text that you don't want to appear backwards. Toggle Mirror on in Design Space. For leather with a coating or special finish, like pull-up leather, don't mirror the design, since the coated side is facing up.

   On the Make screen, select the correct material setting under Browse All Materials, such as Faux Leather (Paper Thin) — this setting automatically performs a double cut and works well for most faux leathers. Set the pressure to More for best results when cutting thicker materials like faux leather.

5. **Cut the design.**

   Move the star wheels on your Cricut's roller bar to the side to avoid marking the leather. Load the mat into your Cricut and press Go to begin the cut.

TIP

Before unloading the mat, check to see whether the leather is fully cut through. If not, press Go to repeat the cut without unloading the mat.

6. **Punch holes.**

   If the Cricut doesn't cut clean holes for jump rings, use a leather punch or your Cricut weeding tool to poke a hole.

7. **Add embellishments (optional).**

   For more glam, add heat transfer vinyl (HTV), glitter, or foil designs to your earrings. For details on using HTV, see Chapter 15.

8. **Assemble the earrings.**

   Attach earring hooks and jump rings using jewelry pliers. Using two pairs of pliers — one to hold the jump ring and one to open it — makes the process much easier. Now your earrings are ready to wear!

Assembling Fabric Flowers

You can craft beautiful fabric flowers for home décor, bouquets, or wearable accessories.

Gather your materials:

- Brayer
- Cricut machine (any model for bonded fabric; Maker series only for non-bonded fabric)
- Embellishments like beads, buttons, floral stem wire, or hair clips (optional)
- Fabric and blade:
  - Bonded fabric (fabric with *interfacing,* or a backing that makes it stiff) is best for reducing fraying and works with all Cricut machines. You'll need to iron the interfacing on the back before cutting. Bonded fabric can be cut with the Fine-Point Blade or the Bonded-Fabric Blade (Maker/Explore only).
  - Nonbonded fabric (fabric without backing or interfacing) is softer, more flexible, and less stiff compared to bonded fabric. It can only be cut with the Cricut Maker series using the Rotary Blade.
- Fabric glue or hot glue gun
- FabricGrip Mat
- Interfacing (for bonding your fabric)
- Iron
- Scissors

Follow these steps:

1. **Create the design.**

   Search "fabric flower" to find a flower design in Projects. Resize it to match your desired flower size. For guidance on determining the best cut sizes for different flower projects, see Chapter 11.

2. **Prepare the fabric for cutting.**

   Use scissors to cut the fabric to fit your mat.

   - **For bonded fabric:** Start by ironing interfacing onto the back of your fabric to bond it, following the instructions on the interfacing package. Place the bonded fabric, interfacing side down, on the FabricGrip Mat. Use a brayer to smooth the fabric and ensure that it sticks firmly to the mat.

   - **For nonbonded fabric (Maker only):** Place the fabric, right (printed or finished) side down, on the FabricGrip Mat unless otherwise specified by your project. This helps achieve cleaner cuts and prevents the mat from pulling at the fabric fibers. Use a brayer to smooth the fabric and eliminate any wrinkles or air bubbles.

3. **Prepare and cut the design.**

   - **For bonded fabric:** Insert the Bonded-Fabric Blade or the Fine-Point Blade into Clamp B. In Design Space, set the material to your specific bonded fabric (for example, Cotton, Bonded). If using a Cricut Explore Air 2, set the dial to Custom. Load the mat and press Go.

   - **For nonbonded fabric (Maker only):** Insert the Rotary Blade into Clamp B of your Cricut Maker, and in Design Space, select the appropriate fabric setting (for example, Light Cotton). Load the mat and press Go.

4. **Assemble the flower.**

   Once cut, gently bend the mat to peel off the fabric without stretching it. Use tweezers for small pieces. For flowers from the Projects library, check the description for assembly instructions. Layer petals from largest to smallest, gluing at the center, and shape petals to create a more realistic appearance.

5. **Add embellishments.**

   Attach beads or buttons to the flower center for extra detail. Use floral wire to create stems, or attach the flower to a clip or headband.

TIP

Stenciling Wood Signs

Painted wood signs are not only popular items to sell at craft fairs but also wonderful personalized gifts during the holidays. Using your Cricut and vinyl, you can create perfect stencils for a variety of crafts. Flip to Chapter 17 to discover how to etch glass with vinyl stencils.

TIP

Start with smooth, unfinished wood or pre-sanded plaques for the best results. Stay away from rough or textured wood to avoid paint bleed and stencil slippage. Make sure that your wood is completely dry before stenciling.

Gather your materials:

- Acrylic paint
- Brayer
- Cricut machine (any model)
- Fine-Point Blade
- Mod Podge
- Sandpaper
- Scissors or trimmer
- Scraper
- Sealant (such as polyurethane), for the optional step of sealing sign
- Stencil brush and paintbrush
- Transfer tape
- Vinyl for stencils (permanent or stencil vinyl)
- Weeding tool or tweezers
- Wood sign or plaque
- Wood stain (optional)

Follow these steps:

1. **Prepare the wood.**

   Sand the wood smooth, wipe away dust, and apply wood stain with a paintbrush if desired, allowing it to dry completely before moving on.

2. **Create the stencil.**

   Design or select your image in Cricut Design Space. Resize it to fit your wood piece.

3. **Prepare and cut the design.**

   After clicking Make, select Vinyl as your material. Use scissors or a trimmer to cut the vinyl to fit the mat. Place the vinyl onto the StandardGrip Mat with the backing down and the colored side up, then begin the cut.

4. **Weed the vinyl.**

   After cutting, use your weeding tool or tweezers to carefully remove the parts of the design that you want to paint, leaving the background intact. Make sure to leave the inner pieces of letters (like the centers of O and A) attached to the vinyl backing. Don't peel away the outer vinyl yet!

5. **Apply the stencil.**

   Use transfer tape to move the stencil from the backing onto the wood. (Flip to Chapter 13 for tips on transferring vinyl.) Press firmly with a brayer or scraper when you apply the stencil to the wood, especially along the edges, to ensure a tight seal and prevent paint bleed.

6. **Seal the stencil.**

   Use a paintbrush to apply a thin layer of Mod Podge over the stencil. This seals the edges and prevents paint from seeping under the vinyl. Let it dry before painting the design.

7. **Paint the design.**

   Use a stencil brush to dab a light coat of acrylic paint onto the wood. Avoid overloading the brush with paint, because this can cause bleeding.

8. **Peel off the stencil.**

   Carefully remove the stencil while the paint is still wet or tacky, pulling sideways to avoid splintering. If you wait until the paint is dry, it can form a solid layer that may pull up with the stencil, damaging your design. Use a weeding tool for smaller pieces.

9. **Seal the sign (optional).**

   For added durability, apply a clear sealant, such as polyurethane, with a paintbrush after you've removed the stencil. This helps protect the design and adds a polished finish.

Creating Vibrant Coffee Mugs

Get ready to make your mornings extra special by creating custom mugs with Cricut's Infusible Ink. This method presses your designs directly into the mug, so they're super vibrant and won't peel off or fade, even in the dishwasher.

TIP

Make sure to use mugs that are specially coated for Infusible Ink, like Cricut's own line of mugs or other sublimation-ready mugs. For more Infusible Ink techniques, see Chapter 16.

Gather your materials:

- Brayer
- Butcher paper
- Cricut machine (any model)
- Fine-Point Blade
- Heat-resistant gloves
- Heat-resistant tape
- Infusible Ink Transfer Sheets
- Lint-free cloth and rubbing alcohol
- Mug press
- Specially coated mugs for sublimation or Infusible Ink
- StandardGrip Mat
- Tweezers
- Vinyl trimmer or scissors

Follow these steps:

1. **Design the mug.**

   TIP

   Create a design in Design Space and resize it to fit the mug. Be sure to mirror your design so it appears correctly when you transfer it onto the mug. The Auto Mirror feature will automatically mirror your design once you select "Infusible Ink Transfer Sheet" as your material on the Make screen.

2. **Prepare the design.**

   Use a trimmer or scissors to cut the Infusible Ink Transfer Sheet to the size needed. Position your Infusible Ink Transfer Sheet, ink-side up, on a StandardGrip Mat, and smooth it down with a brayer.

3. **Cut the design.**

   In Design Space, set your material to Infusible Ink Transfer Sheet and let your Cricut machine handle the cutting.

4. **Weed the design.**

   Remove the transfer sheet from the mat and carefully weed the design by bending the sheet to crack the ink along the cut lines. This makes it easier to distinguish and remove the excess areas by hand without using a weeding hook, which can damage the design. For intricate designs, use tweezers to remove small, stubborn pieces of transfer paper.

5. **Prepare the mug.**

   Clean the mug with a lint-free cloth and rubbing alcohol to remove dust, oils, or debris.

6. **Apply the design.**

   Wrap the design around the mug with the ink against the surface, aligning it carefully, and secure it with heat-resistant tape. Then, wrap the entire mug in butcher paper, making sure that it's smooth and wrinkle-free to avoid uneven pressure. Secure the paper with heat-resistant tape to protect your heat press from ink stains during the transfer process.

7. **Press the mug.**

   Place the mug in the preheated mug press and heat it at 400 degrees Fahrenheit (204 degrees Celsius) for 4–6 minutes.

WARNING

   Use the mug press in a well-ventilated area because it may release some fumes during the heating process. The mug will be *very hot* after coming out of the press. Always use heat-resistant gloves to handle it.

8. **Reveal the design.**

   Using heat-resistant gloves, carefully remove the mug from the press and place it on a heat-resistant surface, such as a silicone mat or thick towel. Allow the mug to cool completely before peeling off the butcher paper and transfer paper, typically 15–30 minutes, to avoid smudging the ink.

Making Decorative Cake Toppers

Crafting custom cake toppers with layered cardstock is a fantastic way to add a personal touch to any celebration. Use 65 lb cardstock for the sturdy base layers and glitter cardstock for a sparkly top layer. You can customize cake toppers for any occasion, like weddings, birthdays, graduations, and baby showers, making every event special and memorable. If you want to make a custom card to go with your cake, check out Chapter 12.

Gather your materials:

>> Adhesives (double-sided adhesive foam squares, craft glue, hot glue, or spray adhesive)

>> Brayer

>> Cardstock (regular, glitter, foil, or poster board)

>> Cricut machine (any model)

>> Fine-Point Blade

>> LightGrip or StandardGrip Mat

>> Support options (bamboo skewers, lollipop sticks, acrylic sticks, decorative straws)

Follow these steps:

1. **Design the topper.**

   Search "cake topper" in the Images or Projects library. Alternatively, create a custom design using text. Choose a bold, thick font for the best results and type your message (for example, *Happy 40th Birthday, Mr. and Mrs.,* or *Happy Mother's Day*).

   Ungroup the text to individually adjust letters or words. In the Edit bar, you can use the Letter Space arrows to adjust the spacing between letters (this is called *kerning*). To adjust entire lines instead of individual letters, click on Advanced > Ungroup to Lines. Make sure that all the letters in each word are connected, or overlapped with the words below, so that everything cuts out as one piece without any small pieces falling out.

2. **Combine the design elements and resize the design.**

   Select all elements and use the Weld or Unite tools to make one cuttable design. Then resize your design so it's no wider than the cake itself, typically 4–6 inches. If you prefer a solid topper with no see-through areas, use the

Offset tool to add a background layer for extra contrast. The offset also helps by providing a base to glue smaller pieces, like the dot on the *i*, that would otherwise fall off.

3. **Prepare the design for cutting.**

   Pick the material setting in Design Space that matches your cardstock type.

4. **Load the cardstock onto the mat.**

   Put your cardstock on either a LightGrip or StandardGrip Mat. Roll over it with a brayer to make sure it flattens down and stays in place.

5. **Cut the design.**

   Load your mat into the Cricut machine and press Go to begin the cut.

   TIP

   After cutting, carefully remove the mat from the machine. Flip the mat over and gently peel it away from the cardstock, taking care not to bend or damage the delicate parts of the topper. If needed, use a spatula tool to help lift delicate cuts.

6. **Assemble the topper.**

   If your design has multiple layers, stack them using double-sided adhesive foam squares to make it pop more. For finer details, apply a small amount of craft glue or hot glue.

7. **Attach the support.**

   Measure and cut the skewers or sticks to match the height of the cake. Glue the supports to the back of the topper with hot glue, making sure they're not visible but still hold it up well. Finally, pop it into your cake!

Cutting Perfect Quilt Blocks

If you love quilting but find cutting fabric challenging, the Cricut Maker machines are your best friend! They're the only models with a Rotary Blade, making fabric cutting accurate and effortless. This is especially helpful if you have physical limitations like arthritis, carpal tunnel syndrome, or poor vision. Let the Cricut Maker series do the heavy lifting and save yourself hours of cutting and sore hands. Then, focus on the fun part — using your sewing machine to piece together projects like a cozy baby blanket or a unique decorative quilt for your home.

Gather your materials:

- Brayer
- Cricut Maker, Cricut Maker 3, or Cricut Maker 4 only
- FabricGrip Mat
- Iron
- Quilting fabric
- Rotary Blade
- Ruler
- Scissors
- Spatula
- Starch or Best Press (optional)
- Tweezers

Follow these steps:

1. **Choose your design.**

   Open Design Space and select a square from Shapes to start from scratch, or search "quilt" in Projects to browse ready-to-make templates.

2. **Resize and duplicate the design.**

   Adjust the size of the square to match your quilt pattern. Use the Duplicate tool to create as many squares as you need.

3. **Prepare your fabric and load it on the mat.**

   Cut your fabric to fit within the adhesive area of the mat, making sure it doesn't extend beyond the edges.

   TIP

   Iron the fabric to remove creases, then apply starch or Best Press to give it more structure. Make sure the fabric is dry before placing it printed side down on the FabricGrip Mat. Smooth it out with a brayer to make sure it sticks well without air bubbles.

4. **Cut the fabric.**

   Move the star wheels to the right to avoid track marks on the fabric. Insert the Rotary Blade into Clamp B of your Cricut Maker. Select the appropriate fabric setting in Design Space based on the type of material you're using (like Cotton or Cotton, Bonded). Load the mat and let the Cricut cut out the shapes for you. After cutting, remove the excess fabric around your squares. Use your hands, tweezers, or a spatula to carefully lift your pieces off the mat.

CHAPTER 22 **Ten Advanced Cricut Projects** 305

5. **Assemble the quilt.**

   Once all your shapes are cut, sew them together following your chosen pattern. For best results, keep an organized layout of your pieces as you sew to avoid mix-ups.

Piecing Together Custom Puzzles

You can create a personalized puzzle from your favorite photos with the Cricut Maker machines. This fun DIY project uses the Print Then Cut feature (see Chapter 18) to transfer a photo onto printable sticker paper. After applying the photo to chipboard, you'll use the Maker's excusive Knife Blade to cut the puzzle pieces.

You can try making this project with the Deep-Point Blade if you're using a Cricut Maker or Explore series machine, but it may not cut as cleanly as the Knife Blade and can cause tearing.

Gather your materials:

- Brayer or scraper
- Chipboard
- Craft knife
- Cricut Maker, Cricut Maker 3, or Cricut Maker 4 only
- Glue
- Inkjet printer
- Knife Blade
- Lightweight chipboard or a cereal box
- Painter's tape
- Printable sticker paper or vinyl
- StrongGrip Mat

Looking to save on materials? Cereal boxes are a great alternative to chipboard. For more tips on working with printable sticker paper and vinyl, be sure to check out Chapter 19.

Follow these steps:

1. **Upload your image.**

   Open Design Space and click Upload. Then select Upload Image to browse your computer for the image you want to use. Choose Complex for the best image detail, then click Continue. Next, select Print Then Cut Image and click Upload. Once the image uploads, click on it and press Add to Canvas.

2. **Attach a puzzle template.**

   Search for a puzzle template in the Images library by typing "puzzle" or directly using the code #M22EA34D1 for a basic design. Many of these puzzle templates cost money or require a Cricut Access subscription (see Chapter 6). You can also find free square and rectangle puzzle templates on my website at www.kerricraftsit.com/puzzle. Select one and add it to your Canvas.

   Some templates have one layer with only the cut lines, and others have two layers: one with the cut lines and another with a solid background. The background piece serves as the base for the puzzle, giving it structure and a solid foundation. You can choose to keep or delete the background piece. If you keep it, you'll glue it to the outline of your top puzzle template later. If the template includes the background piece, drag it off to the side before attaching your photo to the cut line template. This keeps your design clean and ready for assembly.

3. **Resize your image.**

   Decide how large you want your puzzle to be. Adjust both your image and template to be the same size and to fit within the Print Then Cut limits. To make the puzzle as large as possible, enlarge your image until you see a red warning icon in the Layers panel. This means your image is too large. First, click Change Paper Size and select the correct size for your printable sticker paper. Then click the warning icon and choose Auto-Resize Image to automatically adjust the design to the largest size that fits. Take note of the dimensions in the Edit bar and resize your puzzle template to match those dimensions.

4. **Resize the template.**

   I recommend resizing the template to match your image, rather than resizing your image, to avoid distorting your photo. For example, stretching a square image to fit a rectangular template can cause it to skew. Stretching the template is usually less noticeable. Alternatively, you can search for a template that better matches your image's shape to reduce skewing.

   Rotate and resize your puzzle template to match the dimensions of your image. Click the Lock icon at the top of your Canvas to unlock the size settings, then manually enter your image's width and height.

CHAPTER 22 **Ten Advanced Cricut Projects** **307**

If you prefer resizing your image to match the template instead, right-click the image and click Send to Back. With the Lock icon still closed, adjust either the image's width or height to match the puzzle template. Once resized, highlight both the image and the template, then click Align > Align Top. After that, click Align > Align Right to perfectly align your layers on one side.

To remove any excess image extending beyond the template, select a square shape, resize it to cover the overhanging part of the image, and use the Slice tool to cut off the excess. Make sure that both the image and the shape are selected when using the Slice tool, and once you've sliced, delete the excess pieces. Keep in mind that this will remove parts of your image, so make sure that you're okay with losing those details before proceeding.

5. **Align and attach the design.**

   Right-click your image and select Bring to Front so the puzzle template is behind the image. Highlight both the image and the template, then click Align > Center to center them precisely. Once they're aligned, highlight both layers and click Attach. This will keep your image and cut lines together and ensures that the Cricut knows exactly where to cut after printing the image.

6. **Print the photo.**

   Load your printable vinyl or sticker paper into your inkjet printer. Toggle the System Dialog on so that you can adjust the print settings on the following window. Click on Preferences, then adjust the Print Quality settings to High or Best, and select the appropriate paper type. Print your photo.

7. **Apply the photo to the chipboard.**

   Carefully peel the backing off the printed sticker paper and lay it adhesive side up on a flat surface. Align the sticker paper with the edges of the chipboard. Once it's positioned, gently press down from one side to avoid air bubbles. Use a brayer to smooth the paper flat and ensure that it sticks well. If you're using a cereal box, apply the printable vinyl to the blank side of the box for a smoother surface.

8. **Insert the Knife Blade.**

   Install the Knife Blade into Clamp B of your Cricut Maker, ensuring that the gears are aligned. Secure the blade by closing the clamp until it clicks, indicating it's locked in place.

TIP

If it's your first time using the Knife Blade or if Design Space asks you to calibrate it, here's what to do: Click the drop-down menu by your name at the upper-right of Design Space. Select Settings, and then Machines. Next to Machine Calibration, choose your Cricut Maker model, and click Start. Pick the Knife Blade option and follow the on-screen instructions to calibrate.

9. **Cut the puzzle pieces.**

   Attach the photo-mounted chipboard to the StrongGrip Mat using painter's tape around the edges for extra stability. In Design Space, set the material type to Heavy Chipboard and move the star wheels all the way to the right so they don't interfere. Load the mat and press Go to begin the cut. Depending on the thickness of the chipboard, the Knife Blade may need to make 20–30 passes to cut all the way through, which can take 1 to 2 hours to complete. Keep an eye on the machine during this process to make sure it cuts properly.

10. **Remove the puzzle pieces from the mat.**

    Check the cut for completeness before unloading by pausing the machine and lifting a corner of a puzzle piece. Once the puzzle is cut, carefully remove it from the mat. To make removal easier, flip the mat over and gently bend it. Start by slowly peeling off the puzzle pieces to avoid any tearing or damage. Use a craft knife for any final trims if pieces aren't completely separated.

    If you're creating a two-layer puzzle, glue the top piece on. The top piece is a typically a thin rectangle that goes around the puzzle, keeping the pieces inside. Once all the pieces are removed, assemble the puzzle to make sure that it fits together properly. Your puzzle is now ready to be enjoyed!

Personalizing Elegant Envelopes

Your Cricut can neatly address envelopes, making it great for bulk Christmas cards and invitations. For an elegant touch, use the Debossing Tip to add textured designs to the back flap — perfect for monograms or patterns on wedding invites.

Gather your materials:

>> Cricut machine (any model) for writing; for debossing, Cricut Maker or Explore series only

>> Cricut Pens or Markers

>> Debossing Tip (for Maker/Explore series)

>> Envelopes

>> Painter's tape

>> StandardGrip Mat

Follow these steps:

1. **Create an envelope template.**

   In Cricut Design Space, click Shapes and choose a square to represent the front of your envelope. To make a rectangular envelope, resize the square by unlocking the size settings with the Lock icon. Then, adjust the width and height to match your envelope's dimensions.

   To create a template for the back flap, start by selecting the triangle shape in the Shapes library. Resize the triangle's width to match the envelope's width, then use a ruler to measure the height from the point of the envelope to where the flap folds and adjust the triangle's height accordingly. Position the triangle so that it touches the top of the rectangle, then click Align > Center to center it properly. Select both the rectangle and triangle, then click Combine > Unite to merge them into one shape. Now you have a back flap template for adding your return address or monogram.

   TIP

   This template is for visual reference only. Hide it using the Eye icon before clicking Make, or change its Operation to Guide, which creates a non-cutting outline of your shape.

2. **Type the addresses.**

   Click the Text button to add your addresses. Open the Font drop-down menu, use the Filter option, and choose Writing to display fonts perfect for handwriting. Then type the recipient's address in one text box and the return address in another. Adjust the font size to fit the text within the envelope template, and change the Operation to Pen so the Cricut writes the text rather than cutting it.

3. **Align your text.**

   - **Main address:** For the recipient's address on the front of the envelope, select the text you've entered. Use the Align tool in the top menu to center the text within the text box. Then, select both the text and the envelope template. Use the Align tool again to choose Center, making sure that the address is perfectly aligned on the envelope.

   - **Return address:** Decide on the placement of the return address. If you're placing it on the back flap, use Center alignment; if it's on the front top left corner, use Left alignment.

4. **Create a monogram (optional).**

   Use the Monogram Maker in Design Space to create your monogram, adjusting the size to fit the back flap. Set the operation to Deboss in the Operation menu.

5. **Adjust the design for the envelope flap.**

   If you're writing or debossing on the outside of the envelope flap, you need to adjust the design so that it's properly oriented when the flap is closed. To do this, select your design and click Flip > Flip Vertical to flip the design upside down. Then, click Flip > Flip Horizontal to mirror the design so it reads from right to left. This way, when you close the envelope and flip it around, the design will be in the correct orientation and appear as it should.

   TIP: To address multiple envelopes, duplicate the envelope template and text boxes in Design Space and edit the text before starting the print or deboss process.

6. **Attach your designs.**

   Don't attach anything to the template, or your Cricut will treat it as part of the cut. You want your Cricut to write on the envelope, not cut the template shape. Hide or delete the template before attaching elements.

   Highlight all the aligned text and the monogram and click Attach to lock their positions relative to the envelope layout.

7. **Prepare to write and deboss.**

   Stick the envelope onto the StandardGrip Mat (with the flap spread open if you're printing or debossing on it) and tape down the edges with painter's tape. If you're addressing multiple envelopes, consider using a larger mat or placing one envelope in each corner to make it easy to align in the software. In the Prepare Screen after clicking Make, position the design where you want the writing and debossing to appear, making sure that the envelope is aligned with the placement on the screen.

   TIP: For addressing, insert the Cricut Pen into Clamp A and the Debossing Tip into Clamp B.

8. **Address and deboss your envelope.**

   Load the mat into your Cricut and follow the prompts in Design Space, beginning with the writing process. Once that's complete, switch to the Debossing Tip and proceed with debossing the monogram.

9. **Remove the envelope from the mat.**

   After the writing and debossing are complete, gently remove the envelope from the mat. Peel the mat away from the envelope rather than pulling the envelope off to avoid bending or wrinkling.

TIP: For another creative way to address your envelopes, you can use your Cricut to make sticker-style address labels. With Cricut's Print Then Cut feature, you can design and print a whole sheet of return address stickers to apply to your envelopes. For a step-by-step guide on how to make stickers, see Chapter 19.

Index

A

accessories, for heat presses, 59

accounts, creating, 27–28

acrylic key chains, 280–281

Adaptive Tool System, 14

address labels, 254

adhesive sprays, 69

adhesive tape, 129

adhesives, for cards, 158

adjustable settings, of heat presses, 57

adjusting

blades, 64–67

Design Space settings, 216–217

operations, 166

paper size, 245–246

settings, 32–33

advanced projects, 291–311

aligning layers, 198–199

aluminum foil, cleaning blades with, 67–68

Android

calibrating on, 244

connecting via Bluetooth on, 26

installing Design Space on, 30

system and internet connection requirements, 29

updating Design Space software, 70

Angel Policy, 76, 88

applying

etching cream, 236–237

heat transfer vinyl (HTV), 207–210

layers, 198–199

pattern fills, 93

transfer tape to glass, 235–236

assembling cards, 171–172

Attach tool, 111–112

attaching registration marks to layers, 197–198

attachments, for heat presses, 58

auto shutoff, 57

Automatic Background Remover feature, 76

automatic press, 58

auto-resizing images, 245, 246

B

baby bodysuits, Infusible Ink for, 212

baby showers, gift tags for, 127

backing, peeling, 271–272

back-to-school supplies, 176

band promotion, stickers for, 254

base material, for heat transfer vinyl (HTV) projects, 207

bathroom accessories, etching for, 228

beer mugs, etching for, 228

beginner projects, 275–289

birthday banners, 276–277

birthday parties, gift tags for, 128

blade housing, 44

blades, 43–44, 64-68

blanks

about, 60–61

for etching, 229

for Infusible Ink projects, 213, 215, 223–224

for vinyl projects, 182

Bleed on/Bleed off, 247

Bluetooth, connecting via, 25–27

bobby pin, 144

Bonded-Fabric Blade, 20, 52–53

bookmarks, for Print Then Cut projects, 242

borders, adding to stickers, 258–260

borosilicate glass, 230

bouquets, rolled paper flowers for, 138

brayer

about, 41, 129

for cards, 157

for heat transfer vinyl (HTV) projects, 207

for Infusible Ink projects, 213

for vinyl projects, 182

butcher paper, 59, 213

buying Cricuts, 21

Index **313**

C

cake toppers, 138, 303–304
calibrating, 32, 71, 244
candle labels, 288–289
canisters, etching for, 228
Canvas, 33, 80. *See also* Design Space Canvas
cap attachments, 58
caps, 204
car decals, 176
Card Mats, 20, 42, 157, 159
cards
  about, 151
  adding designs, 165–166
  adjusting operations, 166
  assembling, 171–172
  choosing sizes for, 156–157
  creating, 152, 160–172
  Cutaway Cards, 153, 156
  Insert Cards, 153–155
  materials for, 157–159,
    168–169
  mats for, 169–170
  projects for, 160–162
  templates for, 162–165
  tools for, 169–170
cardstock
  about, 129
  for cards, 157, 158
  for Infusible Ink projects, 213
  for Print Then Cut method, 243
  for rolled paper flowers, 139
care instructions
  for heat transfer vinyl (HTV), 210
  for printable heat transfer vinyl (HTV), 272
casserole dishes, etching for, 228
cast-in heating elements, 57
centerpieces, rolled paper flowers for, 138
Cheat Sheet (website), 3, 206
Christmas ornaments, 176
Citistrip, etching coated metal with,
    293–295
clamshell press, 58
classroom stickers, 254

cleaning
  blades, 67–68
  glass, 235
  regular, 63–64
coasters, Infusible Ink for, 212, 225, 285–286
coatings, on glass, 231
coffee mugs, 301–302
Collections, creating, 118
color, of vinyl, 190–191
Color Sync tool, 113, 193
color-changing vinyl, 178
colored glass, 230
commercial licenses, 88–89
community, for Cricut, 9
community groups, 72
computers, syncing Cricut with, 24–27
connecting
  via Bluetooth, 25–27
  via USB cable, 24–25
Contour tool, 112–113
copyright issues, 89
cosmetic bags, Infusible Ink for, 212
cost
  blades, 44
  Creative Fabrica, 78
  Cricut Access subscriptions, 77
  Cricut Essential Tool Set, 40
  DesignBundles, 78
  of heat presses, 58
  standard Cricut Access subscription, 76
Craverland Universal Pen Adapter Set, 45
Create Sticker tool, 76, 257–258
Creative Fabrica, 78, 84, 89, 96, 141, 210
crepe paper, for rolled paper flowers, 140
Cricut
  about, 7–8, 11–12
  buying, 21
  community for, 9
  sending designs to, 119–124
  setting up, 23–38
  support website, 72
  versatility of, 8–9
  website, 21, 25

314   **Cricut For Dummies**

Cricut Access
  about, 75
  alternatives to, 77–78
  standard subscription, 75–76
  subscription types, 77
  tab for, 31
  using Create Sticker tool with, 257–258
  website, 75
Cricut Explore
  about, 15–17
  changing blades in, 65–66
  sticker paper for, 256
Cricut Explore Air 2, 8
Cricut Heat Guide, 271
Cricut Joy
  about, 8, 17–19
  changing blades in, 67
  sticker paper for, 256
Cricut Maker
  about, 8, 12–15
  changing blades in, 65–66
  sticker paper for, 256
  tools for, 53–56
Cricut Venture
  about, 19–21
  changing blades in, 65–66
  sticker paper for, 256
custom bookmarks, 277–278
custom hats, 282–283
custom labels, 287–288
custom puzzles, 306–309
customer service, 72
customizing fonts, 98–99
cut size, choosing for rolled paper flowers, 142–143
Cutaway Cards
  about, 153, 156
  layout guide for, 101, 115
  material for, 168
cutting
  heat transfer vinyl (HTV), 207–210
  for Infusible Ink projects, 218
  troubleshooting, 71–72
  vinyl, 185

D

DaFont, 78, 96
deboss, 20
Debossing Tip, 54, 158
decorations, rolled paper flowers for, 138
decorative vases, etching for, 228
Deep-Point Blade, 8, 44
deleting layers, 106
Design Bundles, 141
Design panel, 80
Design Space
  about, 8, 28
  adjusting settings in, 32–33, 216–217
  creating vinyl stencils in, 231–234
  designing in, 85–115
  designing stickers in, 257–260
  finding settings, 32–33
  installing, 29–30
  internet connection requirements, 29
  multilayered designs in, 191–194
  navigating Home screen, 31–32
  saving for online/offline use, 33–38
  searching for templates, 140–141
  system requirements, 29
  troubleshooting connectivity, 72
  updating software, 69–70
  website, 86
Design Space Canvas
  about, 79
  browsing Projects library, 81–83
  Images tab, 83–84
  key areas of, 80–81
designing
  about, 85
  adding designs to cards, 165–166
  creating projects, 86–87
  finning designs with patterns, 93–94
  guides, 100–101, 103–104
  layers, 104–113
  legal use of fonts and designs, 87–89
  sending designs to Cricut, 119–124
  setting operations, 113–115
  stickers in Design Space, 257–260

Index   315

designing *(continued)*
  templates, 100–103
  transferring designs to vinyl, 186–187
  uploading designs, 90–92
  using designs legally, 87–89
  working with text, 94–100
devices, installing Design Space on, 29–30
die cuts, for cards, 158
die-cut stickers, 262–264
Discover tab, 31
Docking Stand, 21
Double Scoring Wheel, 54
double-sided adhesive tape, 129
double-sided paper, for rolled paper flowers, 139
double-tube heating elements, 57
drawing, with pens and markers, 220–225
drawing and cutting method, for gift tags, 131
dust cover, 64

E

EasyPress
  about, 58
  for Infusible Ink projects, 213
  for printable heat transfer vinyl (HTV), 267
Edit bar, 80
electric quilling tools, 144
engraved pet ID tags, 291–293
Engraving Tip, 54, 61
envelopes, 309–311
Essential Tool Set, 40
etched glass vinyl, 230
etched vinyl, 178
etching
  about, 227
  coated metal with Citistrip, 293–295
  creating in Design Space, 231–234
  materials for, 229–231
  process of, 235–237
  projects for, 228–229
etching cream, 229, 236–237
Etsy, 78
even heat distribution, of heat presses, 57
everyday iron-on, 205

everyday pens, 45
Exclude tool, 111
exterior cleaning, 64
extra fine pens, 45

F

fabric
  Infusible Ink for, 225
  vinyl and, 177
fabric banners, printable HTV for, 266
fabric blank, for printable heat transfer vinyl (HTV), 267
fabric flowers, 297–298
FabricGrip Mat, 42
filling designs with patterns, 93–94
filtering mature content, 33
fine point pens, 45
Fine-Point Blade
  about, 8, 44, 64, 129
  for cards, 157
  for etching, 229
  for Infusible Ink projects, 214
  for Print Then Cut method, 248
  for printable heat transfer vinyl (HTV), 267
  for stickers, 255
  for vinyl projects, 182
firmware, 69, 70
Flatten tool, 112
flexible materials, vinyl and, 177
flock HTV, 205
fluorescent vinyl, 178
foam dots, 129
foil HTV, 205
Foil Transfer Kit, 47–49, 130, 158
FontBundles, 78
fonts
  customizing, 98–99
  installing, 96–97
  saving for offline use, 36–38
  using legally, 87–89
food-contact areas, vinyl and, 177
free subscription, to Cricut Access, 77
frosted vinyl, 230

316   Cricut For Dummies

G

gift accents, rolled paper flowers for, 138

gift tags
about, 127
creating, 130–136
materials for, 129–130
for Print Then Cut projects, 242
projects using, 127–128
tools for, 129–130

glass blanks, for etching, 229

glass coasters, etching for, 228

glass items, customizing with vinyl, 176

glass jars, etching for, 228

glasses, for etching, 230

glitter accents, for cards, 158

glitter cardstock, for rolled paper flowers, 139

glitter gel pens, 45

glitter HTV, 205

glitter vinyl, 178

gloves, for etching, 230

glow-in-the-dark HTV, 205

glow-in-the-dark vinyl, 178

GO2CRAFT All-in-One Accessories Bundle, 177–178

Google Fonts, 96

gridlines, hiding, 33

grocery bags, printable HTV for, 266

Group tool, 106–107

grouping layers, 105

guides, 100–101, 103–104

H

hair accessories, rolled paper flowers for, 138

Halloween treats, stickers for, 254

hashtags, 9

hat attachments, 58

hats, 204, 212, 282–283

headbands, rolled paper flowers for, 138

Heat Guide tab, 31

heat press
about, 56–59
for Infusible Ink projects, 213
for printable heat transfer vinyl (HTV), 267

heat press mat, 59

heat press pillows, 59

heat source, for heat transfer vinyl (HTV) projects, 207

heat transfer vinyl (HTV)
about, 56–59, 130, 203
cutting, 209
cutting and applying, 207–210
finding size and placement for T-shirt decals, 205
layering with registration marks, 199–200
loading, 209
materials for, 207
projects for, 203–204
transferring, 209–210
types, 204–205
washing and care instructions for, 210
weeding, 209–210

heat-resistant tape, for Infusible Ink projects, 213

Help Center (website), 244

high-heat surfaces, vinyl and, 177

holiday gifts, stickers for, 255

holiday ornaments, etching for, 228

holographic HTV, 205

holographic vinyl, 178

home décor, Infusible Ink for, 212

Home screen, navigating, 31–32

hook tweezers, 40

hook weeder, 40

HTVRONT Heat Transfer Paper, 268

I

icons, explained, 2–3

images
auto-resizing, 245, 246
browsing, 83–84
saving for offline use, 36

Images tab, 83–84

Images tool, 141

Infusible Ink
about, 211
blanks for, 223–224
drawing with pens and markers, 45, 220–225
maintenance of, 225

Index   **317**

Infusible Ink *(continued)*
  materials for, 212–215, 217–218
  project ideas for, 212, 285–286
  working with, 215–220
Infusible Ink Transfer Sheets, for Infusible Ink
    projects, 213
inkjet printer, 129, 267
Insert Cards, 153–155, 168–169
Inspire tab, 31
installing
  Design Space, 29–30
  fonts, 96–97
interfacing, 52
interior cleaning, 64
internet connection requirements, 29
Intersect tool, 110–111
invitations, for Print Then Cut projects, 242
iOS
  calibrating on, 244
  connecting via Bluetooth on, 26
  installing Design Space on, 29–30
  system and internet connection requirements, 29
  updating Design Space software, 70
iron, for printable heat transfer vinyl (HTV), 267
iron-on transfer paper, for Print Then Cut
    method, 243
iron-on vinyl. *See* heat transfer vinyl (HTV)

J

jars, etching for, 228

K

Kerri Crafts It, 177, 289
kids' cups, 176
kiss-cut stickers, 262–264
kitchen organization, stickers for, 254
Knife Blade, 8, 56

L

labels, 243, 287–289
laminating sheets, 255, 262
laptop decorations, stickers for, 254
laser copy paper, for Infusible Ink projects, 214

layering
  about, 104–105
  from bottom to top, 194
  HTV with registration marks, 199–200
  with parchment paper, 200–201
  registration marks and, 195–200
  techniques for, 194–204
  tools in Layers Panel, 106–113
  from top to bottom, 194–195
  using, 105–106
  vinyl, 190–201
Layers Panel, 80, 106–113
leather earrings, 295–297
leaves, adding to rolled flowers, 149
Legacy Templates, 101–103
licenses, 88–89
LightGrip Mat
  about, 41
  for Infusible Ink projects, 214
  for Print Then Cut method, 248
  for printable heat transfer vinyl (HTV), 267
  for stickers, 255
lint roller
  about, 41, 59, 68
  for heat transfer vinyl (HTV) projects, 207
  for Infusible Ink projects, 213
  for printable heat transfer vinyl (HTV), 267
lint-free wipes
  about, 41
  for etching, 229
  for vinyl projects, 182
loading
  heat transfer vinyl (HTV), 209
  vinyl, 185

M

Macs
  calibrating on, 244
  connecting via Bluetooth on, 26
  finding hidden font characters, 97–98
  installing Design Space on, 29
  installing fonts, 97
  system and internet connection requirements, 29
  updating Design Space software, 69

318   **Cricut For Dummies**

magnets, for Print Then Cut projects, 243

maintenance
about, 63
calibrating, 71
changing blades, 64–67
cleaning blades, 67–68
firmware, 70
for heat transfer vinyl (HTV), 210
of Infusible Ink projects, 225
mats, 68–69
regular cleaning, 63–64
software, 69–70
troubleshooting, 71–72
of vinyl, 187

Make screen, 123–124

markers
about, 44–47
for cards, 158
drawing with, 220–225
for Infusible Ink projects, 214, 220–225

materials
for cards, 157–159, 168–169
for etching, 229–231
for gift tags, 129–130
for heat transfer vinyl (HTV), 207
for Infusible Ink projects, 212–215, 217–218
preparing for HTV projects, 209
preparing for vinyl projects, 184–185
for Print Then Cut method, 243–244
for printable heat transfer vinyl (HTV), 266–268
for stickers, 255–256
for vinyl projects, 182–183

mats
about, 41
for cards, 169–170
caring for, 68–69
Cricut Card Mats, 157, 159
heat press, 59
for heat transfer vinyl (HTV) projects, 207
LightGrip Mat, 214, 248, 255, 267
setting up, 121–122
sizes of, 42

SnapMat, 122
StandardGrip Mat, 129, 157, 183, 214
types, 41–42

mature content, filtering, 33

measuring tape
for heat transfer vinyl (HTV) projects, 207
for Infusible Ink projects, 213

metal surfaces, 27
metallic cardstock, for rolled paper flowers, 139
metallic pens, 45
mini press, 58
monograms, creating, 99–100, 284
mouse pads, printable HTV for, 266
moving layers, 106
mug attachments, 58
mug press, for Infusible Ink projects, 213
mugs, Infusible Ink for, 212, 225
multilayered designs, in Design Space, 191–194
Multiple Layers feature, 76
My Stuff tab, 31

N

navigating Home screen, 31–32
Navigation bar, 80

O

Offset tool, 259–260
opaque gel pens, 45
OpenType font (OTF), 96–97
operations
adjusting, 166
settings, 113–115
Oracal 631, 178
Oracal 651, 178

P

paintbrush, for etching, 229
paintbrush handles, 144
painter's tape, 41, 230

paper
   paper for rolled paper flowers, 139–140
   resizing, 245–246
   for stickers, 256
paper flowers. *See* rolled paper flowers
parchment paper
   about, 59
   layering with, 200–201
   for printable heat transfer vinyl (HTV), 267
party backdrops, rolled paper flowers for, 138
patterned HTV, 205
patterned paper, for rolled paper flowers, 139
patterns, 93–94
peeling backing, 271–272
pens
   about, 44–47, 129
   for cards, 158
   drawing with, 220–225
   for Infusible Ink projects, 214, 220–225
perforate, 20
Perforation Blade, 54
Performance Machine Mats, 21
permanent markers, 45
permanent vinyl, 178
personal licenses, 88–89
pet ID tags, 291–293
pet-themed gift tags, 128
phone cases, stickers for, 254
photo booth props, for Print Then Cut projects, 243
photos, for cards, 158
Picsvg tool, 78
pillow covers, 204, 212
pistils, attaching to rolled flowers, 149
place mats, printable HTV for, 266
placement, finding for T-shirt decals, 205
planners, stickers for customizing, 254
plate attachments, 58
platen, 57
PNGs, 86
porous surfaces, vinyl and, 177
portable press, 58
portable trimmer, 40
powering up Cricut, 23–24

preferred units, setting, 33
premium subscription, to Cricut Access, 77
Prepare screen, 120–121
price tags, 128
print quality, 246–247
Print Then Cut method
   about, 17–18, 241–242
   Bleed on/Bleed off, 247
   calibrating Cricut for, 244
   for gift tags, 132
   materials for, 243–244
   print quality, 246–247
   process of using, 248–251
   projects for, 242–243
   size limits for, 245–246
printable cardstock, for Print Then Cut method, 243
printable heat transfer vinyl (HTV)
   about, 205, 265
   care instructions for, 272
   materials for, 266–268
   projects with, 266
   pros and cons of, 265–266
   using, 268–272
Printable Iron-On for Dark Fabrics, 268
Printable Iron-On for Light Fabrics, 267
printable iron-on transfer paper, for Print Then Cut method, 243
printable magnet sheets, for Print Then Cut method, 243
printable materials, for Print Then Cut method, 248
printable sticker paper
   about, 129
   choosing, 256
   for Print Then Cut method, 243
   for stickers, 255
printable tattoo paper, for Print Then Cut method, 243
printable vinyl
   about, 130, 179
   for Print Then Cut method, 243
   for stickers, 255
Printable Waterproof Sticker Set, 262
printable window cling, for Print Then Cut method, 243

320   **Cricut For Dummies**

printed pattern vinyl, 179

printer

    for Print Then Cut method, 248

    for stickers, 255

printing stickers, 260–261

Priority member support feature, 76

projects

    advanced, 291–311

    beginner, 275–289

    for cards, 160–162

    creating, 86–87

    etching, 228–229

    for heat transfer vinyl (HTV), 203–204

    for Infusible Ink, 212

    for Print Then Cut method, 242–243

    with printable heat transfer vinyl (HTV), 266

    for rolled paper flowers, 138

    saving, 117–119

    selling safely, 89

    sharing, 117–119

    starting, 80

    for stickers, 254–255

    using gift tags, 127–128

    for vinyl, 176–177

Projects library, browsing, 81–83

Projects tool, 141

protective film, for mats, 68

protective gloves, 59

protective materials, for heat transfer vinyl (HTV) projects, 207

puzzles, 306–309

Pyrex, 230

Q

QuickSwap tools, 20–21, 53–56

quilling tools, 143–144

quilt blocks, 304–306

R

reflective HTV, 205

reflective vinyl, 179

registering machines, 32

registration marks, for layering, 195–200

Remember icon, 2

removable vinyl, 178

resizing paper, 245–246

reusable grocery bags, printable HTV for, 266

ribbon, 129

rinsing off etching cream, 237

rolled paper flowers

    about, 137

    choosing cut size for, 142–143

    choosing paper for, 139–140

    creating, 144–149

    project ideas for, 138

    quilling tools, 143–144

    templates for, 140–142

Rotary Blade, 8, 20, 52, 56, 129

rubbery materials, vinyl and, 177

rubbing alcohol

    about, 41

    for etching, 230

    for vinyl projects, 182

ruler

    about, 41

    for etching, 230

    for heat transfer vinyl (HTV) projects, 207

    for Infusible Ink projects, 213

S

safety features, of heat presses, 57

saving

    for online/offline use, 33–38

    projects, 117–119

    projects off-line, 33

scissors

    about, 40

    for heat transfer vinyl (HTV) projects, 207

    for Infusible Ink projects, 213

Scoring Stylus, 40, 49–51, 130, 158

Scoring Wheels, 49–51, 130, 158

scrapbooks, stickers for, 254

Index   **321**

scraper
about, 40
for cards, 157
for etching, 230
for heat transfer vinyl (HTV) projects, 207
for Print Then Cut method, 248
for stickers, 255
for vinyl projects, 182
scraping mats, 68
sealants, for stickers, 255
searching Design Space for templates, 140–141
seasonal apparel, printable HTV for, 266
selling projects, 88, 89
sending designs to Cricut, 119–124
settings
adjusting, 32–33
Design Space, 216–217
finding, 32–33
operations, 113–115
preferred units, 33
setup
about, 23
creating an account, 27–28
Design Space, 28–38
mats, 121–122
powering up, 23–24
registration marks, 196–197
syncing with computer, 24–27
shadow boxes, 138, 176
sharing projects, 117–119
Shop tab, 31
shot glasses, etching for, 229
showing layers, 106
simple cuts, for gift tags, 130–131
Single Scoring Wheel, 54
size
of cards, 156–157
finding for T-shirt decals, 205
of heat presses, 57
limits for Print Then Cut method, 245–246
of mats, 42
for rolled paper flowers, 142–143
Slice tool, 108, 193–194

smart HTV, 205
Smart Materials, 13, 14, 16, 20, 43
Smart Vinyl, 179, 183
SnapMat, 122
soft brush, for etching, 230
software, maintaining, 69–70
solid-core cardstock, for rolled paper flowers, 139
spatula
about, 40
for Print Then Cut method, 248
for stickers, 255
specialty blades, 56
specialty presses, 59
specialty vinyl, 178–179
spray sealants, 262
stack order, 192
standard method, for vinyl, 181–182
StandardGrip Mat
about, 41, 129
for cards, 157
for Infusible Ink projects, 214
for vinyl projects, 183
starting projects, 80
stems, attaching to rolled flowers, 148
stencil vinyl, 179
stenciled wood signs, 299–300
stencils, 176
sticker paper, 129, 130, 243
stickers
about, 253
for cards, 158
designing in Design Space, 257–260
die-cut, 262–264
kiss-cut, 262–264
materials for, 255–256
for Print Then Cut projects, 243
printing, 260–261
projects for, 254–255
waterproofing, 262
storing mats, 68
stretch HTV, 205
string, 129
StrongGrip Mat, 42

322   **Cricut For Dummies**

stuffed animals, 204

Subtract tool, 110

surfaces, vinyl and, 177

SVG files, 86, 183

swing-away press, 58

syncing Cricut with computer, 24–27

system requirements, 29

T

table centerpieces, rolled paper flowers for, 138

taco method, for vinyl, 182

tape, for Infusible Ink projects, 214

tattoo paper, for Print Then Cut method, 243

teacher gifts, 128

Technical Stuff icon, 3

techniques, for layering, 194–204

Teflon sheet, 59, 267

temperature gun, 59

templates

about, 100–101

for cards, 162–165

legacy, 101–103

for rolled paper flowers, 140–142

text

about, 94–95

adding, 95–96

creating monograms, 99–100

customizing fonts, 98–99

finding, 95–96

finding hidden font characters, 97–98

installing fonts, 96–97

working with, 94–100

thank-you gifts, 128

TheHungryJPEG, 78

thermal tape, 59, 207

thin paper, for rolled paper flowers, 139–140

third-party websites, for templates, 141–142

throw pillows, 266, 281–282

Tip icon, 3

tissue paper, for rolled paper flowers, 140

tools

about, 39–40

blades, 43–44

blanks, 60–61

Bonded-Fabric Blade, 52–53

for cards, 169–170

Cricut Essential Tool Set, 40

Cricut Maker series, 53–56

Foil Transfer Kit, 47–49

for gift tags, 129–130

heat press, 56–59

in Layers Panel, 106–113

markers, 44–47

mats, 41–42

other recommended, 40–41

pens, 44–47

quilling, 143–144

Scoring Stylus, 49–51

Smart Materials, 43

tote bags, 204, 212

towels, 284

trademark issues, 89

transfer tape

about, 181–182

applying to glass, 235–236

applying to vinyl, 186

for etching, 230

for vinyl projects, 183

troubleshooting, 71–72

TrueType font (TTF), 96–97

T-shirts

about, 204

decals, 205

Infusible Ink for, 212

printable HTV for, 266

rule guide, 59

tumbler attachments, 58

tweezers, 144

U

Ungroup tool, 107–108

ungrouping

layered designs, 191–192

layers, 105

Unite tool, 109–110

updating, 69–70

Index **323**

uploading
  designs, 90–92
  patterns, 93–94
USB cable, connecting via, 24–25
UV-activated, color-changing HTV, 205

V

versatility, of Cricut, 8–9
vinyl
  about, 175, 189–190
  color of, 190–191
  cutting, 185
  for etching, 230
  for layering, 190–191
  loading, 185
  maintenance of, 187
  materials for projects, 182–183
  for Print Then Cut method, 243
  projects for, 176–177
  for stickers, 255
  surfaces and, 177
  transfer tape, 181–182
  types, 177–179
  weeding, 179–180, 186
  working with, 183–187
vinyl stencils. *See* etching
vinyl trimmer
  for heat transfer vinyl (HTV) projects, 207
  for Infusible Ink projects, 213

W

wall art, 138, 266
Warning icon, 3
Warped Text feature, 76
washable fabric pens, 45
washi tape, for cards, 158
washing instructions, for heat transfer vinyl (HTV), 210
water bottles, 278–279
watercolor marker & brush set, 45

waterproofing stickers, 262
Wavy Blade, 55
wedding favors, gift tags for, 128
weeding
  defined, 8
  heat transfer vinyl (HTV), 209–210
  for Infusible Ink projects, 218
  vinyl, 179–180, 186
weeding tools
  about, 129
  for cards, 157
  for etching, 230
  for heat transfer vinyl (HTV) projects, 207
  for Infusible Ink projects, 214
  for printable heat transfer vinyl (HTV), 267
  for vinyl, 183
Weld tool, 108–109
wet method, for vinyl, 182
white-core cardstock, for rolled paper flowers, 140
window cling, for Print Then Cut method, 243
Windows PCs
  calibrating on, 244
  connecting via Bluetooth on, 25–26
  finding hidden font characters, 97
  installing Design Space on, 29
  installing fonts, 97
  system and internet connection requirements, 29
  updating Design Space software, 69
wine bags, Infusible Ink for, 212
wine glasses, etching for, 229
wood signs, 176, 299–300
working off-line, 34

Y

YRYM HT Vinyl Transfer Tape, 181

Z

ZIP files, 96–97
Zoom controls, 80

About the Author

Kerri Adamczyk is an avid Cricut crafter, blogger, YouTuber, and now author, and the woman behind the popular `Kerricraftsit.com` and Kerri Crafts It channel on YouTube (she was formerly known as Cricuter). Her journey into crafting began in 2018 when, as a stay-at-home mom, she sought ways to earn extra income while spending time with her two young children. Her discovery of the Cricut machine sparked not just a hobby, but also a thriving business and a platform to help others unleash their creativity.

Kerri began by crafting personalized gifts for friends and family, soon expanding her reach to sell her designs online, at craft fairs, and in a quaint shop in her hometown. Today, her passion extends into teaching, as she shares her expertise through more than 280 tutorials on YouTube, helping a community of more than 56,000 subscribers and garnering over 2.3 million views. In addition to her online tutorials, Kerri manages four vibrant Facebook groups with more than 100,000 members, where crafters exchange tips, inspiration, and support.

Although she holds a bachelor's degree in biology from Westfield State University, Kerri found her true calling in crafting, choosing to forge a path that allows her to make a living doing what she loves. Her expertise extends beyond Cricut, encompassing advanced techniques in laser engraving and sublimation, proving that sometimes the best careers are the ones we make for ourselves.

For more information on Kerri's projects, tutorials, and social media links, visit `https://linktr.ee/KerriCraftsIt`.

Dedication

I dedicate this book to the most amazing husband and dad there ever was, Chris, who has not only accepted my crafting addiction but embraced it with open arms. While I sat writing, you took care of everything — whipping up meals, playing with the kids, always putting everyone before yourself. I couldn't have done this without you. Thank you for always loving and supporting me in everything I do.

To Sierra and Barrett, my OG "Mommy and Me Cricuter Team." You sparked my original interest in Cricut crafting while I searched for a way to work from home so I could live my dream of being a stay-at-home mom and watching you grow. I hope this book shows you that you can do hard things, and that hard work pays off and dreams really do come true.

Lastly, I dedicate this book to my Papa Mike, the first person I call with any big news. Your love and guidance have shaped who I am today. I hope this book makes you proud.

Author's Acknowledgments

A heartfelt thank-you to everyone at John Wiley & Sons, Inc., for making this book a reality. Special thanks to Jennifer Yee, senior acquisitions editor, for believing in me and offering this amazing opportunity. When I first received your email, I thought it was too good to be true — it must be a scam. But once I saw the "@wiley.com" email address, I knew it was the real deal. Having grown up with *For Dummies* books, I never imagined I would one day author one myself. It has truly been an honor.

To Georgette Beatty, my wonderful development editor, thank you for your constant kindness and support throughout every step of this process.

Kristie Pyles, my managing editor, and Kelly Brillhart, my copy editor: Thank you both for your incredible attention to detail and for making sure that everything in this book was perfect.

A special thanks to Alexandra Beauvais, my technical editor. It was a delightful surprise when you stumbled upon one of my Cricut tutorials on YouTube and reached out with such excitement. Your passion for Cricut crafting brought us back together after our college days, and having you as part of this project has been such a fun journey. Your expertise, dedication, and meticulous attention to detail give me peace of mind, knowing that every piece of advice and instruction in this book is clear, correct, and easy to follow.

I also want to thank Amber Bowers, whose exceptional photography skills have beautifully displayed the quality and detail of my Cricut projects throughout this book. Amber has the skills to make simple objects look extraordinarily professional in photographs. Her photos are not only a key part of this book but also enhance my website and YouTube videos. Thank you, Amber, for making my projects shine through your lens.

To my loving family and friends, thanks for being my biggest supporters, always cheering me up and cheering me on when I need it the most. I'm so grateful for your encouragement and proud to share this achievement with you. I also can't forget my fur baby, Maddie, who snuggled by my side, keeping me company during the countless hours I spent typing away.

Lastly, I want to thank the crafting community. You've been my support system since I got my first Cricut machine, constantly inspiring me and pushing me forward. You've helped make this book happen, and I'm so grateful.

Publisher's Acknowledgments

Senior Acquisitions Editor: Jennifer Yee

Senior Managing Editor: Kristie Pyles

Development Editor: Georgette Beatty

Copy Editor: Kelly Brillhart

Technical Editor: Alexandra Beauvais

Production Editor: Magesh Elangovan

Cover Image: Courtesy of Christopher Adamczyk